THE
ENTREPRENEURIAL
BIBLE TO

VENTURE
CAPITAL

THE
ENTREPRENEURIAL
BIBLE TO
VENTURE
CAPITAL

INSIDE SECRETS
FROM THE LEADERS
OF THE STARTUP GAME

ANDREW ROMANS
CO-FOUNDER & GENERAL PARTNER
OF RUBICON VENTURE CAPITAL

New York   Chicago   San Francisco   Athens   London   Madrid
Mexico City   Milan   New Delhi   Singapore   Sydney   Toronto

7 8 9 10   LCR   21 20 19

ISBN: 978-0-07-183035-5
MHID: 0-07-183035-9

e-ISBN: 978-0-07-183036-2
e-MHID: 0-07-183036-7

This publication is designed to provide accurate and authoritative information in regard to the subject matter covered. It is sold with the understanding that neither the author nor the publisher is engaged in rendering legal, accounting, or other professional service. If legal advice or other expert assistance is required, the services of a competent professional person should be sought.

—*From a Declaration of Principles Jointly Adopted by a Committee of the American Bar Association and a Committee of Publishers and Associations*

Author's Note

Under no circumstances should any material in this book be used or considered as an offer to sell or a solicitation of any offer to buy an interest in any individual company or investment fund managed by Andrew Romans or Rubicon Venture Capital. Any such offer or solicitation will be separately made only by means of the Confidential Private Offering Memorandum relating to the particular fund to persons who, among other requirements, meet certain qualifications under federal securities laws and generally are sophisticated in financial matters, such that they are capable of evaluating the merits and risks of prospective investments.

McGraw-Hill Education books are available at special quantity discounts to use as premiums and sales promotions, or for use in corporate training programs. To contact a representative, please visit the Contact Us pages at www.mhprofessional.com.

This book is printed on acid-free paper.

Contents

List of Contributors and Interviewees   **xi**

Foreword by André Jaeggi   **xiii**

Introduction   **1**

(1) Start Me Up!   **3**

Why Now Is a Great Time to Start a Company,
Be a Venture Capitalist, Be an Angel Investor,
or Invest in a VC Fund   **3**

BranchOut: The Textbook Case Study for Superb
Angel Advisory Round and VC Funding   **7**

Add Angel Dignitaries to Your Series A VC Round   **10**

Why Entrepreneurship Is Becoming Increasingly
Important and Why Angel Investing and Venture
Capital Are Here to Stay   **11**

Getting Started   **12**

We've Got to Start a Company   **13**

When to Start Up?   **14**

(2) Angels, Mortals, and Super Angels   **17**

The "Startup Cambrian Explosion"   **18**

Ron Conway, Super Angel   **20**

Accelerators   **22**

Tech Stars and the Rise of Accelerators   24

Online Funding Resources   28

Crowdfunding: Everything You Always Wanted to
    Know but Were Afraid to Ask   28

Practical Ideas and Advice on Raising Angel Funding   35

How to Recruit and Negotiate with Advisors   37

Convertible Note Versus Priced Round   37

Valuation Ranges for Pre-Money Caps on Seed-Stage
    Convertible Note Financings   40

Don't Raise Angel Funding at Too High a Valuation   41

Raising Angel Funding   41

Steve Jobs Rated by His VC   43

The Team Means Everything   44

A Balanced Team   44

Recruit a First-Class Team Contingent upon Funding   51

Choose Your Investors Wisely   52

Building Blocks of Pre-Money Valuations   53

Pitch Lawyers before Pitching Angels   53

Legal Fees for Startups: Fixed Pricing   55

Legal Factors to Consider When Choosing an
    Angel Investor   56

Smart Angels Flock Together   57

Pledge Funds   58

The Importance and Art of Networking   58

Never Turn Down a Smart Strategic Investor   59

3 **How Venture Capital Works**   **61**

Understanding VC Titles   66

To the Victor the Spoils   67

The Stock Market and Venture Capital   69

Where Do VCs Get Their Money?   69

Why Are VCs So Arrogant?   71

Old School Venture Capital: Pitch Johnson on
    the Early Days of Silicon Valley   **72**

Romans Five Forces Venture Model: Incentives
    Are *Not* Aligned   **77**

Corporate VCs   **79**

Family Offices   **80**

The Difference between Venture Capital and Private Equity   **81**

A Perspective on the Difference between VC and PE   **83**

What About Venture Debt?   **85**

This Is Not Your Mother's Venture Debt   **86**

Pick the Right Partner the First Time   **89**

Questions You Should Ask Your Venture Debt Partner   **90**

Venture Debt Terminology and Term Sheets Revealed   **91**

Why Venture Debt Is an Attractive Asset Class   **95**

Fund of Funds   **96**

More Than Matchmakers Between GPs and End Investors   **97**

4   **What to Bring to the Dog and Pony Show!**   **103**

Business Plans   **103**

Executive Summary   **105**

Investor Slide Deck   **105**

Financial Model   **106**

Characteristics of the Best Spreadsheet Models   **109**

Investor Control Schedule   **114**

Demo and Video   **115**

The Pitch   **116**

Five VCs Explain What They *Really* Think About
    Your Pitches   **118**

5   **Practical Ideas and Advice on Raising
VC Funding**   **121**

Getting on the Radar of Your First Choice VC   **121**

How Should an Entrepreneur Approach Negotiation
of the Key Terms?   **123**

How to Negotiate with a Venture Capitalist   **124**

Don't Tell VCs Which Other VCs You Are Talking To   **127**

Confidentiality: No NDAs or Secrets in the Fast Lane   **128**

Bridge Financing   **129**

Living from Round to Round   **129**

Employ an Army of Interns   **130**

Customer Financing   **130**

Dual Tracking   **132**

Venture Fratricide   **132**

6   Corporate Governance: Who's The Boss?   **135**

The VC That Wanted a Board Seat   **136**

Engaging the Board of Directors   **140**

Making Your Board Work for You   **146**

7   Company Building and Growing Value   **149**

Distribution Versus Product   **149**

Skype: Where is Your Button on Kazaa?   **150**

Facebook: The Balance Among Product, End User
Experience, and Advertising   **151**

MySpace: Pimp Out Your Contacts   **153**

YouTube: How to Extend Beyond Your Domain   **156**

The Marketing Myth   **157**

The Blackmail Business Model   **159**

The Nine-Year Overnight Success   **160**

Just Grab the Bird and Lower Yourself Out of
Those Clouds   **161**

How to Come Up with True Innovation That Drives
the Rest   **162**

Picking a Name   **163**

8 Which Way to the Exit? 165

M&A Is the Most Likely Positive Outcome for
Most Entrepreneurs 165

Practical Ideas and Advice When Selling Your Company
via M&A 165

Three Kinds of Business Buyers 170

How Instagram Secured a $1 Billion Valuation 172

Advice on the $300 Million Sale of Adify 173

How Liquidation Preferences and Carve Outs Play in
Exit Scenarios 174

How to Smoke Out the Serious VCs in Your Syndicate 175

Large Trade Sales of Private, Venture-Backed Medical
Device Companies 176

Acqui-Hire Early Exits: VCs Versus Founders 176

Several Perspectives on Acqui-Hires 185

Seek Truth in Facts: Statistics on Venture Exits 186

Fund Physics: Expect Improved IRRs from Smaller Funds 188

9 Do We Need All These Lawyers? 191

What Are the Key Terms in a Term Sheet? 192

No Time Like Right Now to Settle a Legal Dispute 198

Dumb Licensing 200

Letting a Licensee Get Out of Control 201

Sometimes You Have to Go Downhill to Get to the Top
of the Next Hill 202

It Is Better to Be Lucky Than Good 203

10 Ladder to Liquidity: The Secondary Market 205

How Early-Stage Angels and VCs Can Get Their Cash
Back Prior to an Exit 205

To Sell or Not to Sell: The Secondary Market for
Startups 208

The Direct Secondary Market: Selling Some of Your Shares
    for Cash Before a Liquidity Event   **210**

Founders' Preferred: Best Structure for Founder Early
    Liquidity   **211**

Direct Secondary Funds   **213**

When to Take Your Chips off the Table   **213**

The Founders Club Equity Exchange Fund Model   **214**

Afterword   **219**

Acknowledgments   **221**

Index   **223**

List of Contributors and Interviewees

Katherine Barr, general partner, Mohr Davidow Ventures

John Bautista, partner, Orrick

Mark Bivens, entrepreneur and VC, Truffle Capital

Derek Blazensky, founding partner, Cardinal Venture Capital

Paula Brillson, attorney at law, as well as founder and former CEO, Asia Capacity Exchange

Nic Brisbourne, partner, Forward Partners (formerly DFJ–Esprit)

Charles Cella, founder and partner, GTC Law Group

David Cohen, founder and CEO, TechStars

Adam Dell, venture partner, Austin Ventures

Tim Draper, founder and Managing Director, Draper Fisher Jurvetson (DFJ)

Russ Fradin, CEO and cofounder, Dynamic Signal, as well as former CEO and cofounder, Adify

Ben Goodger, partner, Edwards Wildman Palmer

Howard Hartenbaum, general partner, August Capital

Ken Hawk, venture partner and investor, Rubicon Venture Capital, former CEO, Ubidyne

André P. Jaeggi, former Managing Director, Adveq, lead investor and venture partner, Rubicon Venture Capital and Chairman, The Founders Club

Todd M. Jaquez-Fissori, Senior Managing Director, Hercules Technology Growth Capital

Franklin Pitcher "Pitch" Johnson, cofounder, Draper and Johnson Investment Company as well as founder, Asset Management Company

Gary Johnson, head of corporate development, Facebook

Benjamin D. Kern, partner, McGuire Woods

Richard Kimball, cochair of the technology practice Edwards Wildman Palmer

Rick Marini, founder and CEO, BranchOut

Alex Mashinsky, angel investor, Governing Dynamics, as well as founder and former CEO, Arbinet, advisor The Founders Club

Scott Maxwell, founder and Senior Managing Director, Open View Venture Partners

John Montgomery, founder and Chairman, Montgomery & Hansen LLP, as well as founder, Startworks

Antoine Papiernik, partner, Sofinnova Partners

Parag Patel, investor and venture partner, Rubicon Venture Capital, VP worldwide sales, software-defined storage, VMware, former head of corporate development, VMware

Bob Pavey, partner, Morgenthaler Ventures

Jacqueline Reses, head of corporate development and HR, Yahoo!

Matt Rosoff, West Coast Editor, Business Insider SAI

Elton Satusky, partner, Wilson Sonsini Goodrich & Rosati

Steve Schlenker, cofounder and managing partner, DN Capital

Jörg "George" Sperling, partner, WHEB Partners, advisor The Founders Club

Ales Spetic, CEO, Zemanta

Riccardo Zacconi, CEO, King.com

Foreword

A ndrew Romans approached me with his concept of capturing real-life insights into our venture capital ecosystem through interviews with present-day practitioners; I viewed my role as a project supporter but not necessarily as its cheerleader. (Andrew is already enough of an enthusiast himself!) But this "how to" compendium is itself an example of what a startup venture is all about: It is the product of focused enthusiasm plus found resources. I am, in fact, a cheerleader for that.

"Entrepreneurship is the pursuit of opportunity without regard to resources currently controlled." Harvard Business School Professor Howard H. Stevenson enunciated this classical definition in 1975. There are several more recent definitions, usually focusing on risk or business building. But Stevenson captured the essence: the almost obsessive and addictive need of the entrepreneur to strive for achievement against all odds. When talking to venture capitalists and angel investors, this is what they usually claim to look for first in an entrepreneur.

Of course, the would-be entrepreneur needs to have an innovation at hand or some business acumen he or she wants to turn into economic goods, along with a minimum of personal and social competence. The key ingredient, however, is being dogged about this one project.

A quest is not just desirable, it is a must.

At the end of Stevenson's definition stand the resources, which the entrepreneur likely does not have.

That's where venture capital steps in. It's called "venture" capital because money is put at risk with an entrepreneur, but the dollars put forward will not alone make the difference. In a big buyout, some problems may be solved (or drowned) by a lot of money, but not so in a startup. A startup is about building a real business out of a plan. It's about allowing a network to unfold its strength. It's about adding personnel resources to fit the plan. It's about adequately structuring and nurturing a newborn venture into a viable and successful enterprise.

Homework is the key to starting a new venture. A would-be entrepreneur has to ask first: Who is the angel or venture investor that best fits my needs and why? This may not necessarily be the investor with the deepest pockets or the resounding reputation of past successes. There are specialists and generalists, individuals with gray hair who control everything themselves, or those that come in with an armada of young analysts who have never run a business. The natural fit must be tested. Due diligence works both ways, and every individual has a history that can be checked out.

What do I need that I do not have? What is missing in the equation to make this idea a thrilling success? These basic questions pop up over and over again. Their responses lead to answers about the fit—or the misfit—of entrepreneurs with angel investors or venture capital firms. They can provide answers about the timing of adding another venture capital firm. They can help understand why dilution ultimately creates value. Most importantly, these answers should allow every participant in the game to focus on what he or she does best. Venture capital is not only about excellence, it is excellence.

The idea behind this book then is simple: to illustrate and explore entrepreneurship, venture capital, and private equity from different angles. There is no universal panacea for success and there is no shortcut. A flash of wit and a few bucks—even a few very substantial bucks—do not make a business. Only hard work and diligence in finding the right resources can create the ground out of which dazzling businesses do emerge.

Many would-be entrepreneurs complain that raising money is tough, often even unpleasant. Some will gripe, especially when fund-raising is not going well, that it's the fault of bad markets or bad timing or . . . something. Perhaps this book can point out a few other possibilities, along with ways to navigate the terrain. Entrepreneurship and venture capital is an ecosystem that is constantly changing, but beside that evolution some timeless themes appear. I believe this book captures enough of those themes, through practical experiences and true stories, to enable all entrepreneurs and their investors to do better. Define the quest, find the right resources to match the founders' own assets, work hard, and build your own practical experience and success story. If in reading these insights, some entrepreneurs and venture capitalists find better ways to work together, then this project's goal has been achieved. Enjoy the reading . . . and the quest!

André P. Jaeggi

July 2013

André Jaeggi enjoys a front-row seat in the global venture game. Together with Bruno Raschle, he built Adveq from a two-person company into a $5 billion fund of funds, employing about 80 professionals representing 20 nationalities, with offices in Beijing, Shanghai, Hong Kong, New York, Frankfurt, Munich, and a head office in Zurich, Switzerland. At last count, Adveq holds more than 300 investments in VCs and private equity (PE) firms. Time and time again, Jaeggi and Adveq have seen how the movie starts and ends. Like many fund-of-fund executives, Jaeggi sits on several boards of directors of the VCs . . . who in turn sit on the boards of directors of the operating companies . . . that create innovation. Jaeggi is the lead investor, member of the advisory board and venture partner at Rubicon Venture Capital. Jaeggi previously worked with Romans as the chairman of The Founders Club, Andrew Romans' innovative equity exchange fund and liquidity advisory group.

THE ENTREPRENEURIAL BIBLE TO
VENTURE CAPITAL

Introduction

We will either find a way or make one.

HANNIBAL, 217 CE

Raising venture capital (VC) funds, or even putting up with a VC on your board, can feel like making love with a cactus; but if you want to *veni, vidi, vici* and collapse the time to your rocketing exit, VCs in-house might be worth the abrasive side effects and painful legal terms. If you're looking for a perfect term sheet, you may need a space suit to travel to another solar system to find one. The mission of this book is not to diminish the challenges but rather to help all participants in the VC ecosystem be more successful in dealing with those rocky paths. You may also find some new ideas from the Silicon Valley that are making the whole system better for everyone.

This book is meant for:

- Entrepreneurs
- Angel investors
- Venture capitalists
- Investors in the venture capital asset class
- VC ecosystem service providers

You will find here the following topics, recent ideas, trends, and legal matters that will help you:

- Raise angel and VC funding
- Build value in your company
- Sell your company via merger and acquisitions (M&A)
- Understand the quickly evolving secondary market for founders' and investors' early liquidity
- Come up with the idea for an innovative company
- The future of angel and venture capital

This book is not meant for everyone to read cover to cover or from beginning to end. Feel free to flip straight to the topic you find most interesting. Skip around. Some VCs may want to browse through contributions from other VCs or CEOs they know, diving into complex situations, balancing tensions between founders and VCs, crowdfunding, venture debt, venture debt terms, secondary markets, or M&A sections.

My initial motivation to write this book was people asking me to. I often found myself telling a story of how one entrepreneur did something, and my listener would say, "I wish I knew this before closing my angel or VC funding round or selling my company." As more relevant experiences began to repeat themselves, I started to write them down. Eventually, I was motivated to go to the sources and interview individuals whose achievements made their stories particularly compelling. They are the teachers here, and I thank them for their generosity in sharing.

One of my best classes in Georgetown University's MBA program was taught by Adjunct Professor Jonathan Silver. At the time, Jonathan was a founder and general partner at the VC firm Core Capital; he was previously the chief operating officer and managing director at the Tiger Fund, one of the largest hedge funds of its day. Learning business from an active practitioner was exciting. In this book I tap into my network of active entrepreneurs, VCs, and deal lawyers, and let the practitioners teach the class.

Of course, I have my own opinions, but add them only as commentary on the opinions and stories of the VCs that invested in Apple, Intel, and Microsoft, peppered with comments from some CEOs currently leading the companies that are and will be changing the world. Data and facts can help you see how the movie ends, and help you predict what your next movie's script will be.

Start Me Up!

Starting a new company that requires capital to get going is a bold and risky move. I have pulled together stories and advice from key members of the ecosystem in an effort to derisk this endeavor and make everyone more successful. Many of the tactics and tales are timeless, but the appetite for investing in startups oscillates between fear and greed correlating with economic cycles. Tim Draper, the only third-generation VC I know, does a great job of setting the stage with his description of the "Draper Wave."

WHY NOW IS A GREAT TIME TO START A COMPANY, BE A VENTURE CAPITALIST, BE AN ANGEL INVESTOR, OR INVEST IN A VC FUND

In an interview with Tim Draper, founder and managing director of Draper Fisher Jurvetson (DFJ), I asked him to explain his "Draper Wave" that shows historical trends in a cycle between venture capital and private equity (PE). Tim responded:

After the bubble burst in 2000, we had 10 flat years in venture capital. Then in 2008 the world came to an end and I thought: Oh my gosh! We're gonna be hit again! Gradually I realized that just can't be! It can't be right, because eventually these things do come back. I started to analyze history, trying to put this all into perspective, going back to 1957 when my grandfather started venture capital on the West Coast. I created something I call "The Draper Wave" (see Figure 1.1). Venture capital is not a classical sine wave cyclical business, but it is indeed cyclical. It follows waves opposite to those of the private equity business. While venture capital goes up like a shark's tooth (nothing ironic there), then comes down and sort of flattens out, the PE business is simultaneously coming down and then going up like a shark's tooth, flattening while venture capital is revving up again.

Figure 1.1 The Draper Wave

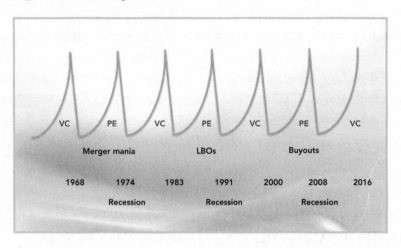

There's nothing scientific here, but the data and the emotional strength of the venture business does follow this pattern. I don't really know what happened when my grandfather was in the business from 1957 to 1965, but let's assume he was trying to solve a big problem during a recession when people are out of work and looking for something to do. They might say, well, you know my boss wasn't that good at what he did. I can do better. Or there's an opportunity here that the company I worked for didn't really take advantage of. So entrepreneurial ideas start happening, and then venture capitalists come in, enabling those entrepreneurs to start employing people. Jobs start to pick up, pick up, pick up, attracting more and more venture capital. Investors begin to see that these are great companies and they pour it on, rising to a crescendo and (often) crashing down. From 1965 to 1974 the big companies became conglomerates, buying other companies, slashing employees. That's how they grew. They'd acquire and fire, acquire and fire, and they made everything much more efficient. That was the roaring sixties that continued from 1965 to 1973.

At that point I think things probably got too frothy and came crashing down, causing the 1973–'74 recession. People were looking for things to do, the computer industry started, and other interesting things happened. Between 1974 and 1983 venture capital boomed again, creating major employment. This peaked in 1983 with Arthur Rock and Steve Jobs (for the first time) on the cover of *Time* magazine, soon before things crashed.

I joined the venture business in 1985 when the headliners were the LBO [leveraged buyout] folks. This was a new form of leverage that improved the efficiency of the system much like the conglomerates had before. They leveraged up, up, up until 1991 when the RJR Nabisco deal brought the house down. The banks decided not to lend anymore; they had lent too easily and too crazily. Of course that led to the 1991 recession.

From 1991 people began starting new companies again, creating the almost decade-long Internet boom; but eventually came the end-of-cycle 2000 crash.

The PE business was really just the LBO business between 2000 and 2008. PE-LBO made the inefficient companies created during 1991 to 2000 more efficient. But once again, in August 2007 the credit crunch brought the cycle crashing down. The venture capital crash followed, and in September 2008 another recession arrived.

We are now about five years into what I see as a nine-year cycle. People are beginning to create new companies, start employing people, and attract venture capital. More and more venture capital is coming out from hiding. I therefore conclude that today is actually an amazing time to start a business and an amazing time to be a venture capitalist. The angels have it right. They were funding these smaller businesses at just the right times. It's all going to pay off very well for them. I don't think we're going to have another bubble until say 2017 or so. This means that we have plenty of time.

I noted to Draper that right now there is more angel investing activity in the Silicon Valley and globally than ever before in history. Accelerators are sprouting up everywhere spawning new ventures, so the sheer number of companies being started and funded right now is higher than ever before in history. At the same time, the dollar amount of money going into first round series A venture capital financings is contracting. I asked, "How do you believe these companies will finance their businesses when the balance has shifted so much?" Draper responded:

What I was saying with the long history is that when there's a need, the investors fill in. Once they start making money in an area, then they pile on, the frenzy begins, followed by the crash. In our present case, the angels were very necessary between 2008 and 2011. The fact that there are more angels than ever before is in general because the venture capital business is growing globally. You are going to have a lot more angels. You're going to have a lot more entrepreneurial successes. You're going to have a lot more businesses that take off because of venture capital. There will be more competitors worldwide, and so the competition will be fiercer. But the markets are also bigger. And so I think everyone will benefit from more venture capital and more entrepreneurship. You will see each of these 18-year generations is going to be bigger than the last until it hits a steady state, which I think will be many generations out.

There are a lot of places in the world that don't really have a lot of venture capital and entrepreneurship, and so there's still opportunity for growth there, East Africa for example. By nature you will see a lot more angels now. I think you are asking where these new accelerator and angel-backed companies will get their financing after three years when their angel funding has run out and they are looking for where their next round will come from. The next round will come from either angels that invest at later stages, venture capitalists, or private equity or hedge fund guys that say—hey, I have to get into this because there's an opportunity. I think where there are good companies there will always be funders behind them. Good companies are only limited by people's imagination.

> *Imagination is everything. It is the preview of life's coming attractions.*
>
> ALBERT EINSTEIN

BranchOut: The Textbook Case Study for Superb Angel Advisory Round and VC Funding

BranchOut is worth examining for a number of reasons. Rick Marini is a very dynamic CEO, the angel group backing the company is unusually powerful, and the value prop is simple and clear: enable Facebook users to connect to existing contacts relevant to their business. BranchOut is basically LinkedIn on top of Facebook.

For a company that has only been in existence for a short time, BranchOut boasts a remarkable constellation of investors, as well as Rick's own choice of VCs. Rick Marini put in the effort and care to recruit over 20 advisors and angels into his deal before going to VCs, creating huge momentum for his company and the VC fund-raise. BranchOut is a masterfully architected super-high-growth enterprise.

Here is Rick's story in his own words.

Every company needs a solid foundation: a great idea, a world-class team, and the capital to fund growth. BranchOut was rare because our foundation was formed very quickly.

In June 2010, I was working with a small team of engineers and a designer who had been with me for years. We founded Tickle.com in 1999 and built it into one of the first social networks. Tickle was the largest personality testing site on the Internet, with 200 million registered users. In 2002, Tickle won a Webby for being the fastest-growing website. In 2004 we sold Tickle.com to Monster World-wide for over $100 million. Our next company was called SuperFan. We built social games and Facebook apps for entertainment companies, like MTV, CBS, Sony, Warner Music, and Universal. So when the idea for BranchOut came, we already had the foundation of a team with experience in viral growth, Facebook apps, and online recruiting. It was the perfect storm.

One day a friend reached out to me to see if I knew someone at a specific company. He wanted an introduction to a sales lead. Having nearly 2,000 friends on Facebook, I searched to see whom I knew at the company in question. Facebook didn't make it easy to find people based on where they work. So I turned to Nate Smith, our director of engineering, asking him to build a widget that iden-tified friends and friends-of-friends by company. Nate's widget worked perfectly, so we immediately decided to pivot the entire company and build BranchOut, the largest professional network on Facebook. On BranchOut people can create professional profiles, search for jobs, and find helpful connections for business oppor-tunities. The opportunity was obvious since Facebook was rapidly becoming the biggest and most visited site online.

One night, very late, I got a call from Michael Arrington, then editor of *TechCrunch*. Mike had heard about what we were up to and wanted to break the story. The next morning BranchOut was on the *TechCrunch* home page and the VCs started calling. We had the big idea and perfect team on day one. Now we just needed the cash.

I had raised $9 million with my Tickle.com cofounder, James Currier, so the process was familiar. The difference this time was that we had so many investment offers so quickly. For example, I went to one of my friends, a prominent super angel, asking for feedback on my pitch before meeting with Sand Hill Road. After seeing the first two slides he stopped me and said, "I don't need to hear any more. I get it. I'm in for a million." I wasn't even pitching him! Clearly this was a big idea and my challenge would be to limit who could participate in the round to those investors who brought the right connections, strategic advice, and vision to build BranchOut into a billion-dollar company.

All of the investors I met with were great, top-tier VCs whom I respect tremendously. Knowing that the lead investor would be on our board and we'd be working as partners, I wanted someone who was the perfect fit. Kevin Efrusy at Accel Partners stood out as just that person. He was the one with the foresight to see that Facebook was the next big thing when no one else saw it. He was tenacious in convincing Mark Zuckerberg and Sean Parker that Accel was the best investor to grow the company. He also invested in Groupon, where he's a board member. I met with Kevin, as well as a number of other VCs, each time checking in on Foursquare so they all saw the number of VCs interested in funding BranchOut.

One day, after an afternoon of back-to-back meetings in Palo Alto, I was driving back to San Francisco when Tim Chang, then partner at Norwest Venture Partners, called and said, "We need to have dinner tonight." He could tell things were heating up and wanted to lead the round. A few minutes after scheduling dinner with Tim, Kevin called and said, "We need to have dinner tonight." I laughed and explained that I was meeting with Tim. Kevin persisted and countered with "Fine, let's have drinks. You name the time and place. I'll drive up from the Valley." So I told him where to meet me and drove to the restaurant to meet Tim.

Tim and I are good friends. We had a great dinner, during which he did something I appreciated and will never forget. He explained, "As a VC I want to lead the round, but as your friend, I can admit that Kevin is also a great fit. If you let him lead, I'll understand. But I want in either way." We wrapped up dinner and I met Kevin at Gordon Biersch, a brewery near my apartment. It was clear he wanted to lead the round. When we got to negotiating the valuation for BranchOut, we literally did it on a napkin. He wrote a number on the napkin and slid it across the table. I crossed it out and wrote a bigger number. He didn't accept, so I proposed a valuation that I knew was fair for both of us. We shook hands, and that was that.

Accel Partners led a $6 million round with Norwest Venture Partners and Floodgate Fund participating. I carved out room for a dozen super angels to also invest, including Shawn Fanning from Napster, Michael Birch from Bebo, Naval Ravikant from Angel List, Dave Morin from Path, Matt Mullenweg from WordPress, Chris Michel from Military.com, Tickle cofounder James Currier, and others. Most of these were friends. I wanted them involved, both for their strategic advice and the potential for them to benefit if BranchOut had a big exit.

Those were the early days of BranchOut. We had the idea, team, and venture funding early on. A few months later we had millions of users, a total of $49 million in venture capital and a product people loved.

ADD ANGEL DIGNITARIES TO YOUR SERIES A VC ROUND

At Rubicon Venture Capital, when we invest in a startup from our VC fund, often co-investing in a syndicate with other tier I VCs, we have the CEO say to the syndicate of VCs, "Wait, I don't want the check for $5 million. Make that $4.5 million, and here's a list of 20 people that will invest $25,000 each after the $4.5 million has been wired." The names on that list are all CEOs and cofounders of major league companies scattered across the United States, Europe, and Israel. Then when we announce the series A financing with big-name VC funds and Rubicon Venture Capital investing we disclose that these additional 20 people also participated." The names on that list are a real Who's Who. VIP entrepreneurs and other people will wonder how a company located in Stockholm, for example, managed to get those people from the Valley and all over the world to invest in that round. This gives you a BranchOut rocket launch. It may be counterintuitive to add angels after the VCs, but it's a brilliant move. And those angels are lucky to get in. At $25,000 to $50,000 being a small amount for them, they don't care if they lose it. If you want to be one of the 20 people on that list, get in touch. We just did one of these this week in San Francisco for a company from Stockholm. At Rubicon Venture Capital we aggregate these angels into a "sidecar fund" so that the operating company only has one shareholder to deal with—Rubicon Venture Capital. This way the cap table is tidy and the angels can add value to the startup they have invested in. It is also exciting for angels to deploy personal capital alongside elite VC funds buying in at the same valuation and terms these professional investors get at optimal risk/reward inflexion points previously not available to angels seeking to deploy small amounts of capital at this optimal risk/reward inflexion point. This practice opens up this previously unattainable investment "product" to retail investors.

WHY ENTREPRENEURSHIP IS BECOMING INCREASINGLY IMPORTANT AND WHY ANGEL INVESTING AND VENTURE CAPITAL ARE HERE TO STAY

The opening of free markets combined with evolved telecommunications, broadband, and the instant spread of ideas is resulting in major shifts in economies. Traditional industries like manufacturing have shifted in large part from the United States and Europe to developing economies with lower total costs of production and new hungry markets to serve. Countries around the world from Chile to China are not passively watching the Silicon Valley. They want Silicon Valleys in their countries too.

The pace of innovation will only increase, and the cost of creating startups continues to fall. A company can launch today with $500,000 in funding compared to needing $5 million to achieve the same results just 10 years ago. In the 1990s when I had a venture-backed startup, I remember paying $50,000 per Sun server and way too much for Oracle software licenses. Now we have Amazon and cloud computing. You pay as you scale. You pay for what you eat as your revenues grow. Ubiquitous open-source code, lower cost offshore development teams and developers everywhere are further driving costs down, while at the same time the cost of developers in Silicon Valley and New York are skyrocketing. Lean Startup dynamics means cheaper, faster, three to ninety day product development cycles with smarter approaches to what is working and not working driven by a process of measure, learn, iterate or pivot.

Marketing is now built into the product. Many startups are just designers and engineers without a sales force but with a savvy marketeer. Today we have over 3 billion people online and a proliferation of mobile web users via smartphones. Most women are online compared to not as many 10 years ago. Smart entrepreneurs can acquire users cheaply and quickly leveraging platforms such as Facebook, Twitter, Google, Apple, Android, YouTube, Pinterest, Instagram, Tumblr, etc. Ten plus years ago this user acquisition required lots of venture capital dollars and took years to reach critical mass.

Companies promote their products and even their funding rounds on social networks and funding websites like AngelList laid over an abundance of angel investors everywhere. This is all combining to increase the volume and quality of tech startups everywhere. The cost of starting a mobile app and a website is around $5,000. Compare that to spending two years of your life in an MBA program and paying $3,000 monthly for student loans for 10 years after you graduate. I agree with Tim Draper: now is a great time to start a company, a great time to make angel investments into tech startups, and a great time to be a venture capitalist or invest in a venture capital fund.

Not everyone needs to move to the Silicon Valley. Technology corridors are flourishing in many places. There are plenty of dead zones, but particularly in the various hot spots, they are highly networked together and are changing the world repeatedly at an increasingly rapid pace.

GETTING STARTED

> *You create your own universe as you go along.*
> WINSTON CHURCHILL

Remember *Harold and the Purple Crayon*? If you're not happy with your life, then draw a door, open it, and walk through it.

Once a professional gets bitten by the entrepreneurial bug, he or she believes there is a real chance of kissing the sky and reaching the stars. Making such a blockbuster success becomes such a passion that one can begin dreams of philanthropy, stopping famine, wars, human trafficking, or whatever you fancy. There are many reasons to become an entrepreneur, but with all of my experience, I would advise that if you really want to just make money, stay away from entrepreneurship, or at least the very early stage deals. Russ Fradin, CEO and cofounder of Dynamic Signal, who sold his previous startup, Adify, to Cox Enterprises, researched data from five Silicon Valley VCs with data going back 15 years and found that only 10 percent of angel-backed deals ever raise VC funding. Of those that do get VC funding, 60 percent fail to return the money raised. Of those that do return the money raised, 30 percent just return the cash one time. Only 10 percent of their portfolios make all the profit for the VC funds. Entrepreneurship is indeed a risky business.

Become an entrepreneur if you must, but admit that this is a lifestyle decision. Some entrepreneurs are risk addicts and can't be helped. I once heard the sage Howard Hartenbaum from August Capital say that when an entrepreneur refers to himself as a "serial entrepreneur" and has no past successes to point to, the "serial" just sounds like "serial killer." My advice is to do it when you are young or in early retirement when you have nothing to lose. If you can't afford to take the risk, don't do it. If you do take the risk, may you at least be good and lucky!

WE'VE GOT TO START A COMPANY

I strapped on a pair of hockey Rollerblades and slipped "Paul's Boutique" into my Sony CD-Diskman and bladed from my apartment on 23rd and Madison in New York City over to Mark Mangan's place on Avenue B in Alphabet City with a stack of Open Systems magazines in my army back-pack. I had gotten the backpack for a few deutsche marks in East Berlin as an exchange student right after the Berlin Wall fell. Now I was working for a UNIX company based in Manhattan but splitting much of my time between the Silicon Valley and Austin, Texas, where most of our developers were. I was only a few months out of undergrad and had started my first real job. The year was 1993. Mosaic (soon to be renamed Netscape) was about to be released.

Open Systems was my favorite trade rag in the UNIX industry. Anyone who was reading it knew about each new product, service offering, or com-pany, months or at least weeks before it would be announced. The magazine did not tell you that, but you could watch things unfold like a soap opera and guess the next product that was needed, and in a few weeks—boom— there it was. Someone did it. When I sat down in my friend's squalid New York apartment, I slapped the stack of magazines on his coffee table and told him, "Dude, we've got to start a company. The combination of http server technology, dialup modem Internet access, and object-oriented software is gonna change everything."

I had already started a few little businesses in high school and college, but now I wanted to start a technology company. I wasn't worried about raising funding. I just had a few new ideas every day and wanted to recruit some cofounders and get going.

Today, when I look at my scattered schedule where I am booked most days in bumper-to-bumper meetings and challenged to keep up with my e-mails, I realize that I cannot be as "smart" as I was in 1993 when I took a few hours each day to read *Open Systems Today*, *Communications Week*, and *Database Inc.* I now obtain information in other ways, but it's not the same. Pre-Internet people read. Internet people struggle to keep up with the social networking noise in their morphing chattering inboxes. My advice to someone who wants to get smart fast on the Internet and technology, cleantech, medtech, or life science is read as much as you can. That probably means blogs more than anything else in the current world.

When to Start Up?

One of the best times to start a business is when you are a student. I started GTX when I was in the full-time MBA program at Georgetown University. It was perfect because I did not need to quit a cash-paying job to start my company. I was personally funded as a student, and I had a two-year runway to graduate and decide to either stick with my startup or abandon it. I took a few independent study classes where I did MBA projects that were 100 percent related to my startup, providing me free, high-quality consulting from faculty and students. For example, my finance professor, Jim Angel, created my financial model; my strategy and marketing plan was crafted and articulated with the help of noted Georgetown strategy professor Paul Almeida. I was incorporating the latest and greatest stuff being taught on campus into my startup, making it very up to date and hip to the latest thinking, across a balanced scorecard of business areas: marketing, sales, finance, accounting, operations, and organizational behavior. In a win-win situation, teams of students, including ex-McKinsey consultants and Goldman Sachs bankers, worked on projects related directly to my startup; they continued to work on real-life issues and my startup benefited from solid and free advice.

I think undergrads are also in a great position to start a company. Universities are communities and natural networks to leverage a product launch, service offering, or new idea. Facebook was started on campus at Harvard. Even Sun Microsystems started on campus (the "Sun" stood for Stanford University Network). Students can market stuff on campus where outside brands may not be able. Students can contact outside companies and distribute their products on campus with their new startup brand stickered or comarketed with these outside products. Many students are willing to work for free or for a very low stipend in order to get experience for their résumés, making it possible to field an army of interns, enabling you to operate without funding or to allow your funding to last longer (watch out for some archaic labor laws regulating compensation for interns in the U.S.).

On the other end of the spectrum is joining a startup when you are older. When Ed Braniff joined my company, GTX, he had taken early retirement in his mid-fifties. Ed had been the CFO for AT&T Systems & Billing, the "minutes" business, accounting for 80 percent of AT&T's revenue at the time. I remember Ed sitting with me and my partner, Phil Anderson, at the hand-me-down table in our scruffy office across the street from Urban Outfitters on M Street in Georgetown, telling us that he could work for two years without a salary, but after that he would need some kind of salary. Phil and I just looked at each other, smiled, and told him he was in.

2

Angels, Mortals, and Super Angels

The term *angel* originated in New York City when the first Broadway plays were financed. Later in the 1920s in Los Angeles when high net individuals came up with the money to produce the first Hollywood films these financiers were referred to as angels again.

Someone that invests as a high-net-worth individual into an early stage company is an angel. Some people say business angels. I just say angels. Today there are more angel investors than ever before and most venture capitalists have moved along the continuum away from early-stage seed investing into raw startups and farther along toward later stage and in many cases private equity investing.

For many who read this book, you will both receive and provide angel financing. In my experience, the first time I raised angel financing was highly personal and meaningful. It was an endorsement of our new company, my partner, and myself.

That means a lot more than just cash to cover costs. For an angel investor, financing a young team is to vouch for them and to do something far more meaningful than just putting cash into the anonymous stock market.

Each time a company reaches an exit, a few or many angel investors are born. Most angel investors are likely to invest locally. This is part of why it is so hard to replicate the Silicon Valley in other parts of the world. A big exit in a provincial location can do a lot to help that region get going.

Many successful entrepreneurs go on to create their own VC funds. Niklas Zennström, cofounder of Skype, first sold to eBay for $2.6 billion in cash and a multibillion dollar earn out and later sold to Microsoft for $8.5 billion, created Atomico, one of the best VCs in Europe. The founders of MySQL in Stockholm, which sold to Oracle for $1 billion, created Open Ocean Capital, Joe Lonsdale, founder of Palantir, a privately held software company in Palo Alto valued at over $10 billion, raised a $400 million fund Formation8 and has become an active venture capitalist.

The list goes on and on, but you can believe that companies like Google, Facebook, Twitter, Yahoo!, Apple, HP, Intel, Cisco, VMware, Oracle, eBay, PayPal, Adobe, YouTube, Admob, Intstagram, WhatsApp, Square, Blogger, Pinterest, Juniper, SanDisk, NetApp, Netflix, Box, Dropbox, Zynga, SalesForce, Electronic Arts, Tesla Motors, SolarCity, Sunrun, LinkedIn, Symantec, Roku, TiVo, Yelp, Palantir, Evernote, etc. have created tons of angel investors by making their young and old employees wealthy. Their pace of buying companies that were founded in Silicon Valley or moved here to be acquired locally continues to create new ecosystems of angels that fund new ecosystems of startups every week. This exit machine combining capital with human capital all located in the same place is one of the reasons things move so quickly here. Many of these folks have invested in my VC fund Rubicon Venture Capital and as a group they source amazing deal flow, add value to our portfolio companies and are well positioned to help us sell our companies at the right time returning cash to our investors and making our portfolio CEOs and founders the next wave of innovation investors.

THE "STARTUP CAMBRIAN EXPLOSION"

Here's a perspective on the current angel scene from Alex Mashinsky, a member of my board of advisors at The Founders Club and a member of our exchange funds with his founder stock. A former competitor, Alex is a successful serial entrepreneur, founder of GroundLink, former CEO of Arbinet, and active angel investor via his fund Governing Dynamics.

In 2011, overall angel investment has for the first time exceeded the total investments by A-round venture funds. This "Startup Cambrian Explosion," is driven by hype from Facebook, Twitter, and other successful startups combined with the highest unemployment rate among 18- to 35-year-old professionals in 70 years. A glut of angel money chasing the next big exit has resulted in thousands of new startups being launched nationwide.

With the explosion of cheap cloud-based services and API infrastructure of hundreds of Web 2.0 platform companies, it now costs less than $100,000 to launch a full beta service on the web or a mobile platform; thus the barriers to product launch have been cut by 90 percent from where they were 10 years ago.

Many of these services have managed to attract over a million users in less than 12 months with no marketing, relying entirely on their social networks and the extended social graph to create a chain reaction of subscription and adoption that in turn drives free but valuable feedback that drives iteration and improvement of the service. The best startups of the past five years have emerged by successfully scaling this model.

These young companies still need capital, so an ecosystem of angel investors has sprung up in all major cities to take pieces of such companies and bet on their future. All such investors hope to be part of the 3:30:300 explosion that came to symbolize the level of valuations startups can expect if they can deliver the hockey stick growth venture capitalists are looking for at the seed, A, and B rounds.

The unseen and devastating part of this explosion is the inevitable death of the vast majority of these startups as they try to leap from the seed stage to the A round safety of venture funding. Like the gazelles trying to cross the Mara River in the Serengeti, many will perish, but the strongest and fastest will make it to the other bank of the river and continue the journey of life.

Over this chasm of A-round death, fast iteration and constant pivoting separates the leaders from the followers. In the words of Steve Jobs, "Innovation distinguishes between a leader and a follower." The best startups win by fast innovation; we all know what happens to the followers.

The problem facing all of these survivors is that there are not enough "A-round ramps" on the other bank of the river to receive all these new gazelles. They all think they are destined for greatness. Only the top stars will be able to leap over the rest of the herd to safety in the ranks of the few A-round investors who still have dry powder to fund new startups.

These survivors are nurtured and supported with A-round funding, recruitment, and networking, and as long as they continue to scale on the hockey stick they can quickly join the ranks of legends like Groupon and eBay, which are the two fastest growth companies in history. If they fail to deliver, they will not receive the coveted B round and may be even abandoned, as less and less capital is available to fund fewer success stories at ever-higher valuations.

The "Startup Cambrian Explosion" is everything we experienced in the 2000 bubble, only 10 times bigger in absolute numbers. Natural selection now works much faster and in a much more brutal way. New startups die within months, and their teams scatter to help others bat for the fences with new ideas. It is not uncommon to meet twenty-something coders who have already been on the teams of 5 or even 10 startups.

I continue to learn new lessons in this new boom. As both a founder and an angel investor in more than 50 companies, I can say that it is harder than ever to figure out which companies will make it and what is a good investment at any stage of the game. But it is a fascinating game, which I love.

We'll discuss later how to find and close angels. You need them. A quick tip to first-time entrepreneurs: stop thinking about VCs and focus on angels; that's where your startup starts up.

ACCELERATORS

In the 1970s, kids went to India or took a gap year traveling in Europe or skiing to find themselves. Now they join accelerators. The growth of accelerators in recent years and months is an interesting shift in the acceleration of startup launches. Initially my view was that an accelerator was a good place to go if you were a first-time entrepreneur or challenged to raise funding. I have changed my view. Now if you are graduating from a high-profile accelerator, you can expect to close funding quickly and command a relatively high valuation. In brief, accelerators are a bit like incubators, but with more of a university program format with bigger advisory boards of mentors. Many folks use the terms *accelerator* and *incubator* interchangeably, but there is a key difference. Incubators are places where multiple startups rent office space and have access to some shared or à la carte services. These companies benefit from the symbiosis and energy of being around other startups and bumping into investors, developers, and other relevant people. Incubators encourage their "tenants" to keep renting office space; so it is more of a longterm location of the startup compared to most accelerators. Many incubators are industry agnostic while some of the best have a common theme like medical devices, fintech, edtech, or mobile apps so that the synergies are maximized. Accelerators by contrast typically have 3-month programs and then move onto the next class of startups. This is part of the "sense of urgency" culture pushing accelerator startups to move quickly and focus on speed. Graduating from an accelerator and moving into an incubator makes sense for some startups.

The basic format of the typical accelerator is that entrepreneurs at very early stage startups apply to one or more accelerator and, if accepted (a bit like applying to the Harvard MBA program), they spend three months going every day to the accelerator, basically running through the accelerator's program. The startups typically get a small amount of funding, ranging from

$15,000 to $150,000, giving up something like 5 to 15 percent of their equity. Most startups that get into the top accelerators end up selling equity to the accelerator at a much lower valuation not to get the cash funding, but to gain the other value delivered by the accelerator. So unlike the incubators which are really shared workspaces or real-estate plays that encourage startups to stay and pay rent, the accelerators are motivated to be done with the current batch after 3 months and get their slug of discounted equity in a new batch of startups and keep the door revolving.

Most accelerators have a list of 50 if not 200 mentors. These mentors cover different topics of importance to the startups, overseeing the balanced scorecard of disciplines needed to launch and grow a successful business. Mentors are not typically paid, but want to help and be part of the ecosystem. Sometimes a mentor may take a personal interest and negotiate some equity for advisory services. Other advisors may make a direct angel investment and join the advisory round. This is really magic for the management team from a provincial location like Nashville with the next big music company but no connections. Through the accelerator, startups get a few months to test their idea, get feedback, iterate, and pivot as well as get culturally educated and connected to local mentors who introduce the startup to tons of insider folks.

The objective is that by the time the startup completes the accelerator program, it is already well positioned to raise angel funding from well-connected angels and to position itself for VC funding. For some who decide not to pursue their startup, the accelerator experience may have saved them from sinking more time, money, and personal reputation into a bad company. At accelerators speed is key. Along the way, the startup gets an education like a mini startup MBA and its strategy is reviewed and improved with the help of some of the most successful entrepreneurs. The experience is like living in a hippie commune, but a startup commune where everyone wants to be Steve Jobs or thinks he or she already is.

We are now seeing the emergence of accelerators in every major tech corridor in the United States, Europe, Asia-Pacific, and Latin America, many only established within the last 36 months, with more on the way. Serial entrepreneurs I know are setting up new accelerators everywhere.

When considering joining a new accelerator, find out what percentage of past companies have gone on to raise significant angel or VC funding, and also take a close look at the mentors supporting the accelerator. With so many tier two and tier three accelerators popping up, many may be bad deals for the founders that join them. I've heard VCs refer to some accelerators as "the blind leading the blind."

The most famous and probably best accelerator is Y Combinator, based in the Silicon Valley. For a while every Y Combinator (YC) company received $150k automatic funding from Ron Conway and Yuri Milner on a convertible note with no cap. I went to the Y Combinator demo day a few weeks ago where 79 companies in the current batch pitched for funding. Almost every company showed a chart of how there first revenues began within a week of starting the program and grew by 25 to 50 percent each week during the 12 week program. This showed me that accelerators like YC are no longer about helping the startup find its strategy, make the initial Minimal Viable Product (MVP) and learn about fundraising, but that YC requires that 90 percent of the startups they accept be at the point of launching a revenue generating product. With that many applicants and the ability of YC to get a big slug of cheap equity, they may as well admit companies they know will be valuable. Showing investors startups that have very high revenue growth is more attractive than investing in the stock market. It shows that some of these accelerators are growth machines rather than incubating risky innovation. A few weeks after the demo day I could see most of these YC graduates completed their funding rounds ranging from $500k to $3m+ at valuations on the high end of the spectrum. Getting into these top accelerators makes more sense to me now than it did just three years ago.

TechStars and the Rise of Accelerators

The other famous accelerator, which some folks argue is even better than Y Combinator, is TechStars. David Cohen, founder and CEO of TechStars tells the story:

Andrew asked me to tell the story of TechStars, so here it is. After founding three companies in Boulder, Colorado, I saw an opportunity to innovate on the classic model of angel investing. The true genesis of TechStars occurred when I realized that I loved angel investing, but I thought that the way angel investing worked kind of sucked. I also cared quite a bit about my hometown of Boulder, Colorado, and soon realized that this passion for building startup communities could translate to other places. The core thesis at the birth of TechStars was to simultaneously bring together potentially interesting companies with a filtering mechanism, leverage the entrepreneurial community behind these companies for a threemonth period, and then decide whether to invest further. In 2006 I took the idea to a friend of mine, Brad Feld, with whom I had made numerous angel investments, and Brad's response was "We had a random meeting, and in 15 minutes I was totally in love with the idea." So Brad helped cofound TechStars from day one along with David Brown, the cofounder and president of Zoll Data Systems, and Jared Polis, the founder of BlueMountain and ProFlowers. We combined our contact networks and recruited 70 prominent web entrepreneurs, venture capitalists, and CEOs to provide mentoring. We launched our first class in 2007 with 10 companies. Two of these were acquired in the same year, and this fueled our growth to Boston in 2009, and with the continued success of our model, we launched Seattle in 2010 and soon thereafter in New York City, San Antonio, Texas, and most recently London.

Part of the premise is that not all entrepreneurs want to move to Silicon Valley. I believe great entrepreneurs are everywhere, and the ecosystem model we provide enables them to flourish closer to where they are. The ecosystems in these cities are strong and continuing to grow, and to overlook them would seem to be silly. At the core of what we do is filtering the companies that get into our programs, and then, once they are selected, we commit to making those companies successful. Less than 1 percent of applicants are accepted. In particular, of the 1,700 applicants to the TechStars' New York Spring 2012 program, 12 were selected.

Here's what we do. TechStars provides each company with free office space and $18,000 in exchange for a 6 percent stake in the company. In addition, a syndicate of more than 75 top venture capitalists backs each company with a $100,000 convertible note, which converts into equity when the company raises a series A. One of TechStars' goals is to improve the entrepreneurial ecosystems in the cities where we operate. There are between 50 and 100 mentors in each city for 10 to 15 companies in each class.

In the first month, the founders engage the mentors and receive feedback on their product or service. The goal of the first month is to orient the team in the correct direction. I like to say that we're trying to get the car pointed in the right direction before stepping on the gas. This is when many companies pivot their focus, market strategy, or idea. In the second month, founders work with their mentors on specific issues like customer interaction, partner opportunities, and product development. In the third month, founders develop a plan for action after TechStars, which includes fund-raising, pitching investors, launching the product, or developing a company strategy.

At the end of the 13-week program, we host "TechStars' Demo Day," which can draw over 500 investors, entrepreneurs, and journalists giving our companies a boost into the world.

You hear about unemployment reaching epic proportions here and there. Rather than look for a job, I would advise young entrepreneurs to join an accelerator, fail perhaps, and get recruited into the deal that works. You might get into the next big thing before the angel round, and just as with an MBA, you are developing an important business contact network. If you consider that there are 79 companies in the YC batch then participating almost guarantees you will become buddies with the CEO and cofounders of a few of the next big high growth tech companies. That in itself should justify spending three months in Silicon Valley.

From the perspective of local governments anywhere in provincial parts of the developed world or developing economies, when you provide funding to an accelerator, you are not just making a cash-on-cash investment, but you are enabling the education of armies of entrepreneurs that are creating the foundation of your future innovation economy. It is not just about how the first 10 startups from a class of an Antwerp accelerator will do, but rather the creation of a population of strong entrepreneurs that may fail once or twice before they hit their first big success. Entrepreneurship needs entrepreneurs more than any of the other ingredients. When I first started doing business with European VCs, it struck me that none of these VCs had entrepreneurial experience themselves. Investing in these accelerators is creating an army of entrepreneurs that will proliferate into the investing side, as well as corporates that will benefit from this training of entrepreneurial skills and culture. Combined with the formula of assembling mentors in key markets, accelerators accelerate the maturation of specific ecosystems in each of these geographies.

The big difference between Silicon Valley and some other markets I have worked in is that the quality of entrepreneurs and investors in Silicon Valley is unmatched. Accelerators like Dave Knox's The Brandery are putting Cincinnati, Ohio, on the map and fostering a lasting startup community in that market with a growing population of educated entrepreneurs. Of the 2,000 accelerators to spring up in the last few years, The Brandery doing great in an unexpected location is just one example of many doing the same. Good accelerators are launching everywhere.

You can now apply to more than one accelerator with a single application at http://gan.co/. Also check out http://ww.f6s.com.

A hilarious and ingenious crack speed version of an accelerator is StartUp Bus. I met its founder, Eoin McMillan, at a VC party in San Francisco. StartUp Bus rotates around SXSW, which is a major startup conference in Austin, Texas. SXSW attracts literally thousands of creative startups launching new companies and products there every year in March. StartUp Bus (http://startupbus.com/) launches buses packed with entrepreneurs from 10 different cities around the country, including San Francisco, New York,

Chicago, and Boston, as well as Mexico City. Each entrepreneur pays $299 for a ticket on the bus, and by the time the bus arrives at SXSW in Austin, each bus must conceive of a new idea and launch a new business. The bus has Wi-Fi and power, and the "buspreneurs" are brainstorming and coding during the drive to Austin.

The cost of my flight from San Francisco to Austin this year was more than $299, so if nothing else StartUp Bus is a low-cost way of getting to SXSW. There are actually events and even services for founders to meet each other to cofound a company. If you are a young entrepreneur, this might be a good way to meet another buspreneur, to become wholly committed to your startup idea, or at least to develop some new local relationships. Part of StartUp Bus's value, as with an accelerator, is the screening of applicants done by Eoin and his partners.

ONLINE FUNDING RESOURCES

Until a few years ago, I did not think much of online funding websites, but I would now advise most entrepreneurs and angels to take the time to put a profile on AngelList (http://angel.co/). I'm sure there are other regional sites like these in other geographies. The good sites help you network to folks you know and the contacts of your contacts. Learning how to persuade your friends to forward your profile to their friends and be noticed is becoming an art. If you can bring more investors or buyers to the table, then it's worth some of your time. Depending on what your business objectives are, you may be socializing your deal not only with possible investors, but also with prospective employees, suppliers, users, customers, and partners.

CROWDFUNDING: EVERYTHING YOU ALWAYS WANTED TO KNOW BUT WERE AFRAID TO ASK

The crowdfunding space is unfolding as I write and promises to be a game changer. Crowdfunding is not really a new idea. Raising funding for the Statue of Liberty in New York City was one of the biggest crowdfunding transactions in history. The people of France gave the statue itself as a gift to the U.S. ambassador to France, but lack of funds delayed the building of the pedestal. Fund-raising efforts came to an impasse until Joseph Pulitzer, publisher of *The World* newspaper and noted for the Pulitzer Prize, leveraged his newspaper to ask Americans to donate. Mr. Pulitzer used his newspaper to access millions of readers and solicited donations to fund the construction of the pedestal. Over 120,000 individual donations, averaging 85 cents each, raised the funding needed to build the pedestal. The funding campaign took five months to complete. Today, the Internet serves the function that the newspaper served in 1884. Crowdfunding is nothing new in this context, just another example of using the Internet to do online what is done in the real world offline.

Howard Leonhardt, founder of Leonhardt Ventures, The California Stock Exchange, and CalXStarts, had this to say about crowdfunding:

> We are about to experience the grandest expression of human creativity and economic growth ever seen in the history of human civilization. Crowdfunding and peer-to-peer microloans are human will expressed in pure form. A person with a vision becomes a dream funded on a mission. It is the explosive combination of democracy and free market capitalism. It allows new ideas to get funded and to be free market tested at a lower cost, with less complexity, in less time than ever before. Experimentation has now become possible for millions that were previously excluded from having any chance for their idea to be tried. Experimentation is the lifeblood of innovation, and innovation is the engine of sustainable job creation. I am confident that this simple breakthrough socioeconomic tool is about to herald in mankind's greatest era.

Equity investment crowdfunding has been in the making since at least the year 2000 but became a legal reality on April 5, 2012, when President Obama signed the JOBS Act into law. The crowdfunding sections of the JOBS Act authorize online "funding portals" or broker/dealers to offer crowdfunding investment opportunities of up to $1 million per year per company raising investment. Investments will be limited to between $2,000 and 10 percent of the investor's annual income, depending on the investor's net worth or annual income. Although Obama shot the starting gun on April 5, all equity-based crowdfunding websites and organizations must be registered with the Securities and Exchange Commission (SEC) and comply with the regulations, which are only now being drafted and were meant to be released in early 2013. While the crowdfunding sections of the JOBS Act gave the SEC 270 days from April 5, 2012, to draft their rules, delays slipped into 2013, and eventually came out with specific guidelines for compliance with the 506(c) offerings. Most entrepreneurs and VCs find the new rules to be more burdensome than the value of going into general solicitation to the public. Further FINRA rule making following the SEC's final rules have clouded the progress of crowdfunding and I personally continue to sit on the sidelines to avoid complications with FINRA and the SEC.

The SEC has been motivated to come up with some rules to protect naive investors from being taken advantage of by con artists gaming the system. It is pretty easy to imagine someone in Miami coming up with a business pitch every week that raises a few thousand dollars, goes bust, and the founder keeps the company car and company yacht. Imagine this con artist going from one crowdfunding website to another, recruiting new accomplices to be the listed CEOs to avoid being caught as a serial failure. Crowdfunding companies want to figure out how to stop that from happening. They are keen to put in place barriers to entry and carve out market verticals for themselves. We will see some crowdfunding sites focus on a single niche like charity, film projects, high-tech startups, individuals' university education, large art projects, or a poets' and painters' pilgrimage to India.

While equity investment crowdfunding is most relevant here, it is worth noting that there are other types of crowdfunding platforms that specialize in different crowdfunding transactions. These fall into four main categories:

- Donation-based
- Rewards-based

- Lending-based
- Equity-based

Each of these types of crowdfunding platforms uses a different approach, but in general people or startups can list their cause, product, or investment opportunity on one of these platforms, leverage their social networks to make some noise and get attention and raise small amounts of funding from many people.

Massolution, a crowdfunding research company, conducted a survey and found that as of April 2012, there were 452 crowdfunding platforms (CFPs) active worldwide. Massolution projects that number could reach 530 CFPs by the end of 2012. North America was the largest market, raising $837 million in 2011. Globally over 1 million campaigns raised nearly $1.5 billion in 2011 (see Figure 2.1 below). A senior executive at Kickstarter told me that they do not believe these numbers are accurate, considering that Kickstarter raised only $100 million of funding in 2011. Kickstarter concluded that these Massolution numbers must include microfinance and other forms of fund-raising that they do not consider crowdfunding. Kickstarter also explained that they do not do equity crowdfunding and that 95 percent of their projects are creative artistic projects such as music and art rather than tech. Note that much of the $100 million number Kickstarter is quoting is pledged but not yet paid out. Despite regulators taking their time to come

Figure 2.1 Growth in Worldwide Crowdfunding 2009–2012, in Millions of Dollars

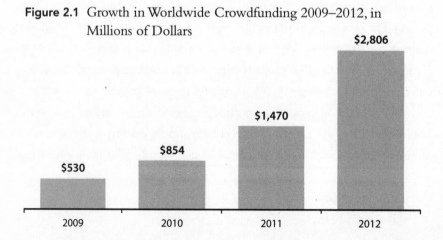

up with regulations for equity-based crowdfunding, this data shows the significance of this new model for fund-raising.

Equity-based crowdfunding is a small cross section of the bigger picture. Rewards-based is even smaller, while roughly half of crowdfunding is donation-based, with another 40 percent being lending-based. Figure 2.2 shows funding by category.

Over $1.5 billion was raised in 2011 via crowdfunding; that number was expected to double in 2012. As a single platform, Indiegogo has funded over 60,000 projects. While investment crowdfunding is still a very small slice of the pie, the potential addressable market is huge.

For example, Fred Wilson from Union Square Ventures points out that if every American family were to put just 1 percent of their investments in crowdfunding, this would bring $300 billion into the venture asset class and blow out VCs, illustrating the potential for crowdfunding to be a game changer. I believe VCs should not feel threatened by this, but instead leverage the trend. VCs might put down 10 percent of the risk capital for a new deal and let 90 percent be shouldered by the crowdfunding unwashed masses.

Figure 2.2 Funding in Millions of Dollars by Category

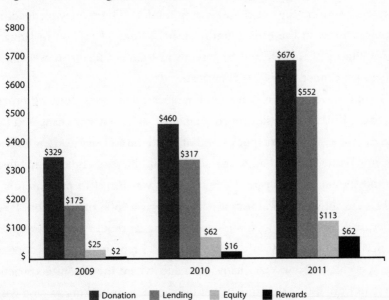

VCs would also be smart to follow the leading trendsetters rising to the top of the crowdfunding platforms as a measure of user validation. Then, when the company is ready for proper $5 million–plus VC funding, the VC is there, incumbent in the deal. In this hypothesis, the fact that the VC would lead the deal would give the crowd confidence to follow the branded VC into the crowdfunding/angel round. This is all good for entrepreneurs, VCs, and angels.

Seeing the game changing rapidly, several hundred reward-based crowdfunding platforms have been launched in recent months to prepare for the changes likely to come from the JOBS Act. Separate from investment crowdfunding, reward-based crowdfunding campaigns are like those found on Crowdfunder, where the investor receives a tangible item or service in return for his or her funds. For example, if your startup wants to raise $500,000 to produce a great new widget, you put a profile and video on Crowdfunder and, if enough people pledge to buy your widget (the promised reward) and the target amount has been raised, then the cash is transferred to the startup. The new company makes the widget and distributes the promised products—the rewards.

Kickstarter was founded in 2009 and is growing nicely. They have raised $380 million for 70,000 projects, giving their projects a 43 percent success rate of meeting the target and raising funding. The money pledged on Kickstarter grew in the early months of 2012 from $4 million in January to $5 million in February and $7 million in March. Indiegogo as a single platform has funded over 60,000 projects.

Beyond rewards-based crowdfunding, investment crowdfunding provisions of the JOBS Act are slow in coming. That said, a few key changes in the JOBS Act took effect more quickly and updated the archaic laws that limited what entrepreneurs could do to raise funding in the past. These are in effect now and should be understood. Previously it was illegal to promote one's angel or VC funding round (often referred to as a "506 offering" or "Reg. D offering") too broadly as doing so would trigger requirements to register the offering with the SEC at considerable cost. I remember participating at funding events in New York many years ago where the organizers strictly forbade us from listing the amount of funding we were seeking to raise with over 500 live investors sitting in the audience. Now there are no restrictions on promoting your 506 offering and conducting general solicitation. There is no longer the limit of 500 shareholders before a company must file IPO reporting with the SEC. This has now been expanded to 2,000 shareholders, and crowdfunding investors will not count toward that number.

This may change when the new regulations have been announced, but it appears that investors making direct investments without the crowdfunding websites must still be accredited investors. The definition of an accredited investor in the United States as listed on the SEC website at the time of this writing is the same now as it was in the 1990s when I was first raising angel funding. Individuals must have a net worth (excluding equity in a primary residence) of $1 million or more or $200,000 of annual income (or $300,000 jointly with a spouse). Depending on the type or stage of the company, different offerings targeted at the accredited investor or unaccredited investor community may be most appropriate. Or as my old friend from London, Tony Fish, explained to me when giving me an update on the crowdfunding scene in the United Kingdom, the user just lies, clicking that he or she meets the criteria of an accredited investor, but no one verifies these claims. Tony is the cofounder of Innovation Warehouse, a shared workspace in East London, and the cofounder of hot startup iNeed, which recently raised funding from a crowdfunding portal.

In either case, more companies will get funded, and we will see more startups launch. The failure rate of startups will remain high, but some of these will get traction and provide better deal flow for classic angels and VCs. Clearly this is good news for entrepreneurs, sophisticated angels, and VCs, although it will be bad news for some naive retail investors. Crowdfunding investors will have some rights to get their cash back if they prove that the entrepreneur misrepresented the opportunity; some investors will lose their investment if the company fails despite its best honest efforts. Hopefully this does not lead to increased litigation risks for the startups involved.

From my perspective, crowdfunding is a wonderful development and will result in many folks finding the seed funding necessary to take the entrepreneurial plunge. I wish all crowdfunding companies the best of luck and hope the SEC does a good job both regulating and stimulating this incredibly important industry.

Practical Ideas and Advice on Raising Angel Funding

Unless you seed fund your business with your own savings or from another business you control that is generating cash, you will first need to raise some funding from angels before you even start talking to VCs. Or, as Mitt Romney said, "borrow money if you have to from your parents to start a business."

So how can you raise angel funding?

First come up with the basic amount of funding you need. Even if you calculate that you need $15 million in funding to bring your business to profitability, you need to come up with an amount for your initial angel round that is realistic within the market. Asking to raise $10 million in a seed round is unrealistic for most mortal entrepreneurs. In the Silicon Valley and New York City, the most common amount of angel funding that entrepreneurs seek is $500,000, $750,000, or $1.5 million. This often will only fund the business for nine months. I personally like to see companies get an initial runway of 18 months, but it is hard to get that much cash put at risk when a startup is still an unproven idea with just a lot of potential. Entrepreneurs are also motivated to not sell too much equity at a low valuation; so they often shorten the runway a current funding round will last as they seek to deploy funding growing the value of their companies and raise more funding at higher valuations minimizing their dilution.

A former VC turned very successful CEO was walking me through his capital history, and in his case his firm raised $500,000 every six months for two years, bringing in a total of $2.2 million before closing a series A with VC firm BlueRun Ventures where he was previously a partner. This demonstrates not putting too much capital at risk until the money is needed and the company continues to prove its investment thesis.

Companies raise funding over multiple rounds. The first money into the company just brings it to the next level where the company begins to increase in value. Then, when it has been proven that the product works or that there is a demand for this product or service, it makes sense to put more money at risk to help the company grow into a real business. This is often referred to as the startup demonstrating "product market fit" and then raising more funding to "scale."

Biotech is a good analog for what is really the same thing in the information technology (IT) world. If someone comes up with a new idea for a molecule that might eventually be the drug that cures cancer, Alzheimer's, or AIDS, the total cost to develop that drug and bring it to market could be $100 million to $1 billion. It would not make sense to invest the full $100 million in the first investment round, only to find out that the drug failed to test well on rats. If it does not test well on animals, then there is no reason to test it on humans. These companies raise just enough capital to run the first tests. If they get good data from these first trials, they raise enough money for the next tests and phase of work.

In the world of IT, raising a $500,000 angel round is often enough money to get some development work done or launch a website or mobile app and see if it can acquire users. Some very experienced or just super dynamic entrepreneurs raise large angel rounds that compete with VCs, and some of these entrepreneurs raise huge angel rounds and leapfrog VCs altogether. Serial entrepreneurs that have been successful in the past can pool together $2 million, $5 million, or even $10 million angel rounds, but this is extremely rare.

Expect to raise $500,000 to $750,000 on your first round. Don't be afraid to raise $1.5 million or $2.5 million if that's what you really need to get going, but realize that's on the chunky side of angel rounds. On the one had the cost of launching a startup has come down radically since the late 1990's, but on the other hand VCs and even top accelerators have moved into later stage investing seeking companies with strong customer revenue or other key metrics of traction. The cost of hiring developers in the Valley and New York has also increased to the point that startups need more funding before they can truly close the classic $3m to $10m series A VC financing. This means entrepreneurs need to be prepared to raise more total amounts of funding before closing VC rounds.

How to Recruit and Negotiate with Advisors

Forming a board of advisors means you can put the members on your website and into your pitch. No need to provide director and officer insurance as required for your board of directors. A board of advisors is easy, and no one needs to worry. You can also drop members from your board of advisors if it's not working. Let them know they can step down anytime they like.

My first advice is to insist that the advisor put some cash into the angel round. Advisors have more credibility if they invest personally when seeking investment from others. The amount doesn't matter. Just have the advisors put in something like $5,000 or $15,000 so that they can say to other investors that they personally invested. You can then frame your deal that you have already closed an "advisory round" with reputable folks and are now seeking to complete the round with another X amount of dollars.

Convertible Note Versus Priced Round

There are two typical ways of structuring angel rounds. The most commonly used method in the Silicon Valley, New York City, London, and most other tech corridors is the convertible note. The second choice is to sell equity in a priced round. Most sophisticated investors such as micro-VCs or super angels prefer to invest via a priced round rather than a convertible note, but can often be dragged into a convertible note financing. At Rubicon Venture Capital we do both. The key moving parts of the note are the cap, discount rate, and interest rate. What happens if the company is acquired prior to a priced round is a fourth important element we pay attention to. I call this the conversion feature.

If an angel invests $50,000 as part of a $500,000 angel round, the money is wired from the angel to the startup's bank account and both parties sign the convertible note. The document states that the angel has lent the $50,000 to the startup as a loan to be repaid with some interest rate ranging from a nominal rate to 15 percent within one or two years. This interest is not repaid to the angel but is just added to the principle that gets converted to equity at the time of the priced round. I prefer the interest rate to look like inflation of 4 to 6 percent. The interest rate rewards angels for how much earlier they invested before the triggering priced round valuation. The document also states that if the company raises an equity or priced financing round within the specified time of one to two years, the loan or debt will convert to equity, typically at a discount to the valuation of the equity financing round or a capped price.

Typically in the Valley, angels form a syndicate to deposit a total of $500,000 or more into the company's bank account on a convertible note with a discount rate of 20 to 35 percent and a cap of $3 to $5 million. Discount rates of 20 and 30 percent are most common. I think 30 percent shows the startup is trying to make the financing attractive to angels and that is a good idea to help close your round and get cash in the door.

Part of the beauty of the angel syndicate is that the entrepreneur does not get into a valuation discussion with each angel. Everyone will convert at the same valuation, which will be fixed by the valuation the professional VCs invest at, which is a valuation accepted by the board typically still dominated by the founders at the time of closing.

Typical individual angel investments range from $25,000 to $250,000 per person. Sometimes larger rounds have folks writing bigger checks, but $50,000 per person is very common. Many entrepreneurs set a minimum investment size, such as $50,000 per person, to avoid months of meetings and conversations to reach the $500,000 target.

Sometimes the first investor to wire funds may be nervous and ask to see a list of other committed angels. Consequently, in some cases it is best practice to have an escrow letter to go along with the convertible note, which states that until a specific amount of cash has been raised, the entrepreneurs cannot touch the money. The specified amount of funding to be raised before the entrepreneurs can touch the cash might be the full target amount of $500,000 or some lower number, such as $300,000. There is also a longstop date in these escrow letters so that the team has until a specific date before they need to return the funds raised if they fall short of the target amount in the escrow letter. You need to be sensible about the longstop date being more than a realistic time frame to raise the minimum amount to trigger the cash out of escrow, but you must have a backup plan to close if you come up short. Only offer this if you must to secure investors' cash before they invest it into another opportunity.

If an angel invested $100,000 of his or her own personal savings into a $500,000 angel round and then 6 to 12 months later the company closed a $5 million series A round with a VC, then the $500,000 of debt would convert to equity with a specific discount to that series A round. If the VCs purchased a third of the stock in the company for an investment of $5 million and there was a discount rate of 30 percent, then the person investing $100,000 would get stock equal to $130,000 compared to what the VC got for $130,000. But when you consider that the VC put in $5 million, the angel has been pretty well crushed down to a relatively small ownership position.

There is also a risk that the startup will do so well with the angel round closed that it will get millions of downloads and start to grow faster than Twitter, and when the VC round happens the pre-money valuation may be $100 million. Then when the angel's debt converts to equity he or she will get totally washed out and own a tiny fraction of the company despite having taken the big risk. Often when the angel is sitting in Starbucks or Peet's Coffee with the founders, the angel is imagining if this goes well it could be the next Facebook. The angel is actually scared about too much early success.

To accommodate these concerns, I suggest hot-wiring a cap into the convertible note. A cap is a ceiling on the valuation at which the angel round of debt will convert to equity. I think a cap of $1.5 million to $5 million is fair. This guarantees that the angel will own a minimum amount of equity at the time that the equity-financing round closes. Not to offer the angel a cap is to assume no risk on the side of the entrepreneur and to put a lot of risk on the angel investor. In recent years, however, it has become more and more common not to have a cap. This is possible when a big angel like Ron Conway offers to invest with a tiny discount rate or no cap. It can also happen when the startup is so hot that the angels all feel lucky and privileged to be invited to participate and get some cash into the deal; they just think they can't lose by getting in before the VCs. No cap on a convertible note is a big mistake in my view. If an angel invests in a note with no cap and then makes introductions to the CEO to get on TV for example and then the business takes off, the angel actually diluted herself as a result of helping the company. So if an angel adds value and increases the valuation after having invested without a cap then she hurts herself for having added value. You can see why smart money only invests at a fixed valuation or specified cap and then adds as much value as possible growing the valuation of the next round. For this reason we at Rubicon Venture Capital would NEVER invest in a convertible note without a cap—never. Always put a cap into your note and encourage your investors to help you quickly grow the value of your business.

When I look at the VC coming in months or years after the angel investors, when the management team is more fully populated, the product is working and has been launched, and customers are paying for the product or service, the increased risk taken by the angels seems a lot more than 30 percent to me. When I see the difference in risk, it makes me think I would be better off investing my cash into the VC who lets the angels take all the early risk and comes in when the startup is much less risky. At Rubicon Venture Capital we often choose to pass on the angel round and wait to invest in the series A financing, because the terms of the angel financing fail to provide us with any motivation to invest early. I'd just rather pay 30% or 20% more and come in at the series A and when I see the founder offering lower terms I just feel foolish investing before the series A.

I don't want to spoil the party of entrepreneurs closing their rounds with no discount rate, no cap, and negligible interest rates, but I think founders should appreciate that the angel is taking a huge risk and adding massive value in cases where the angels become active advisors, recruit partners and board members, and make the introductions to the VCs. Investing in the VC series A or B round, in my view, is the optimal point in the risk/return spectrum for making exceptional 100-times-plus returns. Remember, it is very competitive for any single VC to win those deals.

If your lead angels don't want to do a convertible note, then forget the note and do an equity round. I recently met a new micro-VC seeking to make Ron Conway–style investments in the initial seed round of companies, but specifically staying away from the Valley and New York City, where they think the angel terms are all convertible notes with high caps. Their model is to do priced rounds every time leading angel syndicates and avoid this dynamic of getting crushed by the series A.

The angels should get a fair deal for their investment and hopefully bring consultative value to the company; so if they prefer to take an equity position in the company and they are investing enough cash to justify dropping the note, then you should do it. You can also offer an angel warrant coverage as a kicker on top of the convertible note to pull them across the finish line and be more magnanimous. Warrants are like stock options where a nonemployee has an option to buy equity at a fixed (attractive) price. The legal cost of doing an equity financing is a bit higher, but these are very boilerplate documents, and if you go with a top law firm, it will often defer you paying legal fees until you get to the VCs.

The angels' investment into the convertible note converts to equity at the lower of (a.) the cap specified in the convertible note if that value is lower than the pre-money valuation set by the VCs, e.g., a $3 million cap if the VCs invest at a pre-money valuation of $5 million or (b.) the specified discount to the pre-money valuation set by the VCs, if that pre is lower than the cap. This guarantees the angels' money is rewarded for investing before the VCs. In summary, a covertible note can be super simple and convert at the same terms as the priced round (typically led by VCs) or build in a cap, discount rate, and/or interest rate.

VALUATION RANGES FOR PRE-MONEY CAPS ON SEED-STAGE CONVERTIBLE NOTE FINANCINGS

John Bautista, partner at Orrick, gives his view on valuation ranges for pre-money caps on seed-stage convertible note financings:

For companies raising money for the first time, and doing so under a convertible note structure, I am seeing valuations ranging from $1.5 million at the low end to $5 million at the high end, with $3 million being the midpoint for most deals. This is the pre-money valuation that is included in the convertible note as the cap on valuation determined at the time of conversion into preferred stock. Also, I am starting to see convertible notes at multiple valuation caps. That is, the company first raises money on a convertible note with a lower valuation cap for the first money in (such as $2.5 million pre) and as the company deploys the capital and builds value, then completing a second convertible note round at a higher valuation (such as $4 million pre). This flexibility is one of the benefits of convertible notes. You can raise money at incrementally higher valuations as you build value, resulting in less dilution to the founders. Let's see how mainstream this becomes because it is certainly an efficient way to raise capital.

DON'T RAISE ANGEL FUNDING AT TOO HIGH A VALUATION

One mistake entrepreneurs can make is raising angel funding at too high a valuation. Sometimes I see an entrepreneur who talked his friends, family, and a few angels into buying stock in his company at a super-high valuation. It sounds good that the entrepreneur avoided getting badly diluted at this early stage, but if I introduce that CEO to VCs and they want to invest $5 million at a pre-money valuation of $10 million, the CEO will need to explain to his angels that the value of their investment has fallen by 10 times. And by the way, the VCs are putting down strict terms that give their shares special preferences and privileges. Ideally, each round should show an uptick in valuation, and the pre-money of the next round should be higher than the post-money of the last round. Of course, that's an ideal world. The real world is full of flat and down rounds.

RAISING ANGEL FUNDING

The most likely angels to invest in your company are people that know and respect you. I think it is a worthwhile exercise to make a list of potential angels, starting with your early childhood, and think of where you lived, where you went on vacations, who were your friends, the friends of your parents and siblings, etc. Write down the name of anyone that you think has means. Then go through where you went to school and each place you worked. This will help trigger memories of the wealthy people with whom you have come into contact. Then track them down on LinkedIn and Facebook and, when you go into solicitation for funding, contact them asking them if they know anyone who would be interested in investing. I think it is best not to ask these personal contacts directly to invest in your company, but ask if they know anyone that might invest or even knows your sector and could be an advisor. Many of these people will want to help you. These contacts will help make you as powerful as possible before approaching the purely financial investors. Go for the emotional investors, even your family members. Just make sure that family holidays and get-togethers don't turn into investor relations or board meetings.

Even when this startup plays its course, you may want to keep that list as you may find yourself with another startup that needs angel funding and advisors in the future. I find that a good list takes months or years to develop.

I am a heavy database customer relations management (CRM) power user, so I add all valuable contacts to my database in order to look up angels in a specific country and even search by the sectors they invest in. I think all business-people should use a robust CRM system to organize their Rolodex. Outlook is not good enough for the sophisticated searches you need to perform.

I've heard Ron Conway say he receives five investment opportunities per day, which brings in 30 per week. He then meets with one out of five and invests in two per week. The key point in what he said is that 100 percent of these deals come through people he already knows. This means it is not a good idea to guess his e-mail address and just blast over your executive summary. The correct way to approach him is to be introduced. How can you do that? Go to a lot of networking events and meet a lot of people.

I thought of this when my wife and I were searching for a babysitter. A woman approached her in the park offering to babysit. My wife told me that unless we know someone that knows the babysitter, there's no way we'd leave our kids with her. The same logic applies to angel and VC funding. Schedules get totally filled up. You may as well meet with people that have some filtering on them already.

Often when I meet young entrepreneurs that tell me they raised $500,000 or $1 million of angel funding, I ask them, Where did you meet these angels, and how did you get your deal done? From the Silicon Valley to London, it is typically the same answer—networking events. Sometimes going to a conference is a good way to meet people, too, but these are expensive. If you are keeping your burn rate low, just keep going to free and cheap networking events. It may be frustrating, but meeting one person will lead to another, and that one may give the momentum to get your fund-raising done.

The three most important things in real estate are location, location, and location; in entrepreneurship (a world of pivots), it's management, management, management. Ninety percent of companies will totally shift their strategy at least once. Most companies evolve into something very different from their initial plan. When you invest, you are investing in the team and their integrity. If your investment pivots, you have invested in the team.

STEVE JOBS RATED BY HIS VC

Bob Pavey joined Morgenthaler Ventures in 1969 and has been a partner since 1971. From 1990 to 1992, he served as president and then chairman of the National Venture Capital Association. He was a VC for Steve Jobs. Here are his observations on Steve Jobs as an entrepreneur:

Even before he was the greatest CEO in the country, Steve Jobs showed that he was one of our greatest founding entrepreneurs by "hiring" as his boss and CEO of Apple a truly excellent strategic

leader in Mike Markkula. How many very young first-time founders have that kind of judgment and people skill? The greatest entrepreneurs know what skills they have and what skills they lack . . . and
then they find someone to fill in the holes.

THE TEAM MEANS EVERYTHING

Elton Satusky, a partner at Wilson Sonsini Goodrich & Rosati, is one of the
most active lawyers in the Silicon Valley venture scene and an advisor to The
Founders Club Fund. He related his experience with a good team:

> Everyone knows that the team is important in the Valley, but we did
> one particular deal that really proves that point. The management
> team was very experienced and previously sold a company for $3
> billion. The new company they formed and raised $140 million a
> few years later had absolutely nothing in it, nothing. It only had an
> idea. The money came from a very large syndicate of the bluest of
> blue chip VCs. The idea was that there were a bunch of underper-
> forming, underutilized assets in a number of large corporations in
> a specific area and that with their team's talent and expertise, they
> would be able to get licenses to such assets. The key was that the
> big companies didn't have financial resources or know-how to pur-
> sue the projects. This startup, with nothing but its recent infusion of
> cash, had both of these. It's now a public company.

A BALANCED TEAM

John Montgomery has been a Silicon Valley insider since 1984. He is a leg-
endary lawyer, LP investor in multiple VCs, and author. John is the founder
and chairman of Montgomery & Hansen, former cochairman of the VC
practice at Brobeck, cofounder of Chrysallis, and founder of Startworks. He
is also a friend and an advisor to The Founders Club Fund. Here, John summarizes key ideas from his book, *Great from the Start: How Conscious Corpora-*

tions Attract Success (Morgan James 2012). I recommend it highly as it outlines how to apply the business secrets of Silicon Valley to build a successful corporation conscious of operating in an interdependent economy.

"The best thing you can do for your employees is surround them with fantastic people," says Kip Tindell, cofounder and CEO of The Container Store. Everyone says that it's all about the team, but how can you tell if you have a good one?

Many veteran venture capitalists have a knack for building founding teams that have the right stuff. Gordon Campbell, for example, picked founding teams that shared a common pattern for his mid-1990s Techfarm incubator. He intuitively selected balanced teams and helped them maintain that balance as their companies grew. Understanding what Campbell looked for gives you a framework to assess your team. Let's call them:

The Five Archetypes

Techfarm's portfolio companies usually had three founders of specific, different core archetypes. Three of Techfarms most successful companies: Cobalt Networks, 3Dfx Interactive, and NetMind Technologies, for example, all had three founders: a visionary who saw the company's completed form and knew how to integrate its parts; a technologist with the knowledge and technical skill to translate the vision into a product; and a salesman who matched the product to an unmet customer need. At the concept stage, the visionary was the natural team leader.

The founding trios also shared common *traits*. They were friends who had worked together before. Each was senior enough in his field to see the big opportunity. Each wanted a company based on a sound business model with a clear path to profit. More importantly, the founding teams had the self-confidence and humility to surround themselves with smarter and more experienced people. This combination of archetypes and traits attracted the best employees, customers, vendors and suppliers, consultants, strategic partners, and investors.

The developmental pattern contained *two additional archetypes*: a *money person* and a *mentor*. Each company had an office manager or finance person to provide structure by managing the details. Having someone to ground operations in sound business disciplines freed the visionary, technologist, and salesman to concentrate on building the business. In all companies, Campbell played the role of the fifth archetype, the mentor; he ensured not only the visionary's success but also the success of the entire company. Campbell kept his teams balanced by making sure that they maintained open communication and collaborated freely.

Having all five archetypes present at the beginning is not necessary for a startup to be successful. But Campbell intuitively assessed founding teams for the three core archetypes to determine whether the team was complete. If one of the three core archetypes was missing, the founding team was out of balance, and investing in it was premature.

Venture capitalists like Gordon Campbell are pattern matchers; they compare the founding team of every prospective portfolio company with the developmental pattern of their most successful company. They automatically assess a founding team for archetypal balance. It is critical for an entrepreneur to assess his team and make necessary adjustments to present potential investors with a balanced leadership team. If a company has only a visionary and a technologist, for example, it will probably have trouble connecting its product to customers. Without sales and marketing experience, such an unbalanced, incomplete team will have a lower probability of success. Adding an experienced sales executive will improve the chances of success in both fund-raising and business.

Cobalt's founding team, for example, exhibited Campbell's ideal developmental pattern. Mark Wu was the prime mover, the visionary founding CEO and leader. Vivek Mehra was the brilliant technologist, the founding CTO. Mark Orr was the thoughtful marketing guru, the founding VP of marketing. The three founders had become friends while working together at Apple. They knew one another's strengths, tolerated one another's weaknesses, and had a good sense of humor. They were a natural team. Seniority in their domain helped them see the big, hidden opportunity in the server market. The founders' knowledge about the applicable technology enabled them to seize the opportunity. Campbell augmented the team's strengths with his company-building acumen and served as its mentor. He leveraged his vast contact list to build powerful strategic alliances and expand Cobalt's team with trusted people.

"The core team should be balanced like Cobalt's," says Vivek Mehra, "with a visionary leader, an engineer, and a marketing person. How the team works together is important. The team will grow, but it's best to keep the team small and cross-functional; with three to five people who are not all engineers or all marketing people. Cobalt's founding team was flexible and accepted new people who joined in more senior positions or with more equity. The founders were willing to do what was best for the company by accepting the possibility of playing lesser roles."

3Dfx had a balanced founding team with domain seniority. Gary Tarolli, the CTO, is one of the world's leading authorities on the complex polygonal mathematics at the core of 3Dfx's graphics-rendering engine. Tarolli, then a MIT professor, worked at the bleeding edge of 3D mathematics. With his expertise, 3Dfx had the right technical skills. Gordon Campbell's semiconductor industry experience helped cofounder Scott Sellers translate the vision into products. Campbell led the team as a hands-on executive chairman, and cofounder Ross Q. Smith, in his role as VP of sales and marketing, connected the products to the customers with his endearing Texas drawl.

NetMind also had a balanced founding team. Matt Freivald was the visionary founder who saw the opportunity. Alan Noble was the brilliant engineer who single-handedly coded the complex software necessary to realize Freivald's vision. Mark Richards was the empathetic marketing genius whose natural warmth elicited the authentic customer feedback that enabled Noble to write winning code. NetMind's ability to harness its founders' complementary strengths enabled it to create complex synchronization software with minimal resources. Campbell and his partner Kurt Keilhacker completed the team with their experience building businesses together.

Harnessing the Power of Trust

Gordon Campbell understood the power of trust forged by prior working relationships. He used trust to build a creative, collaborative culture that accomplished great things. Techfarm walked the talk and modeled the fluid teamwork that arises from the familiarity of preexisting trust-based relationships. When Techfarm raised its first venture capital fund, TechFund, in 1997, its team reflected the pattern sought in its portfolio companies—a balanced, senior team that had worked together for years. Campbell was the visionary leader who saw the big picture, designed the investment strategy, and served as the team's mentor. Kurt Keilhacker was the skilled analyst who affirmed Campbell's nose with financial logic. Keilhacker had worked with Campbell since Chips and Technologies and was a trusted partner. Jim Whims was the marketing genius behind the Sony PlayStation, which achieved $1 billion in revenue faster than any consumer product in U.S history. Whims helped connect TechFund's portfolio companies to their customers to drive sales. Koji Morihiro, who was based in Japan, connected TechFund and its portfolio companies with investors and strategic partners in Asia. TechFund also had an office manager and a controller who managed the details. Techfarm's core team evolved over time, but Campbell always maintained the balance among the five archetypes.

Assessing Collective Intelligence

Campbell created a collaborative environment for every group with which he was involved. Once a year he invited the two or three top executives in each portfolio company to his ranch for a weekend retreat. The group warmed up with a fun activity like having a paintball war. There was good food and ample drink, but these gatherings were serious. The collective assembled in the barn, where each company's team solicited solutions to its most pressing problems from the executives of the other companies; they accessed the collective intelligence of the assembled executives to solve their problems. For weeks afterward, the executives were animated with excitement about the business solutions from their peers. These offsites exuded the creative, collaborative spirit of the dynamic cultures of 3Dfx, Cobalt, and NetMind.

Pattern Logic

In the language of the emerging field of social neuroscience, which studies what happens in the brain when people interact, Campbell is a master of social intelligence. Daniel Goleman and Richard Boyatzis define social intelligence as "a set of interpersonal competencies built on specific neural circuits (and related endocrine systems) that inspire others to be effective." Neurobiology has identified a phenomenon called *mood contagion*, whereby a leader's positive behaviors literally trigger corresponding chemical changes in followers' brains that cause similar positive moods. On a neurological level, Campbell infected his companies with confidence. His mentees replicated their mentorships' basis of trust throughout their companies to create environments that promoted optimal brain function.

By intuitively selecting founding teams with a visionary, a technologist, and a salesman with established relationships, Techfarm's companies spent less time in fight-or-flight reactivity and more time enjoying the challenge of realizing their visions. Having whole-brain cultures that celebrated the diversity of perspectives provided by the logic of the technologist, the emotional intelligence of the salesman, and the intuition of the visionary encouraged people to remain in the frontal cortex to solve problems together rather than trigger the defensive regions of the brain like the amygdala and limbic system to engage in conflict.

Social neuroscientists are beginning to understand how the neurons in our individual brains function to form a single system out of a group of people. Scientists have recently discovered several kinds of neurons that play a significant role in organizational behavior. Mirror neurons are the brain's "monkey-see-monkey-do" cells that cause us to recognize others' behaviors and intuitively reproduce them in our own actions. From a neurological standpoint, most leaders unwittingly rely on mirror neurons to create their corporate cultures when they expect the company's core values to be deduced from their own behavior. Because mirror neurons operate on a subcognitive level, the result is a culture that is experienced only subconsciously. As an experienced executive, Campbell was able to help the chief executive officers of his portfolio companies maintain the balance to optimize collaboration and creativity. Simply put, his social intelligence enabled him to organize the people in each company so that they operated collectively and effectively as a single system.

On a fundamental level, Campbell's consistent approach to building balanced teams allowed the culture to become visible at a cognitive level. Campbell's behavior created powerful alignment because the mirror and cognitive brain neurons of the executives in his portfolio companies fired complementarily. His approach created positive neural pathways in his followers' brains that were reinforced by mirror neurons.

Scientists have also found another class of neurons called spindle neurons that seems to be the agent of intuition. *Spindle neurons* are large cells with thousands of connections to other neurons that enable quick judgments and optimal decisions. Effective leaders such as Campbell likely rely on their spindle neurons when they intuitively organize people as a team. A basic understanding of neuroscience will help you emulate Campbell's leadership style.

A friend of mine, Renat Khasanshyn, a venture partner at Runa Capital and an angel investor, told me that if he does not see at least one technical founder on a management team, then he is unlikely to want to invest. He recently made the point that if the founding team cannot recruit at least one developer to "invest" his time to get the product going, then that's a bad signal that he should not take the risk.

RECRUIT A FIRST-CLASS TEAM CONTINGENT UPON FUNDING

When I cofounded The Global TeleExchange (GTX) with Phil Anderson, we knew we were young and needed to recruit a first-class senior management team in order to be successful. We did something very clever, which might work for you. We recruited the very top people we could find and signed employment agreements with them that stated their base salary, bonus, and stock options were all contingent upon our company raising a minimum cash equity financing round of $5 million. We also signed a legally binding vendor financing agreement with Lucent Technologies to provide our company with $25 million vendor financing, but again contingent upon a minimum of $5 million equity financing. So when we went in to pitch VCs we had a clean 55-page business plan with a fully populated management team and funding from Lucent, but this all required a minimum of $5 million cash funding from a VC. There was no way a VC would suggest we close the round for $3 million. The employment contracts stated how much notice each manager would need to give his current employers before starting with us. One might argue these employment agreements were not binding, but in my view the fact that all the equity and salary packages were agreed and we had these signed documents was as powerful as walking into a VC with a stack of signed letters of intent (LOIs). We managed to build a team that we could not afford otherwise and with five captains of industry locked in on our management team. This gave our deal powerful momentum.

When you are deciding which company to invest in as an angel or VC, I would advise you to look first at the management, then at the size of the market, and then after these two look at the idea or technology. When you are pitching to investors, keep this in mind. Tom Perkins says that he always read business plans backward where he would first flip to the back and check the numbers in the financial projections to make sure that the numbers were big enough, but not too much of a hockey stick. Then many investors flip to the management team to see if the execution of those numbers is credible, and then if that looks within tolerance they move on to read the executive summary. If someone came into your office with a search technology like Google that was just so much faster than anything else, you would obviously take it seriously. If you ask the investors of Google what made the company so successful they would probably tell you that it was the technology, but behind a superb management team of Larry, Sergei, and Eric.

CHOOSE YOUR INVESTORS WISELY

Some first-time entrepreneurs confuse the financing valuation and the value of their business. Yes, the valuation stated in the corporate securities documents for your transaction is the value of the business, because that is the price someone paid for it, but in reality this is not the price you would sell the entire business for.

Most entrepreneurs will get to a point where they have a term sheet from some big name VC like Sequoia where Mike Moritz is telling you to take a lower valuation to get him on your board and Sequoia behind your deal. You'll then have another offer from a younger VC with a less established fund offering you more money at a higher valuation with less dilution to you. There will be many factors at play, but in general, you probably should take the lower valuation and get Mike Moritz on your side. The quality of your series A VCs will set the tone for your series B, C, and D that are willing to follow the brand you started with.

An analogue here is deciding to get your MBA at Harvard or University of Texas at Austin when UT Austin is offering a full scholarship and Harvard would require taking out student loans. Austin is fun, but if you're going to spend two years of your life doing group projects with other students, I would advise Harvard over Texas. Don't get caught up in valuations and focus on the end game.

BUILDING BLOCKS OF PRE-MONEY VALUATIONS

There are three building blocks that drive valuations: (1) Financial performance including revenues, growth, and earnings; (2) Product/service/distribution; (3) Team.

Sometimes I hear entrepreneurs say they expect to raise $5 million or $15 million selling a third of the company, so they think they deserve a $10 million or $30 million pre-money valuation even though they have no revenues. My reaction is, if the way we get to a pre-money valuation is based on revenues, product, and team, and looking at you guys you have no revenue, well then the spotlight is going to focus pretty much on your team. Since you have never started a company that was sold for more than $5 million, the team is pretty much discounted to a few hundred thousand, if that. Therefore, the spotlight is going to focus very heavily on your product, and not that much has been invested into the product yet. Ideas without a credible team or product have pretty much no value in the Silicon Valley or anywhere else.

The answer here is to understand how to grow the value of your company quickly, getting cash in the door from investors at key incremental stages in the course of the company's development.

PITCH LAWYERS BEFORE PITCHING ANGELS

If you are on your first deal, you should consider pitching lawyers first. It is always a good idea for a first-time entrepreneur to try to meet three to five big law firms and try to get them to make time for you to pitch your idea to them. This is a good way to practice your pitch and get used to pitching folks that see a ton of deals, ask for feedback, and eventually ask if they know anyone with relevant experience to your deal that might be a fit for advising you. Some smaller law firms may not be able to afford to defer legal fees and will want you to pay a few thousand bucks up front, and then they will do work for you. This may be cheaper in the end than going with a large national or international law firm, but many of these larger firms will defer legal fees until you complete your angel round or even wait until your VC round to start billing you for work done. Much of this work is boilerplate work that does not require more than changing a few things in a form, and it is work that a partner can pass to an associate that has the spare capacity. This is still an investment for the law firm, and if you just send an e-mail with some cryptic ideas about a vague startup you should not expect good results. I recommend early stage entrepreneurs get a polished version of their executive summary and slide deck before contacting a law firm. Exciting these guys about the opportunity is good since then you can list them as your legal counsel and, with luck, they can start introducing you to mentors, angels, and VCs.

Keep in mind that these legal animals count their minutes as if it were opportunity cost of cash. They may even be clocking you while you tell them about your skiing adventure as you try to develop a relationship. A first lunch or breakfast meeting is the way to go after sending them the exec sum and slide deck. Use that time to establish the relationship and try not to take up too much of their time. When you actively go into solicitation, ask if they can make any intros and even feel free to ask for specifics like an intro to Ron Conway and others on your target list. Whatever you do, avoid using a provincial lawyer who really focuses on some other kind of law and does not do angel and VC corporate securities–type work. Any lawyer that has contributed to this book is obviously a good place to start if you are unfamiliar with active lawyers in your area. For my first startup I pitched at least five law firms before deciding with whom to go. I had them all competing to represent me and invest their time and representation in us.

LEGAL FEES FOR STARTUPS: FIXED PRICING

John Bautista, partner at Orrick, explains his pricing structure for startup formation:

> I've moved to fixed pricing for startups (and fee deferrals) for formation and initial financing. This is what I do for companies:
>
> 1. *Formation*: $2,500—which includes company formation, founders' stock issuances (including founders' FF Preferred stock), option plan, offer letters for early employees and advisor, and consulting agreements.
> 2. *Bridge financing*: $5,000 to $7,500—for a convertible note financing on standard terms, which I will help the company negotiate and provide coaching around.
> 3. *Angel equity financing*: $10,000 to $15,000—there is more work here than a bridge financing, with representations and warranties, board composition provisions, stock restriction agreements between the founders and the investors, management rights agreement with investors, and legal opinion provided by Orrick. The fees will be at the higher end of this range if the angels are represented by legal counsel and depending on the number of investors to coordinate closing.
> 4. *Venture financing*: 1.5 times investors' counsel fees. The first thing a company should do is keep the cap on investors' counsel fees to a minimum. The more the due diligence and comments on documents from investors' counsel the more work we will need to do as company counsel to respond. As company counsel, we will draft documents, prepare due diligence, finalize documents, coordinate the closing process with investors, make securities filings, and manage post-closing matters.
>
> I will defer up to $15,000 of fees until the company has raised capital. I work with companies to determine what the capital raise

will be that triggers payment of fees to help them with their cash use. As you will see from the above schedule, $15,000 will go a long way for companies. My view is that greater fee deferrals are usually a red herring; it could mean that the law firm is not working efficiently.

LEGAL FACTORS TO CONSIDER WHEN CHOOSING AN ANGEL INVESTOR

John Bautista went on to talk about what legal factors you should consider in choosing an angel investor:

I was recently asked what "legal considerations" go into choosing an angel investor. These considerations are in addition to determining who is a good strategic fit for you and who will help open doors for your business. On the legal side, you should consider the following:

1. *Lead investor credibility*. Choose an angel who has the credibility to set terms and have others follow with the impetus to renegotiate. For example, if an angel like Ron Conway sets terms with you, it is very unlikely anyone else will try to negotiate different terms.

2. *Convertible debt*. Choose an angel who will do convertible debt instead of equity. Convertible debt is faster, cheaper, and provides you with more flexibility for your first venture round. And a convertible debt round can be done for about $5,000 in legal fees.

3. *Valuation insensitive*. Choose an angel who is fair on valuation. Some angels are looking for big ownership stakes without much investment. At most, you would sell 15 percent of the company in an angel round, and you will want angels who are willing to pay these effectively higher valuations.

4. *Founder friendly*. Choose an angel who is founder friendly who will not insist on a board seat, who will not request voting

rights or blocking rights on your next financing, and who will
not micromanage you.

5. *Flexible terms.* Choose an angel who will sign up for standard
   legal documents, like Orrick's forms, and who won't require
   extensive reps and warranties from you. This will minimize the
   likelihood that the angel will use a lawyer to review documents,
   thus keeping your transaction fees to a minimum.

SMART ANGELS FLOCK TOGETHER

Angels often form angel groups to increase their deal flow, share the due diligence (DD) work involved, and team up to raise larger amounts of capital.
If one angel finds two new deals per week and joins forces with 24 other
angels, then their combined deal flow increases from 2 to 50. By joining
forces, they start to be able to invest enough money to truly capitalize their
startups. Putting $25,000 into a $1 million investment round with several
other angels makes sense. An angel would be smarter to make 20 investments of $25,000 each than two investments of $250,000 each. This is why
I created Georgetown Angels. Our mission is to unite the most powerful
Hoyas to create a formal network of angel mentors to add value beyond just
commodity cash. Our angel group gained a critical mass by uniting accredited angel investors that went to Georgetown University, but has opened its
doors to non-Georgetown angels and includes many angel investors that
have no affiliation with the University. We invest in the best startups we
can find and do not require that anyone on the management team went to
Georgetown. If you are seeking funding get in touch with us. If you went
to Georgetown, or if you want to make angel investments, please find us at
www.georgetown-angels.com.

Typically the angel group creates a new limited liability corporation (LLC) for each investment or a series LLC structure. As angels wire
money into the LLC account, the LLC issues ownership units in the LLC
or series. This way the angel group becomes one single shareholder in the

startup and the startup has a clean cap table and easy-to-manage single share-holder. When it comes to voting rights, the LLC votes and there is no need for the CEO of the startup to track down 15 different angels that are all spending the winter on their sailboats in the Caribbean. Pledge funds can operate on a similar basis. Angels that want to invest across 10 companies, but only have $50,000 to invest can use this structure to spread small amounts of funding across multiple startup investments and benefit from being in a VC fund with small amounts of capital as well as choose which deals they want their money going to. This is new. In the past VCs typically require a mini-mum amount per person ranging from $500,000 to $5,000,000, depending on the fund. The asset class is now becoming more accessible.

PLEDGE FUNDS

A pledge fund is an alternative to a venture capital fund. Rather than raise LP dollars with a 2 and 20 structure, pledge funds take an existing deal in which the pledge fund manager wants to invest and sends that deal out to a net-work of high net worths, family offices, corporate investors, and any other investor in their network. These folks look at each deal on a deal-by-deal basis and only invest in the ones they like. The pledge fund manager typi-cally takes a 20 percent carry on each deal, sets up the LLC to collect the cash and make the investment, and charges some kind of management fee at closing to cover costs and generate some revenue. If you want to raise a VC fund and find it too tough, but you have great deal flow, a pledge fund can be a good way to get started and enjoy deal-by-deal carry, or eventually offer a sweeter deal to the pledge fund LPs if they commit cash to a 2 and 20 struc-tured fund. Expect to see some pledge funds evolve to hybrid-classic funds with some pledge fund LPs and some real LPs.

THE IMPORTANCE AND ART OF NETWORKING

Attending networking events can be tiresome when you are busy and short on time, but if you are an entrepreneur, angel, or VC you must get out there and network. Do not expect rapid-fire good things to come from a networking event. It is the one or two people out of the 30 that you meet that make the event worth the investment.

Networking for an angel or VC is equally important. Imagine you have an opportunity to invest in either VC A or VC B. VC A shows you, the prospective LP investor into the VC fund, that she has received 20 investment opportunities in the past week and is focusing her time on the top 3. Then VC B demonstrates that she has received 60 deals in the past week and is focusing on her top 3 deals. You are likely to make more money investing into fund B. Deal flow is the lifeblood of a VC.

For many entrepreneurs, angels, and VCs involved with The Founders Club, the number one motivating driver to participate is access to more deal flow. We are a deal flow machine wrapped around a perpetually growing trust network. When high deal flow meets trust network and repeat serial entrepreneurs and sophisticated investors, good things start to happen and everyone's luck begins to improve.

One of the motivations for me to write this book is to open a network pathway to you. The more entrepreneurs, investors, and members of the ecosystem who read this book, the more high-quality networking we can establish with one another and the more likely deals will flow among us. This book can be a source of deal flow and investors for all of us.

NEVER TURN DOWN A SMART STRATEGIC INVESTOR

This next story comes from a friend of mine, Ken Hawk, former CEO of Ubidyne and an American entrepreneur who lived in Germany while I was living in London. We met in Berlin at a Founders Club event and now both live in the Silicon Valley.

Ubidyne, after raising a large successful series B during one of the most difficult fund-raising environments in the last decade, had a 5 million euro term sheet from a key strategic investor

(T-Ventures). The management team worked hard to secure the term sheet and saw great value in having one of the world's leading mobile operators as a strategic investor. T-Ventures was flexible on their bite size and the makeup of the syndicate and had offered its CTO as a strategic advisor. Our existing venture investors were split on whether or not to accept their term sheet (which included performance warrants tied to their specific contribution to the company). While none of our investors had ever worked in a startup, some of them were frightened that an investment by T-Ventures would damage our important relationship with Vodafone. The management team did extensive diligence speaking with each of the last 10 investments by T-Ventures, and we found that each of them actually accelerated their traction with other operators. They also confirmed that the promised value add by T-Mobile was delivered above and beyond what they had expected. The best example reference came from the founders of Flarion, who stated the company would never have made it if not for the early investment and support from T-Ventures. Flarion was later acquired by Qualcomm for over $650 million and delivered a spectacular return for their investors.

The T-Ventures issue began to polarize our management team and a subset of our investors. In the end the investors were able to block the deal. In a final meeting in Bonn, our investor actually told the executive management of T-Ventures he saw "absolutely no strategic value" and that T-Ventures should pay exactly the same price as the rest of the investors, i.e., no performance warrants. Less than 18 months later, these same investors had to do an internal 6 million euro round at less than one-tenth the valuation that T-Ventures had offered. The net effects of this strategic mistake wiped out the value of all founder and employee stock options, slowed the company while competitors including Huawei sped up, and gave the blocking investors control of the company.

3

How Venture Capital Works

I can imagine many of my readers know the dynamics of a VC fund because they are VCs or they've raised VC funding multiple times. If you already have a vineyard with a wine named after your favorite dog, feel free to browse this section skipping a bit, but then tune in and read a few sections that may have something for you to consider. For example, you may know how venture capital works, but are you fully aware of the different stages of the VC fund life cycle of your existing VCs and how their positions differ from the new VC leading your next round? Entrepreneurs truly benefit from understanding how VCs work beyond the 2 and 20 structure. The entrepreneur then understands when one VC has an incentive to do one thing while another VC has an incentive to do something totally different. Understanding where the VC is in the life of her fund or the pressures on management fees will help you, the entrepreneur, better understand why the VC is taking the position she is. You can directly and openly discuss this with your VC as a partner in your business and you as a "friend of the fund" and possible LP investor one day in that VC's current or different fund. Understanding some of this in detail can make you more successful.

Venture capital firms are typically organized as limited partnerships with limited partners (LPs) committing the cash and the general partners (GPs, the folks employed as VCs) investing in the fund. The GPs will, hopefully, exit those deals returning the cash to investors with a return and making something for themselves.

Let's take an example of a hypothetical fund to understand the moving parts and changing dynamics or behavior of the GPs. Imagine you and I become partners and decide to raise a VC fund. We are successful and manage to close a fund with LP investors for $100 million. By the way, with most funds LPs expect to see a GP commitment of 1 to 5 percent of the fund. So we should be so successful and rich that we commit $1 million to $5 million of our own savings to demonstrate how much we believe in the fund strategy and prospects for success. If you don't have that coin, there are other ways to finance that GP commitment.

With a $100 million fund, the GPs would take an annual *management fee* of 2 to 2.5 percent of the full amount of the fund to cover not only salaries and office expense but also accounting, travel, conferences, and admin. It's pretty easy to see how a VC GP, after covering all those operating expenses, is not banking much money per year. But, if the fund's investments are good enough that the full $100 million is paid back with a return past the *hurdle rate* (often 6 to 8 percent), the GPs get into *carried interest* or *carry* and then receive 20 percent of all the exits.

The term *carried interest* goes back to the medieval merchants in Genoa, Pisa, Florence, and Venice. These traders carried cargo on their ships belonging to other people and earned 20 percent of the ultimate profits on the "carried" product. Some of today's most popular funds turn away investors and command carry of 25 percent or 30 percent. I think it is sensible for a VC to increase his carry once specific amounts of profits have been returned to the investors. Performance-based bonuses make sense.

The typical life of a VC fund is structured to be 10 years. We can typically invest cash into new companies during the first five or six years. This investment period is referred to as the *commitment period*. After year five (or sometimes year six) the fund would be restricted to only follow-on investments in the portfolio invested in during the first five or six years. The VC's incentive is to identify the 15 or so companies to invest in during the first 5 years compared to investing in a new startup in year 10. If the VC invested in a new company in year 10, that would be effectively asking the LP investor to keep that cash set aside for the first 10 years and then wait another 5 to 10 years for that company to exit, making the time horizon for the LP investor 20 years to exit. In years 6 to 10 the VC is protecting his position and continuing to fund the capital needs of these companies without getting wiped out because he did not reserve cash for follow-on investments.

To understand the pressures on the VC, consider that if the VC is approaching year three or four and still has not managed to get into enough good deals, the VC may become more trigger-happy and be very hungry to get into some new deals. The VC may also want to invest in deals that will require additional funding to use up all the reserve money the VC has. On the flip side, the VC may want to slow down his investment pace or only invest in companies that are completing their last funding round before an exit so he does not need to keep more cash in his fund in reserve for that company.

It is a fair question for an entrepreneur to ask VCs at what stage they are in the life cycle of their fund and what are the dynamics of looking for new investments? Are they looking for deals with large future capital requirements or the opposite? In my experience, when you ask VCs these questions they give you a straight answer such as, "We have room for three more new investments in this fund, and then we'll start making investments out of the new fund" (which may not have been raised yet).

If you join a VC or start a new VC fund, you should expect to go for many years without a bonus. Imagine a Wall Street animal being happy about working 6 or 10 years without a bonus! This starts to look like a labor of love. Some VCs pay themselves the 20 percent from initial exits but face a clawback to pay LPs if they fail to get into carry. Now imagine that there is fierce competition among VCs and it is hard to get into the best deals and hard to get your money out of these companies as many of them drag on for 9 to 15 years before an IPO or M&A exit. Making money as a venture capitalist is hard. No wonder so many VCs quit and become entrepreneurs or angels.

The average time delay between series A investment and exit in 2002 was two years. By 2008 this grew to seven years. The delay peaked in 2009 probably at seven to nine years, but it is quickly coming down again, making VC funds more attractive. Clearly there is a lot of luck involved. VCs might have invested in several companies in years three, four, and five of their 10-year fund; they are now seeing seven years to an exit. Those VCs may not have returned the $100 million by the time they must raise the next fund. In times like these, the VCs exercise their right to extend the life of the fund one or two more years.

After the first five years, funds differ on how they treat the annual management fee, but the 2 or 2.5 percent annual management fee is often shifted gradually onto fees that the VCs charge the portfolio companies for being on the board of directors. If the VCs raise another fund, this may also offset the annual management fee. In general, the total amount of the fund that goes to pay management fees is typically 15 percent of the entire fund. With some funds that fail to raise a new fund after three or five years of raising the first fund, this 15 percent can grow to 20 percent of the $100 million. Some funds simply decrease the annual management fee by a specified amount each quarter starting in year five or six.

Now imagine that the fund is very successful. The VCs raise the $100 million and they invest about $85 million like clockwork, perfectly balancing investment period, cash reserved for the portfolio, and development stage of portfolio companies. They exit, returning $200 million. Sounds great. The first $100 million or $106 million would go to the LPs, proving that venture is still a great asset class. With that done, the fund goes in carry. The VCs receive 20 percent of any exit from that fund, in this case 20 percent of the remaining $94 million. That means the VCs reap a happy $18.8 million from the carry. That sounds good, but now figure this happened over at least 10 years of their lives. That means on an annual basis they made $1.8 million plus the $2.5 million of management fee that was really spent to cover costs in the expensive San Francisco Bay area, New York City, or London. Now figure that there are three or four GPs in the fund who split the carry and expenses. If three GPs split the carry that would mean $6.26 million each, divided by 10 years of work, or $626,000 per year. That's enough to cover school fees for your kids, but remember this was a stellar fund performance that does not happen to most funds.

Experienced VCs would tell you that they raise a fund every three years, so they are stacking fees. When you build a dynasty of multiple overlapping funds, they are always in the investment period. The fees can add up to a good living. But it would seem that many VCs would be better off using their existing skills, partnering with great entrepreneurs, and becoming entrepreneurs.

You can also see that investing into very early stage deals could mean waiting an eternity to get your payoff from an elusive exit or closed IPO market with the guarantee of an economic downturn in each decade in modern times. Many VCs grow up to realize that their best bet is to try to be the last money into a company before a liquidity event. They don't need to reserve follow-on cash because the deal is now fully funded to exit. If they invest in companies that are within two years of an exit, then they can start to return LP dollars and possibly get into carry by year four and five. They are in a better position to go back to the same LPs to invest in their next fund. There is, understandably, fierce competition to invest in a later stage growth company with no product or market risk and investment bankers swarming it to sell or IPO within a year. The internal rate of return (IRR), the main metric VCs and PEs use to measure returns, may not be so high. Many VCs and PEs have grown up to realize it is better to make a 1.2 times return on a $50 million investment than it is to swing for the fences on a risky series A investment hoping it will be a Facebook and return the entire fund. For some, moving the thermometer in the safe direction of getting into carry is the way to go. Other VCs like Accel, who did invest in Facebook, will tell you there is no point in making a 1.2 times investment when some of them will go wrong and over 12 years you deliver 9 to 11 percent IRRs for your LPs. Accel's executives have been saying for years that every single investment they make must have the potential to return the entire fund. So if they have a $400 million fund and they invest $5 million into that company it must have the ability for their slice at exit to return a full $400 million. They figure if they make 15 investments like that, one of them may return the entire fund. Then when the others start to exit they are getting a clean 20 percent of everything and their LPs will be ecstatic.

What one often sees in reality with VCs surfing the dynamics of early versus later stage investing is that they have what is called a *barbell strategy*.

A barbell is a bodybuilder's weight that has a long bar in the middle with two big cannonball weights attached to either end. The big weight on one side represents early stage investments, and the other side represents later stage investments. Mixing how a fund is invested and at different stages of the fund life cycle makes sense.

You can also see that this plays into the many reasons why VCs like to syndicate and share deals with each other to get into the stage deals required to balance a fund based on life cycle. There are many reasons why VCs syndicate that are more important, but having access to a lot of high-quality deal flow from other VCs is a good thing both for inviting other VCs to join your syndicate and for being invited into the syndicate of another reciprocating VC.

Understanding VC Titles

The VCs that you meet when raising money are employed by, or are partners in, a management company called the general partner in the fund. I think it is wise to understand the difference among the individuals of any fund you are seriously talking to. Within a VC firm, not everyone you meet has the power to push your deal through. It is worth considering this because you may convince someone to invest in your company and then find out that person doesn't have the clout to push the deal through the partnership and get your deal done.

Titles are a good indication of who is important in a fund. The top-tier folks are general partners (GPs) or managing directors (MDs), then partners, then vice principals (VPs), then senior associates and associates. Some funds deviate a bit calling everyone a GP or everyone an MD.

You might see the word *managing* in front such as managing partner or managing general partner as an indication of seniority, but as with law firms that person might be more administratively responsible and not necessarily the most powerful or most charismatic partner in the fund. I think that it is important for associates to shoulder some of the workload, but I like to see a partner in the meeting if I am going to a meeting. Focus on the GPs, MDs, and partners.

There are often one or two general partners who have more mojo in the fund and, if they become your champions, they can push the deal through the partnership to get the investment approved. Also if you get one of these senior folks on your board, she will be able to move bigger mountains to raise more funding from other good VCs, IPOs, or M&A transactions, getting you a deal with a company like Facebook, Yahoo!, LinkedIn, or Google.

Many firms have venture partners who are often former VCs from another firm or someone in the ecosystem who is part-time with the firm and focused on some other projects. These are often useful at deal origination and due diligence. Some are on a salary, and some just get economics on a deal that that they bring in. Venture partners are a good way for a small VC partnership to extend its network deeply into specific industries and geographies at a very senior and high-quality level. It's generally a great deal for the venture partner to command some stature in being able to help entrepreneurs access the fund. At the same time, the venture partner might be making angel investments, advising a few companies, buying a company, or finding a CEO role for an already well-funded company. Venture partner status works well for someone in between gigs as a holding place or on a pathway to joining the VC firm when it closes its next fund and the management fee will cover the added expenses of a new partner.

Sometimes you see an entrepreneur-in-residence (EIR). These are normally successful entrepreneurs looking for their next company, working out of the VC office. The VC's perspective is that this entrepreneur's last exit made $500 million for the VCs, so keep him close and that VC will probably be able to lead an investment round in his next venture, or the VCs may hire him to become CEO of one of their existing portfolio companies ready for a real pro. EIRs have strong access to these VCs and are often very dynamic entrepreneurs. That said, the EIR cannot lead and get your deal done, so ask to bring a GP or partner into the discussion.

To the Victor the Spoils

Old-school VCs from the late 1990s used to tell me that a third of their investments are expected to fail. So if they had a $150 million fund they expected to lose a clean $50 million. Then with a third of their investments, "hook or crook" they will get their cash out with a 1 times return—so they'd get $50 million back with no return for the time and effort. That means that the remaining third of their investments costing $50 million would need to return the full $150 million and a return of 40 percent to their investors. The entrepreneur should understand that his business needs the potential to return the entire fund or significantly move the needle toward 40 percent IRR. Your business might make sense and you might be convinced that it will make money for investors, but will it fit into this *venture returns* framework of 10-times-plus returns for the investor?

I see a lot of entrepreneurs focus too much on the economics of the deal or the reputation of the fund and not enough on is this guy smart on my business and what does he really bring to the table beyond cash and the reputation of his fund.

Like wine, venture capital comes in *vintages*. When you see someone raised a VC fund in the Silicon Valley in 1992, you can begin to make an educated guess that the fund did very well. This person would have captured the first dot-com wave where the time between investment and exit was under two years and the IPO market was thriving with big exits for anyone with "dot-com" in their company name. The vintages of VCs leading up to the dot-com meltdown in 2000 performed very well. With such an amazing performance of the asset class every Tom, Dick, and Harry started to opportunistically raise VC funds in 1999 and 2000. For those that managed to close their funds, they found themselves in a parallel universe to the good ones that fostered the good vintages. Their first investments were made and valuations were too high. Now there was too much money chasing too few good management teams and deals; companies had too many copycat competitors; there was no path to exit. The IPO market shut and M&A evaporated as the big buyers' market caps tanked. Just like technology, venture capital has a lot to do with timing. Again, I agree with Tim Draper that right now we currently have a good mix of ingredients for successful VC investing.

THE STOCK MARKET AND VENTURE CAPITAL

Bob Pavey, partner at Morgenthaler Ventures, had this to say about the relationship between the stock market and venture capital:

> The best index for how VC investments will perform is the NASDAQ stock index because it lets us know what price we can sell our companies for (either in an IPO or in an M&A). By the year 2000, every stockbroker and every VC had decided he was a financial genius. None cared to consider that the NASDAQ had risen 100 times—from 50 to 5,000 in the preceding 25 years from 1975 to 2000. When the market goes up 100 times over 25 years, any damned fool can make money in growth stocks. In the last 10 years the NASDAQ has been cut in half—from 5,000 to about 2,500 (and it has bounced off about 1,300 twice). No one feels as smart in this kind of a 10-year bear market. In reality that means we all should be buying around now—but that sure is hard when we are all idiots instead of the geniuses we were 10 years ago.

WHERE DO VCs GET THEIR MONEY?

I met Nic Brisbourne for the first time in 2000 when he was an associate with Reuters Venture Capital. Now a partner at DFJ-Esprit, he's one of the most active VCs in the London mediatech scene. He provided me with great advice as I was developing the model for The Founders Club. In late 2012, data suggested that DFJ-Esprit was responsible for a third of European exits since 2010.

> The quintessential answer to this question is "institutional investors" or "pension funds, insurance companies and endowments." These are all companies that manage huge pools of money, which they invest for maximum risk-weighted return. Generally speaking, they have a high-level "asset allocation" policy that splits their

money across different types of investments with the major groups being equities (shares traded on public exchanges like NASDAQ or the LSE), fixed income (government and corporate debt), cash, and "alternative assets" (which includes venture capital). The idea is that if you have a large pool of money under management you should have a mix of low-risk–low-return, medium-risk–medium-return and high-risk–high-return investments and alternative assets. Venture capital is one of a small number of high-risk–high-return options. The allocation to alternative assets is typically 1 to 5 percent of the total. The good news is that modern portfolio theory is pushing fund managers to increase their exposure to alternative assets, so this percentage is slowly rising.

Venture capital is a part of the alternative assets allocation, usually alongside private equity and property. The bad news is that the portion of alternative assets earmarked for venture capital is highly volatile both between fund managers and within individual fund managers over time, and has been trending markedly down over the last couple of years.

Raising a venture capital fund is similar in many ways to raising money for a startup. The VC writes a pitch deck giving the background of the team and explaining how they will make money, and then they call up potential investors to try to get a meeting and then go and pitch. Institutional investors, or limited partners (LPs), get pitched all the time and many are poor at returning e-mails and phone calls. A typical VC fund has at least 10 to 20 different LPs, so you can imagine that the fund-raising process is often long and hard. Many prospective VCs fail to raise a fund entirely, and for most others the process takes one to two years. It isn't that bad for everyone though—as with startups there are some hot funds at hot periods in the market that get their fund-raising completed in a matter of weeks.

Alan Patricof, one of the founders of Apax and considered by many to be one of the fathers of venture capital, wrote a brilliant post describing the challenges he faced raising his latest fund. He titled the post "You Think It's Hard to Raise Money for a Company? Try Raising It for a VC Firm."

Institutional investors are the most desirable LPs in a VC fund because they typically understand the asset class well and will invest in subsequent funds (assuming good fund performance).

Other investors in VC funds are corporates who want a window into the startup world, often because they like to acquire venture-backed companies, and governments who want to stimulate the startup ecosystem in their country, believing that it will lead to job creation and faster economic growth. Since the credit crunch of 2008, government money has become an increasingly important part of the venture capital landscape as institutional investors have pulled back in a flight from risk.

Venture capital funding is contracting. The data on new VC funds being raised by new and existing fund managers suggests it is time to increase the allocation to different venture funds and avoid the mistake of allowing funds to become too large and be crushed by fund physics. It's not how big it is, but how you use it.

WHY ARE VCS SO ARROGANT?

The best way to deal with VCs is to have some sensitivity about their egos. The first time I raised VC funding I found some of them to be painfully arrogant and difficult. I guess if you can only invest your fund into 15 companies over five years and you see over five deals per day, then over those five years you'll find yourself saying no to a lot of folks. I find that the more junior VCs adjust to this situation quickly in a negative manner. Some entrepreneurs don't take no for an answer and keep pestering the VCs, and this causes aggravation for the rookie VCs. They feel as if everyone is seeking their funding and they are only providing that funding to a very small subset of those they meet. As a result, they begin to feel like the master in a master-slave relationship and the ego, arrogance, and overall frustration begins to ooze. The VC who has been in the game for over 12 years has typically outgrown this dynamic and becomes a cool person again and knows how to manage this constant fund seeking and rejection dynamic.

OLD-SCHOOL VENTURE CAPITAL: PITCH JOHNSON ON THE EARLY DAYS OF SILICON VALLEY

William Henry Draper Jr. cofounded the first Silicon Valley venture capital firm in 1959. Draper, Gaither and Anderson was among the very first venture capital firms west of the Mississippi and the first VC firm in the world structured as a limited partnership, which has become the structure most VCs have followed. His son William Henry Draper III (Bill Draper) teamed up with Pitch Johnson to found Draper and Johnson Investment Company in 1962, acquired a few years later by Sutter Hill Ventures. Bill and Pitch each came up with $75,000 for a total of $150,000. The Small Business Administration (SBA), under the Small Business Investment Act of 1958, contributed another $150,000 to form a Small Business Investment Company (SBIC). With that they were up and running with the ability to borrow another $1.2 million on favorable terms.

Deal flow at that time was so hard to find that Bill and Pitch leased two inexpensive cars and searched the fruit orchards and new developments of Palo Alto, Sunnyvale, and Santa Clara looking for company signs that sounded like technology companies. They literally drove around looking for these companies and walked in the front door telling the receptionist that they wanted to speak to the owners about venture capital. The typical response was, "What's venture capital?"

Sutter Hill Ventures came along a few years later with a strong offer and acquired Draper and Johnson's portfolio. Bill Draper decided to stay on, but Pitch decided he wanted to try his hand at running his own company rather than continue to be a venture capitalist. However, Pitch found himself in demand as a venture capitalist and hit a string of home runs including Amgen (Applied Molecular Genetics, later renamed Amgen), a true world-changer. Amgen employs over 17,000 people and is traded on the NASDAQ with a market cap of over $65 billion as I write. *Business Week* ranked Amgen first on the S&P 500 for being one of the most "future-oriented" of those corporations.

Franklin Pitcher "Pitch" Johnson was cofounder, in 1962, of Draper and Johnson Investment Company, a venture capital company, and became an independent venture capitalist in 1965 as the founder of Asset Management Company. He also taught a class in entrepreneurship and venture capital at the Stanford Graduate School of Business for 12 years and is still active on the faculty there. He is a past director of the National Venture Capital Association and a past president of the Western Association of Venture Capitalists. He has served as an advisor to several eastern European countries since 1990 in the area of entrepreneurship and privatization, and has helped form venture funds in several countries. He is active in educational and cultural affairs and served as chairman of the board of the San Francisco Opera from 1999 to 2008. Pitch is the lead limited partner of Asset Management Ventures, a new fund, and is active in managing his family office and foundation.

I had the honor of sitting with Pitch in his office in Palo Alto, overlooking redwood trees. We discussed his 50 years of practicing venture capital, The Founders Club, the evolution of the secondary market, the Facebook IPO, London and Berlin. At the end our interview, Pitch, who is now 85 years old, gave me "the pitch" of the new fund in which he will be, for the first time, the lead LP, not a GP. Here is how he summarizes his remarkable career:

> My biggest financial success as a venture capitalist was Amgen. In my 50 years of experience as a venture capitalist, the most important thing is finding the right leader for the company. The story there is that the single most important act in Amgen was recruiting George Rathmann to run the company. He had the scientific depth to run a biotech company, the network and skills to recruit fine scientists and a world-class scientific advisory board, the ability to raise capital, and the drive to be a great leader. We needed to convince him to move from Chicago to Thousand Oaks, California. We asked him to bring

his wife, and we basically romanced them. We popped the question in my backyard. I have a picture here in my office of a re-creation of that backyard ask, where the key moment of the company happened. George had a great job at Abbott, so it took a lot of talking to get him to accept our offer and move to Southern California. That moment in my backyard was the key moment for Amgen. There is almost always a key moment in any company's life. That moment was not so much when Bill and I decided we wanted George, but when George said yes.

I completed a degree in mechanical engineering at Stanford and an MBA at Harvard. If you graduate from Stanford, you can go back anytime and take a class just by registering—no need to go through admissions. So when I teamed up with Bill Draper and started Draper and Johnson, I went back and took a course on computers, which didn't exist at the time I was a student. I also took a course on molecular biology, and that opened my eyes to the fact that you could take human genes and put them in other organisms and make human proteins in organisms other than human beings. I was alert to that from the mid-1960s on. Nothing much in biotech came our way other than a company in Berkeley we invested in that worked with proteins and even made some DNA in the late 1960s. Then Genentech got going in 1976. Brook Byers was working for me at the time, and his roommate, Bob Swanson, was the founder of Genentech, but he didn't want to get involved in a deal that his roommate was running since that would be personally difficult. I didn't push him on that, and the timing actually worked out fine, because when Bill Bowes called me up later and said, "I have just formed this corporation and I have a scientific guy from UCLA to run it," I was able to step in. That was Amgen. I joined Bill about three months later, and Bill and I worked together on Amgen for about 10 years before it went public and served together for another 16 years.

Bill Bowes put in the very earliest seed money, and then I joined putting in some money, and we managed to bring in some other individuals and venture capital firms as well as Abbott, who knew what George was doing. At one point we got low on cash and we sold some shares to Johnson & Johnson, who bought in at a pretty good valuation, but we also licensed them some of our technology to keep us funded.

After Bill Draper and I sold Draper and Johnson's portfolio to Sutter Hill and I had some cash to play with, I went around trying to find a company to buy and run. I was tired of being a coach and I wanted to be a player. But in the end, I kept doing deals. One of the deals I loved was Boole & Babbage. They made software you could slide into an IBM 360. Their software could be installed as delivered so you didn't have to make it yourself. It is truly one of the first software companies. As far as staying too long with a company, I was chairman of Boole & Babbage for 29 years. We eventually sold it to BMC, and I still own some BMC stock today.

What lessons can I pass onto other venture capitalists? I tend to stick with CEOs probably a little bit too long. An important lesson is to do the best you can to see if the founder can run the company once it becomes bigger or can be the person to make it bigger. Some people can do a good job supervising six or seven people themselves. The next level is supervising six or seven people that each supervises six or seven people. But sometimes an entrepreneur can't do it anymore. When the pool of talent you're managing is small, you can have lots of personal interactions. As layers of management evolve, it gets harder. A lot of people don't have the capability to supervise operations through others.

Most of the time I was just investing my own family's money resulting from the sale to Sutter Hill, so we didn't have much outsiders' money that we were managing. As a private investment fund, we didn't need to exit quickly or move quickly to shut companies down. I have shut companies down, but I'm always hoping things will work out over time, but even with a nice multiple, the IRR comes under pressure with time. On the other hand, I love the feeling of success, the feeling of building something. The money is the primary reason I'm in it, but I like the creative side. Creating companies, watching them grow, watching them go through adolescence and grow up to become big companies—that's what the excitement is about.

Particularly in biotech, I love it when we create great products that really help people a lot. I'm not at all being insincere. I want to make the money, but if we cure type 1 diabetes in this other company we have been in for a long time, I will have considered that almost a crowning achievement. The IRR won't be so high because we've been in it a long time. The multiple will be pretty good, however, if we succeed.

George Rathmann from Amgen had kidney trouble later, and he had kidney dialysis in his own home eventually, but what kept him alive for a long time was a drug developed under his supervision at Amgen. So that's just one of those ironic and beautiful circles of life.

For most of the way we just managed the capital of our family. We did manage some money for universities and pension funds later, but they often actually approached us and asked us to manage some of their money, which we did; but at least 10 percent of the fund was our family money. The fund that we just formed for now is just me and my wife as the limited partners. We've invested in other venture funds in Poland, Czech Republic, Romania, Russia, New Zealand, and Norway. I only invest in other U.S. funds to help guys I believe in get started.

The new fund in our group, Asset Management Ventures (AMV), has picked an area we think is very interesting. AMV has really sharp information processing people; we have a very sharp doctor; and they are going to do startups and young companies that use sophisticated information technology that serves healthcare markets. They found some deals in that area and some good ones. There will be competition in this sector, but at least those in AMV are specialists. They have the right people to lead those deals.

ROMANS' FIVE FORCES VENTURE MODEL: INCENTIVES ARE *NOT* ALIGNED

Most successful VC-backed companies raise an average of three to seven VC funding rounds. When a company is raising its second or third VC funding round, the CEO, founders, board, and all parties should be aware of the different forces at play. They must understand the different perspectives and effectively negotiate the best outcome for their individual interests, balanced by their fiduciary duties to the company. Understanding what the other party wants is key to being successful in any negotiation, more so in a complex negotiation with multiple parties at the table. I find it useful to consider an analog model to the Porter Five Forces Model, but populated with venture-related forces.

Porter's model puts the client company or the competitive industry rivalry in the center and considers the impact of five different forces. The classic Porter analysis is shown in Figure 3.1. When looking at a B or later financing round for a company, map out a diagram with the operating company raising the financing in the middle, and the various influencing forces surrounding that center.

Figure 3.1 Classic Porter Analysis

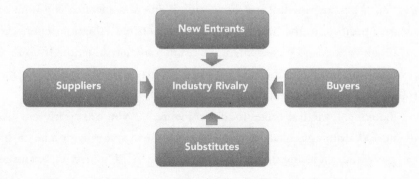

A hypothetical "Romans' Five Forces Analysis" is shown in Figure 3.2. Each company is unique and each situation unique, hence the value in mapping this out and making sure the CEO is on the case.

Figure 3.2 Romans' Five Forces Analysis

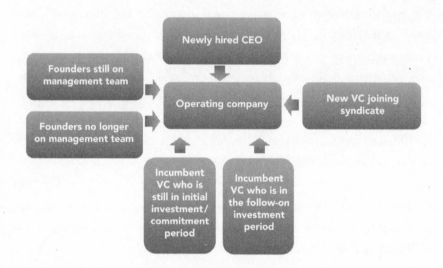

I've seen incumbent VCs push for an up round or a flat round when the new VC is pricing the deal as a down round. The new investor will want to secure a position in the deal with the lowest possible valuation where the existing investors and management will want a higher valuation. If no new investors can be found, the existing investors may push for a down or flat round. This is all about dilution.

Looking at the five forces model in Figure 3.2, you can clearly see that the new VC joining is likely to be pushing for the lowest valuation he or she can get while not losing the deal to a competing VC. The new VC wants to buy as much of the company as possible for the amount of cash committed to the deal. The incumbent VCs want to report to their LPs that assets under management (the value of the LP's investment into the VC's fund) are up and that their dilution is minimized.

Mapping out your own specific deal will show clear dynamics. What becomes abundantly clear with a complicated later-stage venture deal is that each party has a very different set of interests, often directly in conflict. Interests are not aligned! And each different player is going to try to talk the CEO and board into doing what is in that player's interest. The best VCs will support the CEO once the CEO considers all interests and sets the course on a sensible path. The CEO must lead and not be pushed. Go into these situations with your eyes wide open.

The point of the Romans' Five Forces Model is to get to the bottom of the case quickly, understand the different perspectives of each player, set the strategy, and effectively negotiate with the knowledge of the needs and interests of each party.

CORPORATE VCS

I remember seeing an early interview with John Chambers, CEO of Cisco, back when the company was just taking off. He was asked something along these lines, "So, Mr. Chambers, how does Cisco plan to compete with Lucent, which owns Bell Labs, the inventors of the telephone, and has 30,000-plus engineers developing technology?" John responded without a blink, "We have the Silicon Valley, which has more than 30,000 engineers, and one Silicon Valley engineer is worth 10 in New Jersey working for the man. We sometimes invest in the seed rounds of startups to stay close to innovation, but regardless we are here and we buy the great ones when they are ready for prime time."

One of my close personal friends was a transactional corporate securities lawyer working around the clock here in the Silicon Valley on VC funding rounds and M&A transactions. He then joined VMware's internal senior general counsel, doing deals exclusively for VMware. Now they are making investments. It's a natural progression for important corporates that live on new technology and need to keep the momentum of Moore's Law fueling their business.

Corporate VCs investing off of their own balance sheet face issues of consolidated reporting. This means that if corporates own 20 percent or more of the share capital of a portfolio company, then, for GAAP accounting rules in the United States, they must consolidate the financial accounts (revenues, profit/loss, assets, cash flow, etc.) with their own as they are typically publicly traded. That's a nightmare, so the corporates try to keep their position to less than 20 percent. Corporate VCs always position this to the entrepreneur as a selling point, saying that they will never seek to own more than 19.99 percent of the entrepreneur's company. This is reassuring to a first-time entrepreneur, but in reality it means that, despite having deep pockets, this VC may fail to support the company in its moment of need due to this 20 percent accounting rule.

Many of the corporate VCs that survive, like SAP Ventures, break away from the corporate birth parent and raise LP dollars from the corporate and treat it as a strategic LP, seeking financial returns rather than the sole benefactor of market information and a first right to acquire their portfolio companies. The partners at SAP Ventures should be willing to sell a portfolio company to Oracle as well as SAP to get the best outcome for their LP investors and the management teams they back. Investment managers at corporate VCs (CVCs) often do not have 2 and 20 economics and work for a base salary with a bonus, which might be tied more to the performance of the entire corporation than to the performance of the CVC. CVCs that manage to get the corporate to become the exclusive LP do better, and ultimately these funds are better off to diversify their LP base.

FAMILY OFFICES

Most of the wealth in our world is concentrated in the hands of a relatively small number of families. They manage their funds in family offices employing professional teams that typically come up with a specific structure to preserve wealth and expose some of the family fortune to asset classes that have potential to grow the fortune. Unlike VCs who are investing the risky part of their LPs' funds, these family offices are less concerned with growth and more concerned with preserving wealth. They are typically invested in a specific mix of cash, real estate, fixed income/debt, publicly traded equities, foundations, and the alternative asset class of private equity, hedge funds, and venture capital. Often if the size of the family fortune is not large enough, or even if it is sizable, the family may choose to have their money managed by a multifamily office with a larger back office and negotiating power to make more money for their ultrawealthy clients.

Historically, family offices have participated as passive investors relying on institutional fund managers to invest their capital. Family office managers are now seeing an increased opportunity to develop their own in-house teams for direct investment or as an active coinvestment partner with institutional funds. These family-sponsored investors deploy funds through majority and minority investment strategies in real estate, buyouts, venture capital, lending, and financial instruments. The clear trend is that family offices are growing tired of investing into a blind pool VC or PE fund and want an increased ability to select which deal they want to fund on a deal-by-deal basis. We are seeing more and more family offices employ fund managers to coinvest with VCs and, in many cases, compete directly with VCs. It is typically easier to access VCs than family offices.

THE DIFFERENCE BETWEEN VENTURE CAPITAL AND PRIVATE EQUITY

In London, I've heard folks say that any investment round under £5 million is VC and anything above £5 million or £10 million is private equity. One can look at ticket size, but that's not going to be correct in every case.

In general, VCs invest in loss-making businesses and view themselves as value-added company builders. They may invest in a seed or later stage round, but they believe that with their cash and consulting services their investee companies will greatly benefit from their magic wand. VCs typically take minority positions in the cap table (less than 50 percent).

Private equity professionals base their investment thesis around debt, financial engineering, or massive restructuring of their investment targets. They often take controlling positions (more than 50 percent).

If a PE fund commits $1 billion and clubs up with three other funds to get a total of $5 billion in equity financing, and they get a 12 times multiple of debt for the deal (not uncommon pre-August 2007 when the credit crunch hit), they have a $5 billion plus $12 \times 5 = \$65$ billion war chest to buy a huge business. They then make some changes and get out quickly with most of the risk held by the bond/debt holders. With these huge amounts of capital the 2 percent annual management fees are making the top employees of the PE funds super rich and often making angel investments in VC type deals or investing as individuals in VC funds.

For example, imagine that you are a PE fund manager and you decide to buy a European telecom operator. You might decide to buy the company for $50 billion and then divide the company into two new units. One is the utility with steady revenues comprised of the voice and broadband service side. You then leverage that steady utility-like business 95 percent with debt. By the way, that just gave you $50 billion in cash from the debt to finance the entire transaction. You then sell the yellow pages directory services to a global player and pull a few hundred million euros out of the deal on the spot. Then sell your call centers to a conglomerate in India and give them a 5- or 10-year contract, outsourcing that function of the business and taking a few more hundred million in cash. Grease up your chain saw and get busy.

You then strip off the other side of the PTT, which is all the business services that include more Accenture/IBM Global Services type functions. This would ordinarily comprise a few billion dollars in revenue for any PTT servicing both large enterprises and the government. Then the PE firm IPOs or sells that services side of the business; any cash you get for that multibillion-dollar business is pure gravy. The entire investment was covered by the leverage (debt). This really is "get rich quick" stuff.

Unfortunately, there are not that many deals like this running around. VC deals, on the other hand, are all over the place and happen about 1,700 times annually in the United States, 1,400 times annually in Europe, and 300 times annually in Israel. China, India, and Brazil are booming with figures hard to properly track.

All that said, the guys that work in PE typically raise very large funds in comparison to VCs, and so their management fees alone make them more than what most VCs will ever make. When a good PE deal hits, it is epic and everyone gets rich. Most VCs by comparison are struggling and dealing with a lot fewer zeros.

Some VC firms are evolving to become small-deal-size PE firms. They are buying big slugs or controlling positions of companies that are profitable, making changes and coming up with an investment thesis just like the PE deals, but the check size is much more midmarket than the big KKR or Carlyle deals. I expect this to increase because the small business market is so underserved.

VCs are contacted by thousands of entrepreneurs each year seeking to raise funding. The dynamic for the typical VC is that everyone is chasing the VC's capital.

The typical PE is the opposite. The PE team makes outbound cold calls ringing up CEOs of profitable companies, trying to get their foot in the door. These guys also network a lot with each other hoping to get into deal syndicates; so they are often very social. The result is that PE guys often behave like normal people with a friendly personality, while some VCs become aggravated and lose some of their people skills along the way.

I was at a Georgetown University alumni networking event with a PE friend of mine when a lawyer looked at the two of us and said, "I think the difference between private equity and venture capital is that PE guys wear ties and VCs wear jeans." I actually think that's the best description I've ever heard. I only wear a tie when I go to a biotech event or a wedding. A lot of PE guys are still wearing ties or at least suits.

A Perspective on the Difference between VC and PE

Jörg "George" Sperling is a partner at WHEB Ventures and member of the advisory board of The Founders Club, and brings very specific domain and industry expertise in cleantech and semiconductors. His VC experience is from Silicon Valley, New York, London, and Munich. Here is his perspective on the difference between VC and PE:

> I often hear from VCs that they are now also doing "growth-stage" investments. I find this laughable since most of the time they mean "late-stage venture rounds" when they talk about "growth stage."
>
> The difference is significant. While "late-stage venture" companies still need cash to survive since they are cash flow negative, "growth stage" is a subsegment of PE and it refers to companies that are cash flow positive already but still need capital to fuel the growth since they can't secure all the capital they need for their expansion by means of debt.
>
> While this seems to be more an academic discussion about terms and definitions, the difference in the way an investment firm needs to operate is significant. Putting it bluntly: late-stage venture companies badly need cash, so they are out hunting for investors. This means they will find the investors and come to them! Growth-stage companies have slower organic growth or debt as an option to taking on "expensive" equity. This means those companies are not necessarily "in the market" for equity, which means the investors need to find them! So while a typical day for a venture capitalist is to sit in the office and listen to three or four companies who pitch to them, the growth-stage investor is on the road pitching/selling to entrepreneurs who are not dependent on raising equity.
>
> This is a totally different modus operandi, and it also requires different people. It took us years at WHEB to make the move from "venture" to PE, and it would have been totally impossible without a significant team change. Another big difference is the complexity of the deals. A venture term sheet pretty much has three "knobs" to turn: valuation, liquidation preference, and amount of money raised.

A PE deal is never that easy and has many more knobs to adjust such as the mix between debt and equity, deal structure, or the key question whether one needs majority or can live with a minority stake, to name a few of the additional issues. Fundamentally I think the biggest issue is that in venture fund-raising the entrepreneurs are in sales mode and the VC does the selection; for the typical PE deal it's the other way around. For the good PE deals it is still very much a sellers' market.

What About Venture Debt?

Venture debt is a good way to extend your runway to your next equity financing round, profitability, exit, or just fuel growth of the company while minimizing dilution to the founders, employees, and existing investors. At the most simplistic level, the company raises some VC funding and then decides to take out a loan that is repaid typically over 36 months paying both debt and interest. The venture debt (or venture lending as some say) firm also gets a small equity kicker that is typically 6 to 8 percent warrant coverage on the amount of money loaned to the company. That means you may have sold 33 percent of the company for a $5 million equity financing round with your VCs and then borrow another $2 million from the venture debt firm. The venture debt people will get warrants to buy up a small percentage of the company at the same preferred terms as the VCs in that last round, but only for the amount that equals 6 or 8 percent of the $2 million they put in as debt. So net, net, this means less dilution for the existing shareholders.

Sometimes VCs don't like venture debt because they would like to buy more shares in the company and they also want to move more of their fund into your company. So a greedy VC may just say, OK, rather than buying 33 percent of the share capital for $5 million and borrowing $2 million, I will just invest the full $7 million and buy 41 percent—more economics for me! That way all the money is put to work and there is no risk of servicing that mortgage or getting foreclosed on and having a debt equity swap. That's the VC's point of view, which often clashes with the founders'. Often the entrepreneurs don't really understand it; so when the VC just says let's forget about it, everyone moves on. It is useful to have VCs that understand and know the top venture debt people as well as the CEO knowing when to bring this up and have it reviewed by the board as an option.

I have also met many VCs that did not understand venture debt—when it is good to bring in and when it is bad. Forcing a startup to service debt payments when it is still burning cash poses a real risk. Selling more of the founders' stock to VCs and giving up more control of the governance may not be in the best interest of the founders or CEO. Early-stage companies should proceed with caution when raising venture debt, or at least get a real commitment from their equity VCs to weather a storm (entrepreneur beware). In many, many cases it makes sense to talk to the VCs to see whether they think your company is a fit with venture debt.

In some cases, high-growth companies are profitable and paying tax and so the debt simply makes sense on the best debt/equity structure for the company. Sometimes the VC also wants to avoid dilution and is aligned with the founders and management. That is often when VCs bring in the venture debt. Understand what is happening and develop relationships with the major players. Know how to bring in the best ones, as appropriate and when needed. The good ones think and behave like value-added VCs, not bankers on the corner that give you a loan to buy a house.

THIS IS NOT YOUR MOTHER'S VENTURE DEBT

Todd M. Jaquez-Fissori, senior managing director and group head cleantech and technology at Hercules Technology Growth Capital, is one of the best venture debt players in Silicon Valley. He is an experienced equity VC, having practiced at Siemens, Boulder Ventures, and Mayfield. Here is his advice on venture debt:

Venture debt has come a long way from the early equipment leasing models and the popularity of the hands-off low-cost, low-service bank lines. It used to be very much like getting a mortgage or a car loan. You looked for the cheapest provider and you never spoke to the lender again unless you had a complaint. I mean, really, when was the last time your mortgage company called you to offer its help on anything?

Today, as an entrepreneur or even a venture capitalist, you should demand more from your capital providers. Debt provided to startup companies is a strategic and valuable asset and one that should not be minimized, compartmentalized, or trivialized. A smart and talented entrepreneur will see the value in leveraging equity raises and a bright venture capitalist will quickly understand that leverage equals higher returns.

But dumb money is just that—dumb. You need a smart partner with deep pockets who can do multiple rounds and who can work with you through the thick and thin and the ins and outs of venture-backed startups. Demand the same level of experience, knowledge, and skill from your venture debt partner that you demand from your equity partners. This is not your mother's venture debt anymore, so demand more, expect more, and get more.

How Do I Choose a Venture Debt Provider?

How do you choose among various venture debt partners? Your first cut should be banks or non-bank providers of capital. This is easy. You will always need a bank since you need a place other than the mattress to put your money. Banks are not a source of capital. They do not and cannot by law take "risk" as we think about risk in the startup world. Banks are focused on collecting your deposits; they will use a "loan" as a loss leader to get to your deposits. Banks are in the business of lending you your own money first off. They will allow you to use the debt when you have 100 percent or more of that same money in your bank account, otherwise they start to get nervous. In addition, banks have many and sometimes hidden restrictions. They do not or cannot provide more than one loan at a time to a customer. It is not their business. Again note the words—loan and customer. It is a bank. It is a service provider. It is not a partner. It is not a source of capital for the long term. It is not a relationship forged on common goals. It is not a non-bank provider of capital.

Non-bank providers (NBPs) come in a several varieties. Venture debt funds (like a VC fund) have a limited amount of capital to deploy and have to raise a new fund once in a while. Private venture companies usually have unnamed backers, small balance sheets, and lots of leverage. Public venture debt capital companies are "public" for a reason: they have strong performance, strong balances, and a strong understanding of the business; their strength can be assessed from their public numbers, in their companies and in how much they have invested over the years.

The amount of money you are raising and your company's stage of development will dictate who will be interested in providing your capital. Each fund, bank, and entity has a specialty or focus area. What you really want is someone who has the capacity and the desire to provide venture debt capital over multiple rounds, in different amounts and types as you need them. There are very few of these.

So you make your calls, you get a few term sheets if you are lucky in this environment, and then you have to start comparing them. Odds are they will be all over the map. It is important to meet each provider in person; if they aren't willing to do that, find someone else. You are looking for someone who will work with you closely. Who will be your contact? Will the person stay the same? Will I see this person again after the closing? How sincere do you find them?

After looking at terms and talking to a few firms, narrow it down to two funds. Now it's time to really take a look at what value they add beyond the capital infusion. Can they do follow-on rounds? Can they help you connect to other interesting business partners? Do they know anything about your business? Do they understand venture capital and have a partnership mindset? Does this person have the ability to be a strong internal advocate for your business? Do you want to work with this person?

These are important concepts, because when you look at pricing, you get what you pay for. Bickering over what amounts to immaterial dollars on a monthly basis is not a good approach or a good use of your time.

PICK THE RIGHT PARTNER THE FIRST TIME

Today I was speaking with a company that is raising $4 million in venture debt capital alongside of a new equity raise. In an ideal world they should close both the equity and the debt financings at the same time. However, it is a series B round and the company has $3 million in debt from a bank on the books. The bank also demands to be paid off before new debt can come in!

Where does that leave the company? Well, now they have to raise $7 million in new debt instead of $4 million and are paying a new venture debt partner warrants and interest to pay off the last debt provider. That is *not* ideal. This happened because there was not enough consideration made in finding a partner who could grow with the company. It would be like picking VCs with no money left in their fund. The additional problem is that $7 million into the company from a new debt provider might be too big an initial investment for a capital infusion into a new portfolio company. As in venture, without a preexisting relationship, you want to dip your toe in the water. Every situation is different, but a little forward planning, some strategy, and some consideration of the "what-ifs" can make a big difference.

You picked your VC partners for a reason. Hopefully you even chose the partner in the fund that you wanted on your board. You didn't pick them because they were a cheap source of capital. They don't have a magic touch, either. What they do have is years of experience in making mistakes, helping others, extensive networks, contacts, and an understanding of what it takes to help you succeed. They bought part of your company, you created a partnership with them, and together you have a common area of interest—the unfettered success of your company.

You have to apply the same discipline to your venture financing or debt partner. Don't pick a service provider. Don't pick someone you will never see or hear from again. And definitely don't pick someone you don't like to work with. You may ask, well, how will I know? Relationships and references. Work with someone that your peers have worked with. Work with someone your board knows and work with someone that your partners have worked with. Then do your own due diligence. When push comes to shove, you want someone who believes in you, the company, and what you are trying to build. Someone who can stand up to others and say this is a good company and here is why!

QUESTIONS YOU SHOULD ASK YOUR VENTURE DEBT PARTNER

Here are some good questions to ask a venture debt partner:

Philosophical Questions

How do you view your deals?

What is your approach to working with companies?

Will you be my main contact throughout the process and after the investment?

May I have some references to talk to?

Are you committed to actually helping my company?

Is the money really committed even if I don't have cash in the bank?

What would my board/VCs say about me taking venture debt capital at this time?

About Your Fund

How much money do you have to invest in your current fund?

How are your decisions made?

What makes you different?

How many deals have you done?

What do you know about the space we play in?

What is the largest amount that you can provide?

How You Work and What You Do

Tell me about your process?

Do you have the authority to negotiate a term sheet?

What else will you do as a partner for my company?

Can you follow on in future rounds with additional debt?

How long does it take to make a decision and close the round?

VENTURE DEBT TERMINOLOGY AND TERM SHEETS REVEALED

Very much like a traditional equity term sheet, venture debt term sheets explain what the relationship will be, what it will look like, and how much it will cost you at the end of the day. The cost components dominate in a debt deal and appear to be numerous at first glance, but, compared to equity dollars, the price is very cheap. Eighty percent of a venture capital term sheet deals with downside protection and the "what-ifs"; the same can be said for a credit deal. If everything works out, everyone is happy, and everyone gets paid. It's the downside scenarios that the parties also focus on in the term sheet.

Let's examine the most common major terms:

Amount: This is the total amount of the deal and the total amount that you will be paying fees on in most cases. (Note: this could be different from the available amount.) In addition, this amount could include future "options" for additional dollars that might be easily accessed as you will be an existing portfolio company (these amounts will not be included in fees).

Available amount: This is the amount of capital that you can draw down on day one of the closing. It can be equal to the total amount, or it might be a portion of the total. In either case, because the debt fund is "setting aside" dollars for you, you will likely be paying fees on the total amount.

Milestones: Milestones come in many forms and are considered triggering events that release additional dollars to the company. It might be as simple as a date or event, or a significant revenue milestone. Milestones are meant to reduce the lender's up-front exposure. Consider this "dipping their toe in the water." As a CEO, CFO, or founder, you should take milestones seriously, but remember that the lender wants you to succeed and wants to lend you the money. Meet your milestones, and the cash will be there for you.

Proceeds: The cash released to the company sometimes is restricted to a certain purpose, for example, technical development salaries or capital equipment purchases; other times it may be unrestricted and can be used for any general business expenses.

Drawdown period: This is the window of time you have to draw down the capital, after which time you lose access to these funds, as with the expiration date on a coupon. In practice it is much easier to draw down closer to day one than day 365. Most drawdown periods are 6 or 12 months. Sometimes for an extra price you can get 18 months or an automatic 6-month extension with approval. Consider what you need and when you need it.

Minimum draw amount: Typically your debt partner does not want you to ask for $1,000 at a time, simply too much admin cost, so a minimum draw is established.

Term: Stated in months or periods, this is the total amount of time the relationship will be in place. It may or may not be equal to the amortization period. Typical terms are 36 or 40 months.

Amortization period: This sets the number of payments that you will make during repayment. Sometimes if you see 6 months of interest-only with a 36-month term that means you will pay 30 equal payments after the first 6 months, so just be clear about what you are getting and make sure it matches your needs. Another interesting point can be what triggers the beginning of the amortization period. For example, if you have access to $3 million in growth capital and on day one you draw $3 million down, then it is pretty clear—in our example you will pay 36 equal payments. However, what if you wait till day 365 (the last day it is available)? Then what is your payment schedule? It could be either 36 months from that drawdown or more likely 24 months from that period, which is already 12 months into your term. So understand what you are getting into and how it is to be used.

Interest-only period (I/O): This is described as a time period where you will be making interest payments without having to start paying down the actual principal balance owed. This is great for companies who want to save cash, but of course it adds to the cost of the deal and also the risk from the perspective of the debt provider. Like the amortization period, the interest period can be either fixed in time or rolling with each drawdown. If you have a 6-month I/O period and you draw some money at month 3, then you are getting 3 months of I/O; if you wait until month 6, you will not get any I/O period.

Interest rate: The percent of interest you will pay, typically stated on an annual period. The interest rate might be fixed (e.g., 10 percent) or might be stated as prime rate plus 250 basis points (2.5 percent). In either case, there is typically a floor amount of interest that you have to pay; then if interest rates go up your rate might go up as well.

Facility fee: Almost always 1 percent or thereabouts. This is an up-front fee paid as soon as the documents are signed or, sometimes, on the first draw. It is a transaction fee to cover the costs of working on the deal, overhead, and administration.

Backend fee: The backend fee is a final payment due at the end of the term. The fee is a way to defer some of the cost and reduce current monthly payments. As a portfolio company, you may desire to push out some of the cost to a later date thinking to pay it upon additional equity financing or an exit on the company. This increases the perceived risk to the creditor but can be an interesting option for you.

Prepayment: Typically you might find a penalty fee if you pay off the note early because the creditor is losing out on some interest and may try to make it up here. You will likely not trigger this unless you plan on paying off the debt with an upcoming equity round, and most times if you are going to sell the company before total amortization occurs you are not too concerned with this term. It can be stated as a decreasing percentage in each successful year. For example: 3 percent in year one, 2 percent in year two, and 1 percent thereafter.

Warrants: Depending on the stage of the company, the potential exits, and the amount of equity raised, you will find warrant coverage attached to the note, anywhere from 1 to 12 percent. Most early stage deals are around 6 to 8 percent, later stage deals can be 10 to 12 percent because there is less upside built into the warrants. Warrants usually have all the same rights as the current round of finance and will be priced at the lower of the current or next equity round. They are always preferred stock. They are a percentage of the committed amount of the deal and are usually paid up front. Warrants are not a percentage of the company. They usually represent an immaterial amount at the end of the day. Warrants can be replaced with a larger fixed-end-of-term payment as well.

Covenants: Some deals, especially more mature companies or companies with a perceived higher risk, might demand covenants requiring compliance at all times. Noncompliance can prevent additional cash drawdowns or, in worst cases, can trigger default and demand for full repayment. Covenants are usually "guidelines" about what performance is required and accepted by both sides.

MAC clause: Material adverse change (MAC) is a catchall clause that protects the creditor from material changes in the business, shifts in focus, changes in management, and so on. If you go from selling consumer products to a business services company, then you might trigger this clause. It is rarely used and only facilitates a conversation between the parties. It is not as severe as most people believe; equity documents have MAC clauses in them as well.

Equity rights: Simply rights to invest in the next round, often at the creditor's option or with the company's permission.

WHY VENTURE DEBT IS AN ATTRACTIVE ASSET CLASS

Venture debt is a smart asset class. Even if the company goes bust, chances are the venture debt providers get back some or most of the 36 payments before the company implodes. If the loan is not paid, they are the first in line to grab any assets the company owns. For many failed startups, taking possession of a room full of servers might not be worth much, but in other cases there are intellectual property portfolios containing valuable patents. The downside for venture debt is not as severe as that for many early stage VCs. Venture debt firms can also play a more passive role, not taking board seats. One senior investment professional could be in more venture debt deals than many VCs who are limited by the number of boards they can be on and still be effective in their duties. The small equity kicker of warrants spread across a large group of bets means that venture debt lenders hold more lotto tickets to get into a good deal that could provide more returns. The good venture debt lenders are doing well simply by moving a lot of money compared to some VCs that take a long time to invest a $50 million or $200 million fund over 10 years. Some of these venture debt companies are moving $100 millions of dollars every year. Every month they receive cash payments from their portfolio companies. Depending on how the lender is set up, they may have an evergreen structure and can pay returns to their investors and themselves on an annual basis compared to some classic VC structures that go for five to eight years without a bonus.

FUND OF FUNDS

One of the highest points in the food chain in this industry is a fund of funds. Bruno Raschle founded Adveq and was joined by André Jaeggi a few months later, establishing a fund of funds where they raised capital mainly from institutional investors and family offices. With that money they made investments in venture capital, some buyouts, special situations, and private equity funds. It is interesting when one VC firm invests its fund diversely into 15 or 30 companies; but if you really believe in the asset class, it is even more interesting to diversify into 100-plus different VC funds. Fund of funds guys are very data driven and, as you can imagine, very thorough when deciding to invest into a VC fund. They see pretty much all of the VCs that are raising capital for their next funds. Fund of funds are top-notch investors to have because they are very "institutional," meaning they invest and will invest again in the next fund, pending good performance.

More than Matchmakers Between GPs and End Investors

André P. Jaeggi is director and co-owner of Adveq. He founded Adveq's European program in 1998 and led it until his retirement from daily operations in 2009. André is chairman of The Founders Club. He explains that a fund of funds is more than a matchmaker between GPs and end investors:

> When my partner Bruno Raschle and I discussed the possibilities of joining forces in 1997 in order to set up a fund of funds, one thing was clear: the world did not need another fund of funds manager unless we could establish a clear edge.
>
> Our competitive edge was threefold: First, we had access to some of the very best venture fund managers, possible thanks to solid relations with the late treasurer of Stanford University and the treasurer of MIT. Second, many venture fund managers knew Bruno when he was in charge of a pool of corporate money to fund investments and coinvestments. Third, we concentrated on institutional money in order to have a shared long-term view and an alignment of interest around our table.
>
> The fact that Allan Bufferd, then MIT treasurer (today emeritus), and Burge Jamieson, founder of Sigma Partners, accepted positions as our industry advisors certainly opened doors for us in the VC community.
>
> Bruno resigned from a well-paid job, set a target of $60 million for a first venture capital fund, and off he went, raising $66 million, which allowed us to rent a mini-office of approximately 110 square feet in Zurich, Switzerland, and to hire a part-time assistant. Subsequently, I quit my job and went off with a 10-month target of

€60 million to set up a European fund. I raised €96 million. That allowed us to stay in the same office, pay the assistant, and even pay ourselves modest salaries. This would remain the philosophy we kept for the company we later renamed Adveq: secure revenues first, then decide about investments and last maybe serve yourself.

Raising money was, is, and always will be a humbling experience. One hundred phone calls resulted in 10 meetings, which resulted in one commitment.

I remember one special day when we actually secured two commitments from large German institutions.

When showing up at Zurich airport at 6:30 a.m., that gray and windy winter morning, we found our flight to Frankfurt cancelled. Mobile phones not being an option in those days, we called our assistant at home, waking her up, and asked her to call Frankfurt at the opening of business to notify our German hosts that we might have a little delay. Meantime, we hopped in the car for a four-plus-hour drive to Frankfurt. Pulses racing, we were standing and presenting in front of the complete board of trustees of a pension fund at 10:30 a.m. instead of 10 a.m. Whether the presentation was really good or whether they just liked the way we shouldered through, we will never know. But they are still a loyal Adveq LP.

That afternoon we had scheduled a meeting with an insurance company in Munich. Instead of flying, this meant another four-hour drive. Again, we arrived with a little delay, but we could count on their understanding. They too are a loyal Adveq LP to this day. After one more three-and-a-half-hour drive home, we finally had dinner and a big drink at 10 p.m.

Another thing we established early on was a focus on alignment. We were seeing that many of our competitors were becoming asset gatherers. We tried to do the opposite. When you know that you will get an allocation of $5 million to $10 million from those fund managers who consistently provide you with top quartile returns, you don't want to dilute these positions by writing $50 million checks to fund managers who welcome everyone's money. Therefore, we drastically limited the size of our fund of funds. Additionally, we limited the management fee to a cost plus level, allowing us to pay decent salaries; we consequently raised the hurdle rate for the performance fee way above the industry average. That paid off. It still pays off.

Deliberately limiting the size of a fund of funds is not an easy task. It usually creates a huge debate within the investment management community. Ultimately, it is beneficial to all stakeholders: the investors who likely get a better performance, the fund of funds manager who is more likely to achieve his hurdle rate, which can mean big money, and the venture capital manager who has such a limited partner on board. In the early Adveq days, we always asked our managers what kind of limited partners they were looking for. It seldom was the ones with the deepest pockets. It always was those with an understanding of the industry, the ability to cross-compare, and the willingness to share these cross-comparisons.

The core competence of a fund of funds manager is of course manager selection. In a world of very few empirically tested truths, associating oneself with managers who have proven to deliver consistently high-end returns is an issue of survival. What we came up with was what I would call a systematic review of a defined set of soft and hard factors. We collected these factors for all managers we had on our long and short list and, even more important, ranked them against each other. Doing that allowed us to distill a number of return drivers and risk criteria establishing the likelihood of a manager to hit the top quartile. Of course past performance is an element driving potential returns, but things like strategy, operational experience in company building, team cohesion and economics, ethics, the business model of the management firm, and the like are of equal importance. Even with all these factors in place, manager selection still has intuitive moments.

Hardening soft factors in order to be able to include them in a quasi-mathematical model will never reach the exactitude one gets in physics or chemistry. It's more like what one gets out of empirical research in economics or social sciences. But the model can serve as an indicator.

Most fund of funds managers think of themselves as great investors. Maybe they are, but to their customers this is only one side of the coin. The flip side is services. A fund of funds management company is no different from any investment management company. Provided the fund of funds earns a minimal performance for the benefit of its customers, service is what will make the difference. The marketers of a fund of funds ideally are of the same age and background as their counterparts. If in addition to this, one can provide a piece of software easing the clients' processes, then a big step is made from having an agreeable client relationship to almost owning a client.

Next to services come emotions. Tell your clients what they own, even if they own it only indirectly. The fund of funds manager needs to understand what he has in the portfolio. That may be easy with Calvin Klein underwear or a winery in Tuscany, but when it comes to technology and life science, it's a different ball game. Your investment management team must keep up with pertinent technological developments and maintain a high-level understanding of what the underlying companies do. Not all investors in a fund of funds will be interested in the battery pack of a Tesla car, but they can be emotionally involved in the idea of the Tesla and willing to go along for the adventure of the new.

So, who and what are fund of funds? To a large extent they make their living from bundling money from institutional customers and deploying it carefully based on intensive data analysis. The fund of funds can be a lucrative business based on the stability of long-term customer contracts. Yes, size matters, but that works both ways. Size is a must in order to be recognized as a serious player; but size may dramatically impair performance by limiting investment choices. As long as performance, realized performance that is, remains as slow to show as it has been over the last decade, the fund of funds' investment equation will not change. What may change and seems to be already changing is a shift from classical fund of funds to segregated accounts and service agreements. The acid test will then be whether a fund of funds has the guts to tell a large potential customer that he is better off investing a smaller amount than simply playing the "asset class." Because the fund of funds is not just an asset class, it is still at the heart of financing and building businesses.

4

What to Bring to the Dog and Pony Show

Entrepreneurs need a business plan or some set of documents to use in communicating with venture capitalists. I personally do not enjoy reading business plans as I find them too lengthy. Some VCs love them and some hate them. I am generally not in favor of entrepreneurs spending too much time drafting business plans, but many VCs will disagree with me. What I think every entrepreneur does need in the way of investment materials is an executive summary (Word document saved as a PDF), investor presentation (PowerPoint or other slide deck often saved as a PDF), financial model (Excel), demo (live working product), and investor control schedule (Excel).

BUSINESS PLANS

Bob Pavey, partner with Morganthaler Ventures, discusses his expectations for a business plan from entrepreneurs:

> We VCs insist on a business plan from our entrepreneurs, not because we expect them to make that plan but because this is the most efficient way for us to communicate about the opportunity and how to capitalize on it. In 42 years in VC I have only found one entrepreneur who made every plan he gave me: Paul Levine, CEO

of Atria Software in Boston. Paul was a sandbagger, and I came to find that I really love sandbaggers.

Every entrepreneur should have some basic documentation when fundraising. VCs differ on how they like to receive information, but here are some basic guidelines. In ancient times (the 1990s), entrepreneurs drafted 55- to 60-page business plans that went into great detail on every element of the business.

The new world of the business plan reflects several new imperatives:

- Launch quickly to see if there is any interest in your product or service.
- Measure the results and interview your early users.
- Pivot if the users don't like it.
- Iterate if they like it.
- Measure feedback to guide the next version of your product or service.

This is much more in line with Eric Ries's *The Lean Startup*, a must-read book. Many Internet sectors are changing so quickly that it makes more sense to get a product in front of users quickly to make sure that there is some interest in this product, rather than just conducting research and building products because users promised they would use it if you made it for them.

The docs I like to see for a deal are:

- A one- or two-page executive summary
- A 10-slide PowerPoint (PPT) investor slide deck
- A longer version of the same slide deck designed for a 20-minute pitch
- As many backup slides as you want for answering questions and taking a deeper dive on any topic asked by the investor
- The financial model
- An investor control schedule
- A demo or video reel

Executive Summary

The executive summary can be one to four pages, depending on the nature of the business. One to two pages is usually the way to go. More than that and it should include some images or screenshots that are taking up the space. I like to see some kind of breakout box on one of the margins, but it is really up to you to craft the layout. You should be able to find lots of examples and adopt something clean and crisp that you like. Don't go below font 10 in Arial and don't make the margins too thin. This document is much like a résumé and should print nicely. The purpose of the executive summary, like the purpose of a résumé, is to get you the interview. In your case, its purpose is to get you the meeting or conference call where you can make your 30-minute to one-hour pitch. Don't think of the executive summary as much more than that.

A little strategy of mine in making a killer exec sum is to first make the PPT investor slide deck. You put all your effort into that, and then you basically take the slide headings (the title of each slide) and use that to be your sections, bolded words for the exec sum. Rather than have the slide with its bullet points and images, you have a bit of text. This can be very powerful, because one needs a few minutes and patience to flip through a slide deck, but now you see all of your killer deal selling points laid out right on one or two pages. I always get excited when I see my PPT slide deck transformed into a two-pager. The effect is left hook, right hook, boom, boom body blow, Mohammed Ali head punch, knockout! Seeing the points back to back with short time delay enables these punches to add up. Seeing them in slide format allows a bit of time to pass between the points. If things are going well the prospective investor sees the exec sum, sees or hears the pitch, and then later, when reviewing the exec sum, feels the investment thesis momentum.

Investor Slide Deck

Drafting of the investor slide deck is something that should involve everyone associated with the company. You are not just preparing yourself for a fund-raising exercise; you are actually inventing the company, its culture, and everything you are making. Hoping that you enjoy the entrepreneurship game, this is almost a time to stop and smell the flowers. This should be an area that the CEO enjoys. Now is when you are pulling the best out of each person you have managed to recruit to be in that room.

Every deal is unique, so trying to give you a list of the 10 things every investor slide deck must contain is putting restrictions on your creativity before you even get started. However, a few topics that go into most investor slide decks are:

- Market
- Value proposition
- How it works
- Distribution
- Team
- Competition
- Key milestones
- Deal (how much you are seeking to raise)

FINANCIAL MODEL

A financial model is an Excel spreadsheet showing historical financial data, typically three to five years of forecasted revenues and other financial data. I like to see an income statement, operating cash flow, and balance sheet. For most startups, the only thing that matters is the income statement and operating cash flow.

A good financial model should show key assumptions in blue font, which indicates the user can change the numbers in those cells and the change will proliferate through the entire set of financials (fins). For example, if you have in your assumptions the number of salespeople working for the company in year three and then you have another assumption of the number of large accounts each salesperson is expected to sign up each quarter, the number of users per new account, and so on, these changes drive the revenues and the costs.

I like a set of fins that have a very simple tab demonstrating the revenues, costs, net income, and cash position each year, but that these numbers are being driven by other tabs in the spreadsheet that are very detailed with assumptions the user can play with. The potential investor can therefore see what his or her investment will make if the total number of users or customers is cut by 90 percent and see how much cash the company would be losing or generating in worst, base, and best-case scenarios—but with the ability to play around with numerous key assumptions and not just the number of customers.

I always add in a tab that shows the expected exit value associated with a certain performance of the company in year three or five. The assumptions might allow the user of the spreadsheet to change the exit multiple on sales or EBITDA. The investor could put into the spreadsheet $5 million to be invested, for example. That would drive assumptions in headcount, that would drive revenue and cost assumptions, and then the spreadsheet would show the internal rate of return (IRR) on that investment with the assumption of the company being sold for 3 times revenue. The prospective investor could then change that to a multiple of 1 times revenue to consider the worst-case scenario for how much she would make or lose on the deal.

Taking the time to build this out is not an exercise in trying to impress your would-be VC. It can save the VC time in trying to do this modeling to come to a decision on how much the VC likes the deal.

I never feel that I truly understand a business until the CEO or CFO walks me through the financial model. The exercise of challenging the team on each assumption and the responses and arguments they throw around begin to help me or the investor get comfortable on each element that will drive the ultimate performance of that business.

The very quick snapshot of the fins should go into the exec sum for most businesses just to give the investors a sense of what the potential is and how big you are thinking. Depending on the deal and the market conditions, which are constantly changing, one should be careful about not forecasting numbers that are too small and not too big. I've seen plans asking to raise $10 million in funding and then five years later they are forecasting $10 million in revenues with $2 million EBITDA. The flip side is showing that a perfect storm of your hopes all come into play in year 3 when Mark Zuckerberg is promoting your product to all of his users and you are generating more cash than the U. S. Federal Reserve Bank mints during a recession. You and your cofounders can get high and teary eyed when you truly believe in the assumptions of your financial model making you a $1 billion company in year three, but it is the experience of the VC that this has never happened for any of their deals.

That's the thing. The VC has been involved in many deals and has been on the sidelines following the scoreboard of many more. What the VC knows is that very few of these hockey sticks ever come to pass. This is what venture is all about, and this is what we are all working on, but there is a balance in showing this high potential without looking naive. As a rule of thumb, showing top line of revenue of $80 million in five years will mean the business should have potential to reach an exit price that will provide an acceptable return to the VC. Now I can hear some partner at Andreessen Horowitz reading this and saying, "We expect a minimum of $100 million of revenue in three years," but I'm just trying to help here.

The process of drafting and editing the fins should give the entrepreneur a true understanding of his or her business and the ability to defend it under crowbar scrutiny from the most aggressive investor. No one style of fins will please all investors. Try to observe how your audience is reacting and know when to pull back from the details and start drawing a diagram on the back of a napkin. Don't force-feed the numbers if you have not gotten past the first step where the big lightbulb epiphany has gone off for them and they say something like, "So, this is really all about sales execution, hmm." Showing your headcount and payroll tab is just tormenting the VC if you have not yet sold your value prop and distribution strategy. A good set of fins should be intuitively understood by a professional investor, much like a good iPhone app. If you are CEO, do not plan to hand this over to your CFO and be clueless on your model. Every CEO should be able to walk an investor through the fins and defend them under scrutiny. CEOs must stay on top of the numbers.

In sum, keep it simple, but with a layer of complexity available for review upon request.

CHARACTERISTICS OF THE BEST SPREADSHEET MODELS

When it comes to financial models, Scott Maxwell's views are worth considering. Scott was chief financial officer of the Global Equity Division at Lehman Brothers and a managing director at Insight Venture Partners before founding OpenView Venture Partners in Boston. OpenView raised a $140 million fund in January 2009, which sounds like pulling a rabbit out of a hat with the venture world in complete shatters at that time. You may remember the infamous Sequoia slides were the shot heard around the world in September 2008; the last quarter of 2008 disappeared into a wormhole. I'm impressed with anyone closing a fund at that time. Here is Maxwell's advice on characteristics of the best spreadsheets:

> Companies that really want to build a great economic model build spreadsheets that help them to understand and manage their business from an economic perspective. The spreadsheets can be used for many purposes, including answering questions like:
>
> - What will my business look like several years from now if we stay on the same trajectory?
> - What happens if we add more resources or reallocate resources in a different way?
> - What happens if we are able to improve the key drivers of our business performance?
> - What are the capital requirements for the business under different scenarios?
> - What is the best scenario for us?
> - How do you know that you have a great spreadsheet model?
>
> The best spreadsheet models have several characteristics:

1. *The model is predictive.* Most importantly, your spreadsheet model can actually predict the actual economic results of your business. If you really want to test your spreadsheet model, then run it on the last 12 months and see if you can predict your results from the last 12 months using the model.

   If you have a new business or new components to your business model, then you won't be able to figure out if your model is predictive (you won't have the data), but you can still make reasonable estimates, use those estimates in your spreadsheet, and try to pin down more accurate estimates as the data becomes available. This will allow you to start developing an understanding of what you might be able to achieve, and you can iterate on the estimates over time to develop a more predictive model.

2. *The key economic drivers are separated, clear, and measurable.* For the most part, your economic drivers are the three to seven key components of your model that drive the majority of your economic performance. They should demonstrate the key resources that you pay for and how your customers respond to the market interactions created by your key resources. In other words, your key resources generate market interactions that drive your customer results and that relationship needs to be clear in your economic model.

   The best models truly clarify the few important economic drivers, allow them to be viewed and changed separately, and the drivers themselves are measurable. You need to make sure that you have drivers that you actually measure operationally so that you can monitor and manage the performance of those drivers over time, and use the measurements to update your economic model.

   For example, if your sales and marketing resources are a key driver because they generate new customer revenue, your model estimates the relationship between your sales and marketing resources and the new business that they generate; you can then track and manage the true relationship over time. If your customer attrition rate is a key economic driver, your model estimates the attrition, and you can track and manage your customer attrition rate over time. If your new customers drive more help tickets, and therefore the need for more customer service staff, then having this relationship in your model would be beneficial.

The key point is that identifying your key drivers, measuring and managing them, and then updating more accurate measures in your spreadsheet model is key to both having a great spreadsheet model and also key to maximizing your economic performance. You will better understand how your business works and be in a position to better manage it.

3. *Your level of confidence in your drivers is clear.* It is relatively easy to model your resources (a.k.a., expenses, headcount) and to manage to those resources. Your confidence in predicting your resources over time should be high if you are good at managing your resource levels. Understanding how those resources stimulate the market and result in revenue to you is more difficult, particularly if you have a new business model or new parts of your business model.

Understanding your confidence level for your key drivers is really important. By better understanding which of your economic drivers are hypotheses (low confidence estimates) versus which are well understood (completely calibrated drivers), you can then work to better understand the drivers that are less well understood and you can do some sensitivity analysis on the drivers that are hypotheses (more on this below) so that you can better understand the possible range of your future economic performance.

4. *You can do a sensitivity analysis,* particularly for the drivers that you are less confident in, so that you can see the range of pos-

sible outcomes going forward. You also can use this sensitivity analysis to help you to prioritize the economic drivers that are most important to your performance so that you can work on improving them.

As an example, if the relationship between sales and marketing resources and new customer revenue is an important driver, you can adjust the number (a.k.a., parameter of the model in your spreadsheet) that describes that relationship and then see how that change creates different future results. A more sophisticated sensitivity analysis would be the ability to have different numbers at different points in time so that you can see the effects of phasing in improvements (or deterioration) of new customer revenue per unit sales and marketing resource.

5. *Your investments are separated from the core economics of your model.* This is a somewhat confusing point to a lot of people, but you can have a great economic model without being a profitable company. You can also have a profitable company while having components of your economic model that are not very good. A huge part of the difference between your economic model and your profitability is the investments that you are making in your business.

    For example, the most important investments for most growth companies are:

    -   *Sales and marketing resources* so that you can acquire more customers (current sales and marketing expenses aiming to generate more customer revenue in the future).
    -   *Product development resources* so that you can attract more customers or generate more revenue per customer in the future (current product team expenses aiming to generate more customer revenue in the future).

    From your spreadsheet model perspective, the key is to be able to see your core economic model results separately from the investments that you are making in your business. You need to do this so that you can make sure that the core economics of your business are sound. You also want to make sure that each of your investments and the result that you expect from them are sound. Not keeping your investments separate and distinct will just muddy your understanding of the business.

6. *Your spreadsheet model can be evaluated with real-world questions,* particularly for models that have multiyear projections. You want to make sure that you are not predicting crazy results in your model, so make sure that your model calculates some real-world numbers so that you can use your management judgment to make sure that your model is reasonable.

   For example, how many people do you need to hire in different departments in order to execute according to the model? If you need to quadruple your staff every year, you probably have a problem. Also, is there enough market to realize your results? (If not, you might want to consider something else!) Can you reasonably raise enough investor money to execute against your model?

7. *You can gain clarity around the economics of building your competitive advantage.* While some of your competitive advantage won't cost you extra money, you will generally have extra resources associated with helping you create competitive advantage. It is important that you clearly separate these resources in your spreadsheet if you want to understand what your effort associated with creating competitive advantage is costing you.

   For example, if you have a competitive advantage around customer service, you may have extra or more expensive customer service staff to ensure that you have great customer service. If you have a distinct positioning around "easy to use," then you may have extra user experience staff or extra user interface or design staff to ensure that you have the best user experience.

Knowing what you are spending on building and maintaining your competitive advantage is helpful; separating out your resources may also help you to think through additional resources that you need to truly create competitive advantage.

8. Finally, *your spreadsheet model should be as simple as possible.* The simpler the model, the fewer the cells, the easier time you will have managing your economic model. You will have fewer things that you need to think about and remember; it will be easier to make sure that your model is accurate. A simple model will also help you to develop rules of thumb that will help you to manage your business without needing to revisit your spreadsheet.

It is really difficult to create a spreadsheet that contains all eight of the above characteristics and is also as simple as possible, but if you put the time into it, you will get there.

INVESTOR CONTROL SCHEDULE

This is a highly confidential document you should show only to your most trusted advisors and friends. The Investor Control Schedule (ICS) is a spreadsheet that shows the name of every investor you have contacted or are considering contacting in the future, including angels, VCs, family offices, and strategic partner cash investors. It helps you keep control of your funding process. You will inevitably meet some do-gooder or shark at a cocktail party who says he is really close with the GPs at Accel and Kleiner and wants to make some introductions for a fee or just for good karma points to help you along. You should make sure that if that person is introducing you to anyone at any fund you have control over the process and you know who is contacted when and by whom.

The ICS should show the name of the investor, the first and other contacts at that fund you are in touch with, who made the introduction, who is the point person at your company talking to the investor, what materials you have sent (i.e., the exec sum, slides, fins, long investor slide deck, etc.), the date of the last contact with the investor, the stage you are at with the investor (i.e., passed, meeting scheduled, in discussions), the range of low to high on amount this investor might invest, and then a notes section.

I like to color code them using color like light blue background for the ones that we are in positive discussions with, another color for the ones in our top five short list, yellow for new hot leads (like the first meeting is scheduled but has not happened yet), and brown for those that already passed. I then clean up the sheet once a week or so, putting all the brown ones at the bottom and the hottest leads at the top. I used to make the ICS an advanced Excel doc that fed results into a summary dashboard at the top showing the number of investors contacted, the number that had passed, and other key information, but unless you are a professional fund-raiser with paying clients you don't need that kind of automated data.

Demo and Video

Depending on the nature of your business, sometimes a demo speaks more effectively than a PowerPoint slide deck. Often it's best to show a working demo of the product. I think most VCs pull up their chair and get a little excited to see a working demo. Investors often discount what they hear and assume that you have not done the work yet to create a working product. If you have the working product, flaunt it and show some substance. You may want to make sure you have Internet access before arriving for the meeting. If you have a Mac you may want to carry around an adaptor for the PC projector interface.

I see more and more companies putting little video reels on their website to explain what their product or service does for end users, both in B2B and B2C segments. Entrepreneurs are getting good at putting their pitch into video, either filming themselves on stage pitching at some demo day or making a YouTube or Vimeo video where they show some animation or themselves moving their mouse over their Internet browser and using their product. I see these videos on their home pages, on investor websites like AngelList, Gust, and even CrunchBase and Vator.tv. Most crowdfunding sites require the video, and that's the main substance of your pitch. In general this is good. Ideas come to life in these demo video reels, ideas that are harder to convey in an executive summary, investor slide deck, or financial model. Truth be told, I often hit the gong 5 or 10 seconds into video reel pitches people send me. I prefer to kill my curiosity by jumping around an executive summary and situate the key points like stage of a deal and avoid loss of time with a two-minute drumroll introduction on some video reel. The best way to pitch me is to state your business quickly and to the point. I like bullet points in the e-mail as briefly as possible letting me know what you want, how much funding has been raised to date, the names of any reputable investors you may have in the deal, revenues, stage of the deal with key milestones, details on the team, and so on. The worst is an e-mail asking to meet for a coffee or drink with an exotic claim and a Gmail e-mail address. I don't have time to do a Google and LinkedIn search to understand the significance of a person's or company's name. My e-mail load is such a problem that I do not enjoy creativity or beating around the bush. Please, come straight to the point.

THE PITCH

The pitch is incredibly important. Have a few different versions of your pitch: a *30-second pitch* you can use when meeting a prospective investor or anyone at a networking event; *a two-minute pitch* you can use to follow up the 30-second pitch if your listener wants to know more; and then *your full-on 20-minute meeting pitch*. In fact, you should have multiple versions of each of these pitches, based on your audience and the situation. For example, someone at a casual BBQ might ask you what you do. You should have a version to tell folks without going into a full-on "give-me-a-term-sheet" pitch.

Even in your 20-minute pitch the first 30 seconds need to be good enough to buy you another two to five minutes. Those two to five minutes should be good enough to get you the 30- to 60-minute meeting. The two-hour meeting can follow that.

The first 30 seconds are incredibly important. Trying to speak quickly to jam it all in the 30 seconds is not what you want to do. Clarity and precision are your friends.

Hollywood is a good analog. In 1975, the biggest moneymaking blockbuster movie of all time was *Jaws*. Two years later it was *Star Wars*. Some guy probably sitting by a pool in L.A. said to some other Hollywood guy, "Imagine *Jaws* on a spaceship, but the shark is a space monster chasing a young woman with a hot ass running around in her underwear: *Jaws* meets *Star Wars*." The movie, of course, was 1979's *Alien* with Sigourney Weaver. The point here is that the pitch was very much dumbed down and the recipient of the pitch was instantly sold. Keep your elevator pitch very simple; resist the temptation to get complicated and spew too much detail. Nic Brisbourne recently blogged advice suggesting entrepreneurs *not* say "We are company A meets company B." His logic is that this is distracting and VCs would like to know who you are, not whom you are similar to. LiquidSpace recently pitched me saying we are Airbnb for meeting rooms. It's clear for them, but I agree with Nic that entrepreneurs should simply state their business without an analogue that can distract the brain of an investor.

I had lunch with Rolf Ehrhardt, founder and CEO of BioCision, recently in San Francisco. Rolf is a serial entrepreneur that raised nearly $20 million for his last startup; for his current startup he's has been raising multimillion-dollar rounds of debt and convertible note cash, all from angel investors. At his last company they had very complex, whiz-bang technology, biotech chemistry meets biology, led by a team of Stanford PhD wizards. He said that he had delivered his pitch to nearly 100 VCs explaining the brilliance of his technology, how it works on so many different layers, will revolutionize the way clinical trials are managed, blah, blah, and a lot more blah. Then he took a meeting with one VC alone without bringing any of his scientists and said, "Rather than conduct a clinical trial on animals and then humans, we just do the clinical trial in a test tube but with human cells in the test tube." He dumbed it down. A term sheet was signed within a week, and cash was in the bank a few weeks later.

The pitch and the investor materials are important. Just like finding a good name for your company, these things take work. Get help if it is not in your skill set. By the time you are pitching investors you should have advisors or mentors on board willing to help you. Ask them if you can meet with them to practice and refine your pitch.

FIVE VCS EXPLAIN WHAT THEY *REALLY* THINK ABOUT YOUR PITCHES

Matt Rosoff, former West Coast Editor for Business Insider SAI, conveys some venture capitalists' feedback on pitches:

- *Introductions matter.* Josh Kopelman of First Round Capital says that the person introducing the entrepreneur is a big deal. If he doesn't trust the referral, he won't even take the meeting.

- *Keep it short.* Rothrock has seen more than 10,000 pitches, and the best ones are short and to the point. Kopelman also told about his successful pitch for Half.com, which gave users an online marketplace to sell used books. He simply asked how many people had read a book by a popular author. Nearly every hand went up. Then he asked how many wanted to read it again. Nobody raised a hand. Done. The rest was details.

- *Answer questions quickly without getting defensive.* Both Rothrock and Bill Maris of Google Ventures said that entrepreneurs need to answer questions quickly and simply. VCs are trying to assess risk, and if you don't help them, they can't help you. Maris is particularly turned off by people who get defensive during Q&As. He ends up concentrating on their attitude instead of their company.

- *Be a good storyteller.* Kopelman says that most successful entrepreneurs are great storytellers. They have to be able to get investors to believe in their crazy idea, and then convince employees to sign on and press to write about it. Senkut agreed; it's easy for entrepreneurs to inspire their first few employees with stock options or founding titles. But inspiring the fiftieth or hundredth employee requires a great story.

- *Avoid buzzwords.* Lots of buzzwords are immediate death, says Kopelman. As he put it, he didn't pitch Half.com by saying it was an online peer-to-peer marketplace for monetization of underutilized printed matter assets (or words to that effect). If he had, it wouldn't have worked.

- *Know the people you're pitching.* Rothrock said that entrepreneurs should know everything about the VCs they're pitching: where they live ("as long as you don't drop by"), their dog's name, their hot-button issues. Senkut agreed: do your research and try to make personal connections.

- *Don't forget the financial info.* This may seem obvious, but Rothrock said that he sees a lot of pitches with no financial information about the company. Big mistake. Think big or don't bother. Howard Hartenbaum of August Capital points out that VCs need to be convinced that they're investing in a company that has the potential to be huge. A business might be perfectly successful if it gets to $80 million in revenue in five years, but it won't help the typical VC fund return its investors' money. If you can't convince yourself that your company has huge potential, seek money elsewhere.

- *"Stay in touch" means "no."* So says Maris.

- *Forget saving the world.* One audience member asked whether VCs give a little slack to startups that are trying to do good. "I discount them," said Maris. It's not that VCs are all individually callous, although some are, but their job is making good investments for their limited partners. For this goal, there's only one fair way to measure the value of a company, and that's the discounted value of expected future cash flow. There are other sources of funding, like the Gates Foundation or Google.org, for companies that are more socially oriented.

5

Practical Ideas and Advice on Raising VC Funding

A good CEO is always fund-raising. Seek opportunities to get to know VCs. Make all of them want to invest in you and decide which ones you like. Think of VCs as potential partners.

Never e-mail more than one VC at the same firm. It's tempting to just blast all of them with your executive summary and pray that one of them will get excited by your multibillion-dollar opportunity, but don't do it. That's basically like putting ketchup on your sushi. It's just not cool; so don't do it.

GETTING ON THE RADAR OF YOUR FIRST-CHOICE VC

Ales Spetic, CEO of Zemanta, gives the following advice on reaching your first-choice venture capitalist:

> It was summer 2008. Slovenian startup Zemanta just launched its blogging service after nine months of development. In one year we managed to win Seedcamp in London, fund-raise without a product, and launch a service without any meaningful experience or connections. Yet for a group of Slovenians no mountain seemed insurmountable.

I was hired as a CEO of the startup less than a year before to "bring some kind of adult supervision," as one of our investors put it. In that summer we hit a wall. We were based in Ljubljana, Slovenia, well-known in London, however no traction or connections in the United States. So for us a natural step was to find those connections, and I believe the best route for startups is through great investors. So we decided to find an investor in the United States. There were a few names that would be a great fit; however, our eyes were on one of them in particular: Fred Wilson and Union Square Ventures!

Fred Wilson already invested in Twitter and Zynga at that time, and there was realistically little chance for his investment somewhere in Europe. When we started to talk to people about our idea of trying to get Fred on board, everybody was pretty skeptical: "There is no way that Fred Wilson is going to invest outside New York!" "Slovenia?" "No way!" and similar comments were pretty common.

So here was the plan: we decided to go on a covert offensive. We started to systematically call and talk to anyone that might have an influence on Fred Wilson. Not to get an intro, just to start massaging an idea around him. And on June 7, 2008, Fred blogged about Zemanta: "One of my favorite VC quotes comes from Bill Kaiser of Greylock. He once said, 'When I hear about a company once, I often ignore it, when I hear about it twice, I pay attention, when I hear about it for the third time, I take a meeting.' It happened to me this week."

At that time he didn't know that he was a subject of a carefully orchestrated campaign that culminated in a big green flashing dot on his radar. Of course we were lucky, however we did do our homework! That blog post was a trigger for us to start working on an intro, and also gave our investors, particularly Saul Klein, a great excuse to start talking to Fred.

The grand finale happened a few weeks after that blog post. I was on a family vacation in Croatia, when I got a phone call: "Fred is

in London and he wants to meet you!" I said I would come immediately, though I didn't know at that time that it would take me
seven departures and landings in one day to get to London on time
during the high tourist season. But I did it.

On one side of the table there was the most famous guy of
early stage investing, and on the other a first time startup CEO
from Slovenia. My heart was pounding. The meeting lasted for an
hour. Then he met with our investors, and in one day, he gave me a
call, "We want in, here is our term sheet." Simple, powerful, and as
professional as can be. In a few weeks we announced the investment
from USV and Fred joined our board.

How Should an Entrepreneur Approach Negotiation of the Key Terms?

Nic Brisbourne, partner at DFJ-Esprit, gave the following advice on
negotiation:

> The most important term in the term sheet is without doubt the
> valuation. My advice here is to follow standard practice and let
> the VC be the first one to come up with a number. Letting
> the other side go first is textbook best practice for negotiations—
> you never know, but you might just get a higher valuation than you
> were expecting. Most VCs will press hard for some kind of indi-
> cation prior to putting in an offer, and if you feel you have a good
> handle on market rates for your type of company then giving an
> indicative range can help the process along, but I would avoid giv-
> ing a precise figure.
>
> Advisors have the best feel for market rates. When they are lead-
> ing a deal it is common practice to guide investors with a valuation
> range. It is much less common in deals without advisors, and I think
> that is because, in these situations, the board is less confident that
> they will peg the range at the right level.

In some situations there is a genuine floor beneath which the current shareholders aren't willing to take in an investment. In that case it is worth telling prospective investors as soon as they get serious.

Beyond valuation, my advice is to stick pretty closely to standard market practice. If the term sheet being offered is plain vanilla (i.e., one times participating preference share, weighted-average anti-dilution, standard consent rights), then the best approach is to agree to it quickly and focus on getting to completion. If VCs start out with standard terms it is likely because they want to do a quick and fair deal, and trying to move the terms from fair to entrepreneur friendly probably won't work. If, on the other hand, the term sheet is full of nonstandard clauses that advantage the investor, then I would work hard to get the deal back to market norms.

The third and final point is that if there is anything nonstandard that is important, you should put that on the table early. I would avoid being aggressive, but at the point when the investor starts talking about issuing a term sheet it is worth saying something along the lines of "one of the things we would really like to see is XYZ." Then (if she is so inclined) the investor can build your request into her models early and hard-to-change expectations won't get set in the wrong place.

HOW TO NEGOTIATE WITH A VENTURE CAPITALIST

Katherine Barr is a general partner at Mohr Davidow Ventures, a $2 billion Silicon Valley venture capital firm founded in 1983. Katherine focuses primarily on investments in web and mobile consumer and business services. She also guest lectures a yearly negotiation session at Stanford University. She gives this advice on negotiation:

As a former professional high-tech negotiator and now general partner at a venture capital firm having seen thousands of pitches, I have a number of observations to share with entrepreneurs.

Preparation

Negotiating a good outcome starts with being prepared. This seems obvious, and yet in my previous job I would still get calls from senior tech executives along the lines of, "I need your help preparing for my negotiation. Our meeting is in 10 minutes and we're circling the block!"

As entrepreneurs, you are incredibly busy. However, taking the time to review and edit your deck prior to a meeting with an investor is definitely worthwhile. Financials tend to contain the most common mistakes, as well as statistics related to technically complex products. For example, my colleague was somewhat baffled when one company pitching their product showed graphs that indicated they were technically inferior to their competition, as well as when he was pitched an idea that defied the laws of physics.

"Gamification"

Gamification may drive engagement in your app, but too much of it in negotiations could push your potential investors to say, "Game over." I've seen companies try to play venture investors off each other, going back and forth a number of times to tweak valuations and terms. In each case, the entrepreneurs ended up having the investors decide not to participate in the round. You are setting the tone for how you want to work with your investors (and vice versa!) from the very first conversation you have with them. And when the going gets tough, which it invariably does, it's preferable to have a strong working relationship with your investors so that they don't try to "game" you the first chance they get. It's also a very small world and everyone talks to each other. Your behavior will follow you almost anywhere you end up.

Specifically, don't overstate other investors' interest or their progress to a term sheet. For better or worse, word travels quickly among investors, and it will be quite easy for you to be "discovered" if this isn't true. A few years ago, I was pitched by a young, rather inexperienced entrepreneur. In an attempt to hurry the investment process along, he actually named a couple of earlier stage, smaller funds that had supposedly already given him a term sheet. I happened to be having lunch with one of those investors later that day, and this company's name came up. The other investor said, "We passed after the first meeting because we have a competing investment." That was not the reason I declined the investment, but regardless, it was not the best judgment on the part of that entrepreneur.

Valuation

Valuation can be a delicate subject in venture negotiations. Venture funds are typically sensitive about getting a particular range of ownership according to the stage of the company.

At an average of 20 percent ownership at the time of exit, a $700 million venture fund would need at least three $1 billion exits—which are not very common across the entire venture industry—to just return the money to its limited partners. It would then require at least three more $1 billion exits to get to a 2 times overall multiple on the fund, which is on the low end of target multiples for venture funds. This is why venture firms require a particular percentage ownership, and the earlier the company, the more ownership they require given the amount of risk (and increased likelihood of failure) for any particular company. This is also why venture firms aren't incentivized by small exits—they don't move the needle on a fund.

Also, beware of valuations that get too high. This can provide a fleeting ego boost for entrepreneurs, but if you miss your milestones prior to the next round, you might end up with a flat or down round that will be dilutive to you. Remember that the investors, while not happy with a flat or down round, can always invest more money in the company to bump up their ownership again.

Communication

When you are in term sheet discussions, it's generally most productive to discuss the business terms with the investor before passing documents over to the lawyers to start redlining them. You definitely want to get advice and guidance from your attorney in the background, but it's important to have a direct conversation with your potential investor about the terms that are important to you and why.

A common mistake is having your attorney insert nonstandard terms that you haven't discussed with your potential investor. This can destroy trust, which isn't good for your working relationship moving forward.

For example, board composition is a topic you should discuss with your potential investor. The investor will likely assume that you are fine with the typical board construct of two common, two preferred, and one independent board member. If that is not the construct you want, explain your reasoning (including interests and concerns) that underlies your thinking.

Regardless of the outcome, it's important to be able to engage in a constructive and candid way from the start, and you should expect the same from the investor. Together you are setting the tone for how you are going to work together through the ups and downs of multiple years to come.

DON'T TELL VCs WHICH OTHER VCs YOU ARE TALKING TO

It is tempting to tell one VC like DFJ that NEA is very interested in your deal. It may be true that you have had multiple meetings with NEA and the discussion is going well; but you should realize that, if you tell DFJ that you are talking to NEA, it is very possible DFJ will pick up the phone and call NEA, which happens to be located directly across the street on Sand Hill

Road. If NEA gets to the point that they decide not to pursue the investment, then that decision may spread like cancer to DFJ and you are dead with both of them. On the flip side, if you get NEA confidently to the table to lead the deal you may be able to leverage that and let NEA know that you really like DFJ. You could explain the unique value that the partner at DFJ brings to the party and use your deal-making skills to form a strong syndicate of two reputable VCs. You should be very cautious not to mention the names of the other VCs you are talking to until the time is ripe to suggest syndication. When you feel confident that the VC you like is really in, it may be the right time to ask whether they are thinking of forming a syndicate. Even with you controlling the flow of information, these VCs are clustered together and already sit on boards of other companies together. Chances are they are already sharing ideas about your deal. It's always better when the VCs bring up the syndicate idea themselves.

Confidentiality: No NDAs or Secrets in the Fast Lane

Never ask a VC to sign a nondisclosure agreement (NDA). That will just show the VC that you are on your first deal. The entrepreneur in me finds this VC position to be downright insulting to entrepreneurs. Microsoft cofounder Paul Allen's Vulcan Ventures even has a disclaimer on their website (or at least they did the last time I looked) which asserts that by submitting your investment materials to their deals@ e-mail address, the business plan or whatever you send them becomes their property and they can develop the business if they choose to. I don't like to sign NDAs because it takes time. Entrepreneurs should not be afraid of VCs, but try to understand them, be cautious, and keep the partnership a happy one.

As in any negotiation, when raising funds from angels or VCs you need a strong Best Alternative to The Negotiated Agreement (BATNA). If you can pull more VCs to the table than you can close with, supply and demand will land your deal in a fair place, and you should have a choice of which VC you want to partner with.

BRIDGE FINANCING

The CEO of one of the The Founders Club companies told me that he was going to close an internal round for $5 million with existing investors with a closing date of August 30. I advised him not to close an internal priced round at the end of summer, but to approach his strongest investor and close a bridge financing round for $1.5 million on August 1. The money would come in on a convertible note with a small discount to the next round. That cash would then last the company for more than a year. Meanwhile the company could remain focused on closing sales, and then starting September 1, they could go out to new investors and find a new cash investor to join the syndicate before Christmas.

Pricing on any transaction is the match point between supply and demand. If that CEO had sold equity in the middle of summer, the finite amount of stock for sale would remain constant, but the demand curve would be limited by the fact that many investors were on vacation. Closing the bridge and hitting the fund-raising pavement hard on September 1 would drive up the demand and the strike price. Clearly this was in the CEO's interest and that of the existing investor syndicate. Discount rates that may be negotiated by existing investors often get ripped up by a new investor driving the terms of the next round.

LIVING FROM ROUND TO ROUND

Knowing you have cash in the bank to last only six months can be stressful for someone with a mortgage and a house full of kids, not to mention 30 employees. Some CEOs sail a little too close to the wind and find themselves running out of cash quickly. Getting new cash in the door almost always takes longer than expected. I've seen everything from terrorist attacks to volcanoes create a crisis for a CEO sailing too close to the wind.

CEOs want to grow the value of their company as much as they can before selling equity to angels or VCs. Then, when they close VC funding, they want to grow the value of their company as much as possible before going out for more funding. They want to increase their valuation and minimize their dilution, while being able to raise the cash they want, when they want, so that they don't have to put on the kneepads to seek more funding without time to focus on the business. The real advice is to make sure that at all times you have socialized warm contacts for your deal. Your main benefactor may not come through just when you want.

EMPLOY AN ARMY OF INTERNS

I first witnessed the intern mob when doing due diligence on one of our portfolio companies in Berlin. Smeet, a virtual world gaming social network company, had recently completed a VC round with Partech International and Hasso Plattner Ventures. Hasso Plattner is a person, the founder of SAP; so Hasso Plattner Ventures is a kind of Steve Jobs Ventures in Germany.

Although Smeet had just closed a round, the office was jam-packed with employees buzzing around like bees. When we got into an office with the door closed, I said, "You guys have an army of employees in here. What's payroll on a monthly basis?"

They all laughed and said that they were nearly all interns. Smeet had a cool office just off Oranienburgerstrasse in ultra-hip East Berlin; that was their only real expense. They had a near racket going with all this free labor, probably pulling ideas and viral growth from these young digital natives.

CUSTOMER FINANCING

Sometimes the best source of funding is providing a customer with a product or service. Give customers exactly what they want and they may pay you cash to make it, and then you are funded.

This works particularly well for B2B software companies, but it can work for B2C companies that launch via a B2B2C strategy then focus on B2C on their own, while having the initial customer white label the product or service.

Approach a company that you think needs your product and explain that you can make the product or solution for them in three, six, nine, or however many months, but that you will need X amount of dollars per month to fund this development. It may be that paying $30,000 or $50,000 per month to your startup is a bargain for this company, either in the money it will save or value it will receive from you. So rather than sell equity in your startup to a super early stage angel investor, go out and get a customer that needs what you want to build. This customer will pay the costs of developing your first product, act as product manager, and work with you on the exact functional requirements for you to pass to your developers. At the end of the development period, you have a first happy customer, the customer gets a free or discounted license, and you earned some professional services revenue.

Now, if you want to go to angel investors you have a working product, revenue, and a team in place with a happy reference customer. You may find that you are better off without the angel investor and just start selling the product through agents and distributors. I saw a couple of Ukrainian software developers do this. Telenor, the incumbent Norwegian telephone company, needed a billing system for its voice over IP (VoIP) consumer service. Telenor had expensive billing systems generating call detail records (CDRs) for its PSTN conventional telephone service, but they did not work for the new voice over broadband service the company was deploying. This was many years before Vonage.

The Ukrainians developed the solution for Telenor but negotiated an agreement where Telenor paid the monthly costs to make the product over six months, then had a license to use the software along with a service agreement paying continual revenue to the Ukrainian developers. The developers then continued to evolve the product, also embedding an open-source Asterisk SIP–based softswitch. They kept bolting on product after product until they had basically built a telecom software product suite that other companies like Broadsoft and Sylantro in the United States built by raising $50-million-plus venture capital funding. Make sure as you structure these agreements with your customer that you still own the intellectual property (IP) and that the customer is not an owner of your business. These Ukrainians were able to offer the product to customers at a fraction of the cost of their competitors because they were not under any pressure to return the VC funding. They were off to the races.

DUAL TRACKING

Dual tracking means simultaneously doing two things, typically seeking financing and talking to buyers at the same time. This can also mean talking to angels with one deal structure and VCs with another at the same time.

It is alarming to many entrepreneurs that they see another company getting $5 million or even $18 million series A for a deal that is earlier stage than theirs and that addresses a smaller market. What the entrepreneur has overlooked is that the other guy who got funded made a 10 times return for the same VC on his last deal, has the same management team back again, and is addressing the same industry where the entrepreneur's team are proven Jedi masters. Sometimes the folks raising big series A rounds are entrepreneurs in residence (EIRs) and have been brainstorming with the VCs for 6 to 18 months before closing that round.

VENTURE FRATRICIDE

Howard Hartenbaum, a general partner with August Capital, explained "venture fratricide":

> I just tend to stay away from companies where there are a lot of direct competitors. If or when several get funded, there is "venture fratricide" as the multiple companies compete uneconomically using their venture cash, resulting in trouble (and sometimes failure) for the entire segment. I'm not saying that one won't succeed, just that a crowded space makes me nervous (my normal state of mind) to consider an investment.

What I mean by venture fratricide is that VCs see another VC invest in an interesting company and they think to themselves, "I want a company like that," so they go and find a similar company and finance it. Then a couple more VCs do the same thing, and suddenly you have four companies funded in a space and they all compete for customers, employees, and partners and all become uneconomic.

6

Corporate Governance: Who's the Boss?

When you raise money, the money wants a certain degree of control and a voice in the governance of the company. Some of the anecdotes contributed to this book illustrate how some real-world investors suffer from not having sufficient control or even a board seat.

As an entrepreneur, it is important to plan from the very beginning for how you will share control and give up more and more over time to investors. In each financing negotiation, the two primary cards on the table are valuation and control. You can expect that the VCs leading your series A will want something like two board seats. The VCs leading each subsequent financing round will each want one board seat. Many capital intensive deals that go through multiple rounds and raise over $100 million in funding end up having very large boards where the founders may have one or no seats and the CEO, now probably a hired CEO, has a seat and is slave to the group of seven or eight VCs who probably can't agree on anything.

Suppose you founded your company with five board seats, with an option to increase the board to seven or nine. After series A, you have two seats for founders, two for the series A VCs, and one mutually agreed-to outsider. Then you raise series B, C, and D. That's three more VCs to accommodate. Let's discuss options to manage this.

The trick is to put some constitutional rules about governance into your company bylaws at the time you establish your company. These documents, created with your cofounders, can state that the board will comprise five seats and can be expanded with board consent to seven, nine, or eleven (mind you, eleven is a circus). You can then put in some language that says that two seats are reserved for founders, one for the CEO if not a founder, one for a mutually agreed-to outsider. As the board grows from five to seven, you should push to not let it grow bigger while operating as a privately held company. If you do, your job as CEO will be painfully full of trying to call all these people up on weekends.

As your board grows, you can transform some board members to board advisors. In my experience, these advisors, depending on their personalities, may have as much power at the table under the title of advisor as they did as full board members with a vote to cast.

If you are the founding CEO, make sure that the agreements you have in place consider the very real possibility that you will hire another CEO; so if the bylaws state that one seat on the board is reserved for the CEO, that may not be you. People die, get reborn, move on. Keeping two seats for founders is not stupid.

THE VC THAT WANTED A BOARD SEAT

This next story comes from a friend of mine with a VC fund based in Silicon Valley. I'll keep the identities of my friend, the company, and the CEO confidential, but the lesson is clear. Here are his words.

> The deal in question was in a space that was definitely outside of our comfort zone, namely life sciences. However, our investment philosophy was based on leveraging our extensive Asian limited partner and corporate networks to bring added value to our portfolio companies. Since our firm was based on geographic connections, our investment focus was sector agnostic. Despite our internal bias to shy away from life science investments, we decided to proceed with this

particular company for a number of reasons. The CEO and founder told a story about the company that was rational and covered many of the key elements in our decision-making process. The company addressed a large target market; there was a cohesive and seemingly complete management team in place; there was a clear path to liquidity within three years; IP and licensing agreements appeared solid; the financing round was large enough to substantially reduce financing risk until the expected IPO. In addition, one of the members of our investment committee, let's call him Joe, was adamant that this was an excellent investment opportunity. Joe's support was notable because Joe was notoriously pessimistic or skeptical depending on your point of view. So we went forward with the investment and amazingly, everything that was planned in the PowerPoint slide decks and due diligence materials in terms of projections and timelines all happened according to plan. This never happens. The only odd thing about the deal was that there were no investor directors on the board of directors. We had a board observer role but not a board seat. The board of directors consisted of two company officers and five independent directors. The justification for this board arrangement was that the company planned to exit via IPO and it was better to have a public company–style board in place from the start. The CEO also made the argument that since we weren't normally life science investors it would be better to have a board composed of experienced life science professionals. Remember that this company was not a pure early stage startup when we invested. Since this investment was pitched as a later stage company we acquiesced to the board structure without too much pushback. Things went swimmingly for a few years. A top-tier investment bank was selected to be the lead underwriter; the S-1 was filed as well as the concomitant revisions; the company was set to go public. But at the last minute the bankers wanted to adjust the IPO valuation downward. This is where the trouble begins.

The CEO was angry about the reduced valuation. Although he would never admit it, this was a huge blow to his pride. So the

CEO decided to switch underwriters. A competing investment bank promised that it could take the company public at the original, higher valuation. The CEO can pitch this switch to the board as the responsible course of action and in fact the only correct course of action from a fiduciary standpoint. From a practical standpoint, though, it sends a terrible signal to the markets. I have no experience as an institutional buyer of IPO shares, but I can't imagine wanting to purchase shares in a company that dumped its industry gold standard investment banker at the last minute in favor of a lesser-known bank of lower prestige (remember this was back in the days when investment bankers were not considered evil).

Long story short: the IPO never happened. The company was able to raise enough money in a private placement to do one phase III clinical trial. The trial results were inconclusive, and the company was left in a position where it didn't have enough cash to complete another trial and it was damaged goods so it couldn't raise more money. At this point the company still had $20 million of the invested capital remaining. The CEO wanted to pivot the company's focus toward other compounds in its IP portfolio, and he wanted to recap the company reflecting the new startup nature of the enterprise. This is where the situation turned ugly from my standpoint. The proposed recap was at a completely arbitrary valuation put forward by the CEO, and he still did not want any investor representation on the board of directors. The other option was to go forward with an orderly shutdown, return the remaining cash to the shareholders, and auction off the IP assets. Needless to say I was strongly in favor of the wind-down option. I wanted at least one investor representative to be present in board committee meetings where the wind-down and IP asset sale plans were formed. There was no chance this would happen. Without getting in to all the gory details, the end result was that preferred shareholders received 15 percent of their original investment in cash and the CEO purchased the IP assets for a few thousand dollars.

The one critical decision, that I think would have turned out differently had there been a different governance structure in place, was the decision to switch investment banks. If the IPO had gone forward, we would have taken the hit on a lower valuation but we would have raised enough money to give us a do over on the phase III trial. There was simply not enough weight given to financing risk at the board level. I strongly believe that a board composed of only management and independent directors will almost always defer major business decisions to management. I also think it's common for founder CEOs to not fully appreciate the need to raise money when you don't need it because when you do need cash it can be difficult to find. I think George Soros calls this "concept reflexivity."

The wind-down of the company would also have been done in a more transparent manner if there were investor representation at the board level. I'll never know if the IP assets could have been sold for any meaningful amount of money. Technically we probably could have won some kind of moral victory in litigation, but we would have been burning our own money on the legal costs. However, the manner in which the wind-down was conducted certainly left a bitter taste, and to this day it's the only instance where I ended up disliking an entrepreneur we backed.

Myself excluded, I don't think there are any great lessons to be learned from this story. I think most seasoned investment professionals would shake their heads at the decision to not have investors directly represented at the board level. What's more interesting to me though is why the CEO was so adamant about not having investors as board members. It is clearly more convenient to run a company with a board that rarely disagrees with management. It is also true that serious board level disagreements are almost always between management board members and investor board members. I can only speculate, but I think the CEO didn't want the hassle, or was afraid, of acrimonious board meetings and he didn't value the input from investors whose expertise was primarily financial. As with most things in life, reflecting on this experience leads to more questions than answers. In terms of boardroom behavior, what is the proper balance between the need to have harmonious board relations (and yes, I do believe that board meetings should be harmonious the great majority of the time) and the counterbalancing requirement to have board members who will play the role of bomb thrower at the appropriate times. Also, should VCs always be experts in the fields in which they invest? My opinion is no, but that is clearly self-serving.

ENGAGING THE BOARD OF DIRECTORS

John Montgomery, founder and chairman of Montgomery & Hansen LLP and founder of Startworks, gives this advice on engaging the board of directors:

Do you understand boardroom dynamics? Is your executive team prepared for two tiers of management and reporting to a board of directors?

To manage successfully, your team needs to adjust its behavior to fit the characteristics of each tier. The board of directors is a deliberative body that operates by consensus to guide management. On the other hand, executives are action oriented and driven by a military-style chain of command, with the CEO directing the actions of the other executives. Successful CEOs lead their executive teams but guide their directors to reach consensus in the boardroom; they also develop good board processes to enhance the board's critical guidance and oversight functions, and to facilitate consensus.

A board of directors is a small, tribe-like unit. Boards generally select the strongest leader to be the chairperson because tribes automatically align themselves behind the natural leader. When the strongest leader is the chairman, the board will run smoothly because there won't be a power vacuum. Many companies fail because the founder did not understand tribal leadership dynamics. Most founding CEOs serve as the initial chairperson of their board but unwittingly create a power vacuum because they are still developing leadership skills and don't understand boardroom power politics. A power vacuum on a board of directors is disastrous because it invites conflict when other directors try to fill the vacuum.

The best way for a first-time CEO to ensure that his company has a functional board of directors is to find an experienced executive to serve as the chairperson. An experienced mentor usually makes an excellent chairperson. The best time to bring in an independent director to serve as chairperson is long before raising venture capital.

Encouraging Whole-Brain Thinking in the Boardroom

Montgomery continues:

A board of directors led by a first-time CEO as chairperson often loses the capacity to access its collective intelligence when venture capitalists join the board. Without a strong leader to keep the balance, venture capitalists often redirect the focus to making a return. Not only will these directors fill any power vacuum but they will also tend to focus more on financial results than on how the business is functioning as a whole. A balance of perspectives in the boardroom can prevent the board from devolving into a left-brain, spreadsheet-logic-dominated monoculture. A company's long-term survival depends on the chairperson's ability to maintain whole-brain thinking in the boardroom and keep the company focused on fulfilling its vision. When the board focuses primarily on making a financial return, the power of the company's purpose is lost. Employees feel the subtle shift and become dispirited. Meaningful employment devolves into a job, and the culture disappears. Companies die when the board allows its primary focus to shift from realizing the vision to financial engineering.

Several factors facilitate such a shift to a primary focus on financial return. First, it is easy to forget the importance of vision and culture because traditional accounting does not recognize them as assets. Second, filling a power vacuum often precipitates this shift. Third, replacing the founder with a new CEO almost guarantees this shift.

The best way to preserve culture during a management transition is to articulate its key elements and create a succession plan that will enable the new CEO to inherit the culture and maintain it. With a succession plan, employees avoid the anxiety of deducing a new culture from the behavior of the new CEO. If the new CEO preserves the positive aspects of the established culture, he is more likely to win the support of the team and prevent the company from devolving into a financial-engineering game.

Establishing a Good Board Process

"If venture capitalists were truly brilliant they would all be entrepreneurs running companies," says Derek Blazensky, the founding partner of Cardinal Venture Capital, as cited by John Montgomery. "Venture capitalists are, however, brilliant pattern matchers who see the same issues across their portfolios of companies. A great venture capitalist recognizes these patterns and contributes his pattern-matching expertise to boards of directors."

Board Composition

Effective CEOs proactively manage the composition of the board of directors. According to John Montgomery, Blazensky further states:

Until a company raises outside professional money and has fiduciary duties to the investor stockholders, a startup should have an informal advisory board instead of a formal board of directors. If the founder's relatives are directors, the company should invite them off the board before the company composes its formal board of directors. The term sheet for the series A financing will require the company to establish a formal board.

After the series A financing, the ideal board has five directors. Generally, the common stock has the right to elect two directors, who are usually the founder, who came up with the brilliant idea, and the CEO, who may or may not be the founder. After the series B financing, the company will have two venture capital directors elected by the preferred stock.

To keep the board focused on building the business, it is critical to have an outside, independent person as the fifth director. The ideal independent director contributes management expertise from several tours of duty as a CEO. The independent director should have had operating responsibility and made the numbers for several years at a world-class company. Such an independent director can be extremely helpful on the operations side of the business but is usually less helpful in fund-raising.

Frequency of Board Meetings

Again citing Derek Blazensky, John Montgomery notes that the best practice is to hold eight board meetings a year, including four official board meetings. Startups don't need more than four formal board meetings in a year because most board-level discussion is about strategy and operations. The board uses official meetings to approve stock option grants, budgets, and other major items.

Here is Blazensky's recipe for an effective board process: An operations review meeting should follow each of the four official board meetings. The foundation of a functional board process is having the five key directors meet four times a year in formal board meetings and four times for operations review meetings. The board should always schedule the next year's meetings well before the end of each calendar year. Monthly meetings set up the CEO for failure because it's difficult to accomplish enough between meetings. Monthly meetings distract management from running the business. If the series A term sheet requires that the board meet monthly, however, the company should sign that term sheet and take the money. The term sheet is not the place to fight frequency of meetings.

Conducting Effective Board Meetings

Montgomery further cites the ideas of Leo Quilici, Cobalt's CFO, and Derek Blazensky: "The CEO should start organizing the next board meeting two weeks ahead of time to give the management team enough time to prepare their presentations," says Quilici. "A CEO must maintain good communication with his board," says Blazensky, "proactively educate and presell each director before every board meeting because directors hate surprises."

"The CEO must manage the board and not allow the directors to drive a board meeting," says Quilici. "If the CEO fails to drive the meeting, the board may conclude that the CEO is not driving the company either and may act to replace him. Finally, the CEO should never ask for direction at the board meeting because his job is to lead the company and to tell the board what the direction is. The CEO shouldn't worry if the board disagrees with the direction because it's his job to determine the direction."

A well-run board has already reached consensus before the meeting on all matters requiring a vote, including approval of a budget, an expense or revenue plan, or an executive hire. A CEO should never call for a vote unless he already knows the outcome. Each director should have already approved the budget or other item before the board meeting. Great CEOs ensure the desired result by proactively reaching consensus in advance.

The senior management team should attend board meetings, especially operations review meetings. The VP of sales should discuss sales, and the VP of marketing should discuss marketing. Hearing the perspective of each member of the executive team helps the board gauge performance. It's usually a bad sign if the CEO doesn't invite the management team to board meetings. On the other extreme, it's a bad sign if the CEO creates a human shield by inviting half of the company because the board will not dare to address really hard issues with 30 people in the room.

Board Responsibilities

Again according to Montgomery, Blazensky says that directors have the responsibility to extend the duties of care and loyalty to all stockholders: "Being informed helps directors speak candidly and exercise the duties of care and loyalty." A great CEO prepares each director before each board meeting so that the director can privately give feedback and guidance about the company's next moves. Directors need enough time to be thoughtful in private to come to the board meeting prepared with ideas.

The board's activities are not as clearly defined as its fiduciary responsibilities. "A good board," notes Blazensky, "will help develop the business strategy." The CEO's job is to drive the company's strategy and guide the company. The CEO should constantly remind the directors of the vision in almost every communication and update them whenever it changes.

"A great board also assists with fund-raising," adds Blazensky. "The CEO should share his fund-raising strategy and ask the board for help and input.

"The board should also help draft the annual budget and the revenue plan and design the right incentives to inspire the team to climb the mountain. Proper incentives establish the metrics by which the company's progress will be measured. Reaching the goals should allow the company to afford to make the incentive payments. Boards usually adopt incentives too quickly and base them on financial metrics like cash on hand or the size of last year's incentives rather than true performance metrics. For example, the incentive structure should reward maintaining the largest accounts and discourage losing them. An effective board designs appropriate management incentives. The independent director is usually the right person to lead the compensation committee because he understands the pressure that management is under in operating the business. Because he is usually not a significant investor, he doesn't want to keep salaries artificially low to make his money last longer but rather wants to keep the business on track to reach its goals. His prior executive experience is also helpful in designing effective management incentives.

"The board helps attract the best available executives that the company can afford to hire. An effective board also removes the underperformers who don't fit the culture or who fail to meet the performance criteria of the incentive program. To encourage honest feedback about the CEO's management skills, some boards meet occasionally without him present. The board can candidly discuss the CEO in such sessions and circle back with him to discuss any issues that are raised."

"A good board of directors also helps engineer the exit transaction," concludes Blazensky. "The board's responsibility is to look out for the interests of all the stockholders who invested in the company. Investors make money only when a business is sold or goes public. A good board helps the company prepare for such an exit."

Making Your Board Work for You

Mark Bivens, entrepreneur and VC with Truffle Capital, had this to say about working with a board:

Fred Wilson ran an excellent series recently on his blog about startup boards of directors. The series began with several posts of Fred's typically concise and valuable insights, and subsequently featured guest opinions from a number of experienced practitioners in the ecosystem.

One of Fred's pearls of wisdom on board meetings struck me as particularly relevant for startups here in continental Europe: "Board meetings should not be held for the benefit of the board; they should be for the benefit of the CEO."

This message resonated with me when I think about board meetings in many venture-backed startups here. VCs often dominate the boards of European startups, certainly in terms of influence if not in full legal voting majority. Board composition in European companies is closely correlated with the company's corporate form. In Belgium and the Netherlands, for instance, the common BV corporate entity has a two-tier structure, with a board of supervisory directors separated from the board of managing directors. In France, a startup may have a single tier structure (conseil d'administration) but frequently adapts a two-tier one as it matures (directoire plus conseil de surveillance). Because of the absence of management in the supervisory board layer of a two-tier structure, this organ is commonly controlled by the VCs.

This is certainly not a problem per se. However, a VC-dominated board can create an environment in which the management team comes to regard the board meeting as a reporting obligation to plow through, i.e., a quarterly or bimonthly chore. A European VC tilt toward under-capitalization—or at least the reluctance to fund outsize financing rounds that give even those companies with a high burn rate an extended cash runway—can keep startups on a tight financing leash and thus also reinforce the headmaster/pupil dynamic.

The consequence is that board sessions turn into operational update exercises as opposed to truly open exchanges on the most important strategic issues facing the company.

So how to avoid this trap?

Both the VCs and the entrepreneurs are responsible. As VCs, we should communicate clear expectations and board meeting rules of engagement to entrepreneurs at the time of the deal. We should also take care to isolate the important but operationally oriented reporting items to a place outside the boundaries of the board meeting.

Entrepreneurs, and this can be uncomfortable, need to learn how to (politely) say no to VC requests to add nonstrategic topics to the board agenda. Rather, they should be strict in prioritizing the most important strategic topics for discussion and should view each board meeting as a chance to share (as Fred called it) "the issues that are keeping them awake at night."

Then we'll all get a good night's sleep.

7

Company Building and Growing Value

Success in entrepreneurship is certainly not all about raising funding. If anything, one mistake some entrepreneurs make is raising too much funding, becoming addicted to spending money and failing to get their business on a clear path to profitability. Each time an entrepreneur raises funding, it lifts the liquidation stack of how much of the exit consideration will need to pay off the investors before founders and management get into the money. This section examines a few key lessons from very successful venture-backed exits whose elements can be embedded into new ventures resulting in rapid growth and building value in the business. Many of these elements are best considered at the time of idea inception or as early as possible thereafter, rather than after-the-fact efforts to incorporate into the business model.

DISTRIBUTION VERSUS PRODUCT

There seems to be a trend of entrepreneurs focused on product more than distribution. Steve Jobs was superfocused on the product and perfection in its design. And, of course, there is Mark Zuckerberg's relentless obsession with making the product better, believing that the rest of the business then falls into place. Despite these two great success stories, I like a deal with a killer distribution strategy. There is no question that a great product makes a company, but let's work hard to guarantee success by finding a way to acquire initial users. In the telecom world we called this cost of user/subscriber acquisition.

Amazing product or service offerings, with no clue on how to acquire users, often scare me. They win from time to time like Angry Birds, but that's a big leap of faith until real users have validated it. Even Facebook had the Harvard student community responsible for its successful launch. What is your Harvard?

Let's look at a few killer success stories and consider product versus distribution.

SKYPE: WHERE IS YOUR BUTTON ON KAZAA?

Skype was quite undifferentiated in a crowded space where the barriers to entry were super low. If you went to a Voice on the Net (VON) show where the Voice over IP (VoIP) community assembled, you'd find 200-plus companies offering a similar softphone. Skype launched the company by putting a button on Kazaa. Cofounded by the two Skype founders, Kazaa was basically a copycat of Napster. At the time of Skype's launch on Kazaa, Kazaa had 11 million unique visitors per day. Kazaa users were stealing their music, movies, TV, software, games, and porn using Kazaa's peer-to-peer (P2P) technology. Users would download the pirated file, simultaneously sending/uploading it from their PC. These users were clearly enabled with fast broadband connections, all-you-can eat bandwidth subscriptions, and not afraid of peer-to-peer technology running on their PCs.

I hear the banner ad on Kazaa said something like, "Don't pay for your music, why pay for telecom?" I don't know what the button actually said. Tell me if you know.

After six days of the banner ad being up, tons of users downloaded Skype and e-mailed their friends to also download Skype and connect with them to get the free magic phone call. I've heard they pulled the ad after six or seven days because they were crashing their servers with user growth.

Skype is probably the most highly networked effect company in history. Skype had a great but undifferentiated product, but a unique and magic distribution channel that sparked atomic growth. The company then executed flawlessly refining the product.

Index, one of the main VCs behind Skype, told me that what appealed to the VCs was the serverless nature of the Peer-2-Peer technology architecture. So for them it was not all about the button on Kazaa. I don't disagree, but for me it was all about matching the launch of Skype with the button on Kazaa. My point still rings clear: make a killer product, but match it with a killer distribution strategy.

With all the existing communities and social networks, if you work hard at it, you can manifest a killer distribution strategy and find your button on Kazaa. (By the way, the name of the VC fund started by the Skype founders is Atomico . . . as in radioactive growth.)

FACEBOOK: THE BALANCE AMONG PRODUCT, END USER EXPERIENCE, AND ADVERTISING

Buddies of mine at Deutsche Bank in San Francisco set up an afternoon meeting with an early Facebooker recently. We spent five hours together in our first meeting, which started in DB's boardroom on the forty-fifth floor overlooking the sun-covered fog blanketing San Francisco Bay. We continued a few hours later in the bar at the St. Regis Hotel. The meeting was with one of the first guys to join the advertising sales team at Facebook. Later a product guy from Facebook joined us. I tried to get an understanding of what is the secret sauce or magic dust that these guys could bring to my portfolio. What kind of special advice or super value could they bring coming freshly out of Facebook? For example, a company that recently pitched me sells stuff online, and 60 percent of their traffic (Internet visitors) comes from Facebook, another 24 percent comes from Twitter, and only 10 percent comes from Google. The CEO has mastered social media and knows how to motivate women to click on the Like button on Facebook and tweet things promoting his business in return for giving these users reward points to get discounts and group purchase deals on products sold on his site. So basically he's figured out how to transform his users into chimps clicking on Facebook buttons, promoting his products to their friends and followers on Facebook and Twitter. Google hardly fits into his customer acquisition strategy, which helps explain why the value is moving to Facebook and Twitter.

When I met the real Facebookers, I was expecting to learn more of these black arts secrets of how to leverage Facebook. What I learned was very different. I got the impression that the movie about Facebook was accurate in the sense that Zuckerberg was and remains totally uninterested in money and is totally obsessed with the product being super cool for the user. For example, the advertising Facebooker would come back with a $50 million purchase order from a big brand advertiser like Bank of America (B of A). The bank wanted to offer credit cards tailored for young students. B of A hoped to acquire customers for life by skinning the entire website Bank of America red. When presented with the B of A deal, Zuckerberg rejected the idea of reskinning his website in the colors of a bank.

Domino's Pizza loves to sell pizza to students. The company agreed with the Facebook ad sales team on a dynamic advertising campaign where a pizza would fly out of the box and move across the Facebook screen; the user could click on the pizza to make it a kind of video game ad. Zuckerberg responded by allowing Domino's Pizza to have a small text ad in the bottom right corner of the screen, more subtle than Google AdSense.

Zuckerberg did not just let the advertising team run wild with his company. If you look at Pandora and Last.fm, these music websites change the entire background skin of the site to some laundry detergent advertiser. There is absolutely no shame in this, but that's what happens. The Facebooker told me that with every other company he had worked at, the advertising customer paying the cold cash was king. At Facebook the product sensibility was, is, and will always be king. The fact that Zuckerberg does not care about money also keeps the culture pure. My guy at Facebook joined the month before they decided to open up Facebook from university users only to the general public. This was a big risk to allow your mom and dad to join Facebook and become friends with you when up until that point it was students only. They watched the user base grow from 8 million to 54 million in 12 months. Before then the advertising team could get meetings with brands, but they struggled to get good deals. The advertisers told these Facebookers that they were not MySpace and that most of the advertising budget to reach this youthful demographic was going to MySpace. That changed when Facebook got to 54 million users. After that, $50 million advertising deals were not uncommon. These guys grew sales from zero to $4 billion in four years. That's a lot of traveling. They crushed MySpace.

MYSPACE: PIMP OUT YOUR CONTACTS

Let's look at MySpace. There was a time when VCs were critical of Peter Thiel investing in another social network after MySpace became the category killer and fed off the carcass of Friendster. I had something of a front-row seat with the MySpace story because of a buddy of mine, Jay Stevens, the first MySpace employee to be located outside of the United States. He grew MySpace's international operations and business, and lived around the corner from me in London.

MySpace was founded in 2003 and acquired by News Corporation in 2005 for $580 million and generated $800 million of revenue in 2008. That is a very short ride from launch to blockbuster exit. The secret to its success was a killer distribution strategy over a very crappy product.

At the time MySpace came along, Friendster was the dominant social network. What MySpace did well was appeal to music bands with a light value prop. They said to music bands, "Hey, make a MySpace page for your band, upload a few of your songs, then e-mail your fan base to listen to your music for free. Only upload songs you want to give away for free and put a link to buy the album. So if you are a small band in Denmark and all of a sudden you get a million downloads in China, you don't have to worry about paying bandwidth costs or IT when hosting the songs on your own website. MySpace pays for all of that for free, and in fact you hardly need a web developer or anything."

The bands made MySpace pages and e-mailed their fan base to visit their MySpace pages. Even a bad high school band has over 1,000 e-mail addresses for its fan base. Good ones have millions of e-mail addresses. In the fan base of any band are lots of other bands. If you had a small band and you went to an Arctic Monkeys concert, you would hear the band on stage telling you to download a copy of tonight's concert for free at www.MySpace.com/arcticmonkeys. The bands in the audience signed up and e-mailed their fan e-mail lists, which in turn contain bands on those e-mail lists, and so the radioactive message spreads. Bands could play gigs three nights a week, spreading the word about MySpace, touring from city to city. Huge. Think of how much money a company would need to spend to get users to come to their website. MySpace paid near nothing.

That is how you found a company and two years later sell if for over $500 million.

One amazing marketing thing Jay did in Europe was produce parties. When he opened the Italian market, he rented out a warehouse and organized a one-night disco, filling the building with bands, all you can drink open bar, and canapés. It was free to attend, but in order to be on the list to get in the front door, one needed to have a MySpace profile. He leveraged the great relationships MySpace had with bands to pack these parties with five or more different bands in the same building at the same time to attract "the kids" to come. These parties might happen on a Tuesday night and, by Friday the same week, every digital native in the country would know who MySpace was and consider it cool. Despite the huge talent Jay and the MySpace team brought to bear, being owned by Rupert Murdoch was just not cool. I hope Justin Timberlake can turn it into something great again.

Even when MySpace was king of social networks, with 25 million users and a huge lead over Facebook, every time I met folks from MySpace, including Jay, they were talking about leaving. They would motor on about their great ideas and what they wanted to do, but being owned by Rupert Murdoch meant that the employees of MySpace lacked any equity incentive to make a fortune there. The ship had already sailed, and being owned by News Corp just infected the entire company with cancer. No CEO came along to inspire anyone. Facebook not only charged them as the underdog, but MySpace didn't put up much of a fight.

I invested in a viral comedy website called ComedyBlaze.tv and created a MySpace profile to acquire hundreds of comedian users per day, along with their video content. By mastering the MySpace product early on, I could see what worked and what didn't. I was not in the demographic to care about having a MySpace profile, but used it for my other business. My memory of the MySpace product is shockingly bad, super clunky. It's hard to believe the company had such amazing traction with such a weak product. Rather than enable the user to set the background image on a MySpace profile, I needed to have my developers make the MySpace profile using html.

By the time MySpace made the product good, then excellent, the war was already lost to Facebook. One of the Facebookers told me that the reason they beat MySpace so handily is that each Facebook user was verified as being who they claimed to be. On MySpace, I would receive invites from some hot girl in a bikini asking to be my friend, but I could tell that it was probably some big, fat, hairy man or some Indian dude in a call center, gaming the system for some spam junk-mail client. With Facebook, you could tell that your friends were indeed your friends. Facebookers I know credit this as one of their success ingredients.

Clearly, building an amazing product that sells itself is the current trend. The product itself is the sales and marketing department, with virility and distribution networks built into your product, coupled with smart execution strategies. The takeaway with MySpace was a weak product combined with a strong value proposition and brilliant distribution strategy. When folks talk about MySpace as a loser to Facebook, I think of the company that launched a website and two years later was sold for over half a billion dollars in cash. That is a huge success story and a role model for venture-backed success.

From 2005 until early 2008, MySpace was the most visited social networking site in the world. In June 2006, it surpassed Google as the most visited website in the United States. In April 2008, MySpace was overtaken by Facebook in the number of unique worldwide visitors; it was surpassed in the number of unique U.S. visitors in May 2009. Since then, the number of MySpace users has declined steadily. As of February 2013, MySpace was ranked 220th globally and 133rd in the United States. In June 2009, MySpace employed approximately 1,600 workers. Since then the company has undergone several rounds of layoffs and, by June 2011, MySpace had reduced its staff to around 200. On June 29, 2011, MySpace was sold to Specific Media and Justin Timberlake for approximately $35 million.

YOUTUBE: HOW TO EXTEND BEYOND YOUR DOMAIN

YouTube is the premier example of what I call "an extend" or "extensible" company. You can upload a video of, say, your startup pitch to YouTube, then embed that video into your website. Users can come to your website and watch your video while the video is being served up and hosted by YouTube at zero cost to you.

YouTube is not restricted or confined to its own website domain, but extends and embeds to millions of other websites that each have their own daily traffic. It is massively viral. Everywhere you go on the web, you see YouTube, without the need to go to www.youtube.com.

Today you can design ways of embedding virility and fire pace spreading of your value prop over other existing networks, fan bases, existing communities, and so on. It's hard to match the YouTube embed model, but a lot of websites can create widgets and drop them onto other sites or enable any other website to go to your URL and embed your widget onto their website. If you can drop your value prop into the checkout process of Amazon or eBay or some other hugely trafficked partner, then you are on your way.

I obsess about finding "my button on Kazaa" with all of my digital companies. Entrepreneurs should manifest their Skype-Kazaa, MySpace–music band fan base, YouTube–extend distribution buttons. I find it useful to connect CEOs that can swap traffic or coach each other on how to find these digital distribution channels. The reason I like BranchOut so much is the very obvious distribution channel it has carved out for itself on Facebook.

THE MARKETING MYTH

Adam Dell, venture partner at Austin Ventures, observes:

> Allocating too many resources toward marketing and away from product innovation can be the death knell for an early-stage startup. Some companies rely on various forms of advertising to build their business with channels ranging from TV to radio, billboards, and display ads. If you look at best companies that have been built over the last 10 years in the technology space, they are businesses that have built their brands by virtue of the caliber and quality of the value proposition that they deliver to their customers.

Adam cautions entrepreneurs that paying someone to get the word out about your business diverts finite energy and resources away from your product and customer experience:

> Companies like OpenTable, ZipCar, PayPal, and Facebook built their brands based on the activity of what they do rather than by spending money to tell people what they do. Startups should think at a very foundational level of their business how to incorporate the very act of using the product or service as a means of spreading the message. Virility is something you build into the business from day one, not something you add later. OpenTable is viral by its nature, given the dynamics of network effects. ZipCar is another example, which enables members to share info about car location and routes. These companies are able to build their businesses much more efficiently with a sense of control over their own destiny. Facebook is obviously all about sharing.
>
> Companies that start to market themselves through paid channels become addicted to this method of growth. Not only will the effectiveness of these paid channels change over time as the dynamics of a given advertising channel change, but the energy and focus

of a small organization such as a startup is sucked away from innovating around the product or value proposition. The key is to design
products or services that grow tentacles that move the value proposition beyond a small set of customers.

Focus energy and resources heavily on product innovation, customer delight, getting your tentacles into the customers, and make
them your evangelists.

Take a look at the funding history of OpenTable in Table 7.1. This is an
example of the number and sheer volume of the funding rounds for a company that eventually gets to an IPO on NASDAQ. They started with a seed
round of $75,000, and then raised over $100 million. It took over 10 years to
reach an IPO.

Table 7.1 Funding History of OpenTable

Investment Firm	Participating Round Number(s)
American Express Co.	3
Angel Investors LP	1, 2
Arba Seed Investment Group	1
Archery Capital	4
Benchmark Capital	3, 4*
Brainstorm Ventures International	
Comdisco Ventures	4
Draper Richards	2, 4, 5
Epoch Partners	4
IAC/InterActiveCorp	
ICON	3
Impact Venture Partners	3, 4
Individual Investors	1, 2
Integral Capital Partners	4
Lettuce Entertain You Enterprises	3
Prescient Capital	1*, 2*, 3
Stafford Capital	1
Undisclosed Venture Investor(s)	6

Investment Firm	Participating Round Number(s)
Upstart Capital	4
Venture Frogs LLC	2
W Capital Partners	
Worldspan	4
Zagat Survey LLC	3

★ = Lead investor.

Round	Round Type	Date	Amount	Post Valuation (MM)
1	Seed	Apr. 30, 1999	$0.75	$3.10
2	First	May 17, 1999	$2.00	$9.00
3	Second	Jan. 3, 2000	$10.00	$30.00
4	Third	Sep. 21, 2000	$42.00	$130.00
5	Fourth	Feb. 7, 2003	$7.00	N/A
6	Fifth	Oct. 28, 2004	$15.00	N/A
7	IPO	May 21, 2009	$31.40	$483.79

THE BLACKMAIL BUSINESS MODEL

Steve Schlenker, cofounder and managing partner of DN Capital, had this to say about "the blackmail business model":

> Worst business model: We referred to this one internally as "the blackmail business model." This was shortly after the rise of Wikipedia and the launch of Wikia in the States. A U.K.-based company that will remain nameless had the idea of hiring students to go around to small businesses who did not have web presence and say that for a nominal charge (circa £100, all payable to the student), they would create wikis that would immediately give the businesses a web presence that they could then market to their customers, provide updates on menus or services or pricing or hours, etc. The company then intended to call each business a few weeks later, par-

ticularly after the businesses had marketed their wikis to their regular customers, and say, "You do realize anyone can update a wiki, including your competitors? If you pay us a monthly service fee, we will monitor what is being updated on your wiki and make certain comments you don't want are not posted." Felt like something straight out of Palermo. Needless to say, we passed.

THE NINE-YEAR OVERNIGHT SUCCESS

The story of Riccardo Zacconi, CEO of King.com, is a good illustration of different life cycles a company goes through. The first cycle was bootstrapping with his own cash and total commitment to getting a real product out the door and launched. The next phase was closing angel funding and taking the company immediately into a profitable state. This is where King.com differs from many businesses that become addicted to angel and VC funding. With just a modest amount of angel funding, King.com grew to a substantial casual gaming business distributing games on all the major online portals and countless other Internet partner websites. The company grew its teams in Stockholm, Hamburg, Milan, Malta, and Los Angeles. Riccardo is Italian and lives in London as the CEO. By January 2005, King.com was profitable and managing high growth and scale. In September 2005 Index Ventures and Apax invested 34 million euros ($45 million), both investing in the company and buying shares from Riccardo and his cofounders in a direct secondary transaction. The founders took half of that cash out for themselves and left the other half to grow the business.

By April 2011 the company had 110 employees, strong investors, management, and a wide book of game titles and intellectual property. They leveraged all of this when they relaunched their business on Facebook. Before April 2011 King.com had 300 million game plays per month. By June 2012 this had grown to 3 billion game plays, becoming the fourth largest games developer on Facebook. By January 2013 King.com had 6 billion game plays and 400 employees. It would seem to me that the real King.com story may only now be starting.

I think Riccardo's tale has many lessons, a key one being that even when you think you have gone past bootstrapping and are in major scaling and high-growth mode with everything working, you may still need to iterate, pivot, and keep innovating to become wildly successful. I see a lot of CEOs tell me how they plan to raise large chunky angel rounds, meaning $5 million to $10 million, all from angels, and then bypass VCs and do a deal with a private equity player like Riccardo did. When I hear this, I think that this CEO is not having any luck with VCs and there is just not enough cash to fund all the deals attracting angel funding. In Riccardo's case, he truly managed to design a capital efficient business model without the need for venture capital funding. He went from bootstrapping and angel funding to private equity bypassing the VCs. Nice work!

JUST GRAB THE BIRD AND LOWER YOURSELF OUT OF THOSE CLOUDS

This next story comes from a friend of mine, Paula Brillson, attorney at law and founder and former CEO of Asia Capacity Exchange (ACE), whom I got to know as a competitor in the late 1990s and early 2000s. I wanted to include at least one story from the Internet telecom boom-and-bust period, as it is a relevant part of history and shapes how entrepreneurs and VCs behave today. Paula Brillson is a transactional attorney and an advisor to small businesses and entrepreneurs from corporate matters to contracts to intellectual property and an avid blogger (www.brillson.com).

> Back in 2000 my startup company, Asia Capacity Exchange, (an innovative online exchange for buying and selling bandwidth as a commodity) was evaluated at $80 million by Morgan Stanley and we received a firm offer letter for their investment. After only one year of operation and minimal sales in our pipeline, by today's standards that would have been a real triumph. However, as first generation Internet entrepreneurs, our heads were way up in the clouds, and when we were approached to go on a road show with

Deutsche Bank at a valuation of $140 million, we couldn't resist. Following the road show we sent a letter to Morgan Stanley declining their offer and we anxiously awaited the letter of intent from Deutsche Bank.

Our dot-com bubble burst when the technology-heavy NAS-DAQ stock market index went from an all-time high of 5,132 on March 10, 2000 to 1,840 in March 2001—a drop of 64 percent in 12 months. Once this first thread was pulled, it didn't take long for the company to start unraveling. Not only did Deutsche Bank decide to withdraw their verbal offer, but within the coming weeks, one by one our customers (also Internet startups) began to default. By September 2002 the index was below 1,200 and investors had lost $5 trillion in the meltdown. We quickly saw our evaluation drop to $60 million and below, and suddenly the air was very thin up there in the clouds. While very few industry analysts could have predicted the collapse of the market or the demise of Enron, who were also operating a bandwidth exchange as a way to disguise losses and create false profits, Enron's collapse led to complete loss of credibility for our emerging bandwidth exchange industry. The lesson to be learned here is that a bird in hand is worth more than many in the bush and that as a startup company, just grab the bird and lower yourself out of those clouds.

How to Come Up with True Innovation That Drives the Rest

All that we are is the result of what we have thought.
THE BUDDHA

Apple may be relevant to your company's approach to innovation. Allow employees to try 10 ideas, see which ones attract continued support, winnow out one, and give it the company's focus. That selection funnel within a firm starts to become a formula for innovation. It is much like the VC's funnel where 3,000 investment opportunities turns into calls and meetings with 300 companies, follow-up meetings with 100, and 5 to 10 investments per year. Startup teams can review ideas just like a VC fund and drill down to one idea to focus on.

Many people retweet words of wisdom from Steve Jobs, but it's worth saying here that if you just listen to your customers, you will only give them more, faster, cheaper, but never true innovation. Josh James, CEO of Omniture, sold to Adobe for $1.8 billion, said, "Don't listen to what your customers want or you'll get hit with a wave of oncoming traffic from competitors that are bigger than you." That makes strategic sense. "Art is listening to the user. Science is measuring and acting on the data," says Deep Nishar, SVP, products and user experience, LinkedIn.

Steve Jobs said, "Some people say, 'Give the customers what they want.' But that's not my approach. Our job is to figure out what they're going to want before they do. I think Henry Ford once said, 'If I asked customers what they wanted, they would have told me—a faster horse!' People don't know what they want until you show it to them. That's why I never rely on market research. Our task is to read things that are not yet on the page."

PICKING A NAME

Benjamin D. Kern, partner at McGuireWoods, made the following observations about choosing a name:

> You don't need to be a corporate lawyer to get a company up and running. Pick a name, register with the secretary of state of the state in which you intend to operate, put some software code or a couple of patents in the company, and watch the value of your stock grow.
>
> Three out of four of these things should be easy, and they are. So why do first-time entrepreneurs usually get it wrong?
>
> If you get more than three notices per month about expiring domain names that you've registered and since forgotten, you're

probably an aspiring website billionaire. For the last decade, choosing a domain name has been one of the first steps in kicking off a new company.

Entrepreneurs check domain names, and sometimes spend several hundred dollars registering them, or spend thousands trying to buy them at auction. They may spend several hundred more dollars in registering a company name with a state's secretary of state. But a decidedly smaller number of entrepreneurs check the U.S. Patent and Trademark Office's public records for trademark conflicts. And fewer still engage a search firm or a lawyer to do an organized trademark search, or spend the moderate additional money that it would take to file a trademark intent-to-use application.

But the trademark can trump a domain name or a company name. If you register a domain name or corporate name that conflicts with someone else's trademark, you may not be able to use the name to identify your products, and could potentially be forced to give up the domain name.

Failing to do appropriate trademark research is a mistake sometimes made by experienced leaders as well as first-time entrepreneurs. Among the companies that make these mistakes, the lucky ones are those who can change their branding or name strategy at a reasonable cost.

One recent, public example came in the case of New Century Bank, whose "New Century" name proved uncomfortably close to another bank that was in financial difficulty. New Century Bank chose to transition to the name Customers 1st and registered the domain names customersfirstbank.com and customers 1stbank. com. The domain names were available, but the trademark space was a crowded one. After an expensive rebranding process to change the name to Customers 1st, the bank was sued for trademark infringement and became subject to a court order prohibiting the use of the name.

8

Which Way to the Exit?

I made most of my money selling too early.

J. P. MORGAN

M&A IS THE MOST LIKELY POSITIVE OUTCOME FOR MOST ENTREPRENEURS

Merger and acquisition (M&A) is the most likely positive outcome for most angel- or VC-backed technology startups and therefore worth understanding from the first moment you begin to conceive your new venture or as you move along the journey to exit. For acquirers M&A is about a lot of things. Is a dollar spent on acquisitive growth better than a dollar spent on organic growth? M&A is about revenue growth, innovation, augmenting the DNA of your employees and core leadership team, lowering attrition, and increasing the "coolness" of your company to appeal to new recruits. M&A is about confidence within a company, confidence in the macroeconomic environment, defense, economies of scale. M&A is about animal instincts.

PRACTICAL IDEAS AND ADVICE WHEN SELLING YOUR COMPANY VIA M&A

It's rumored that Google had a chance to sell to Excite for $1 million and turned it down. I turned down an offer to sell my company for $6 million when I owned 50 percent of it with no investors. Instead of selling, I gambled, raising trainloads of VC funding. I went for it. More on that later.

When you go to networking events and conferences, lawyers and accountants will tell you tons of things you need to prepare and tidy up before selling your company.

The best advice I hear on selling your company is this: don't focus on *selling* your company, but rather focus on *building* a great company with strong revenue growth and very happy customers and partners. If you do that well, buyers will find you.

Keep talking to bankers and analysts about your business. These bankers have regular meetings with the big balance sheet buyers like Google. When they visit these acquisitive companies, they want to differentiate themselves from the other bankers. They want to be able to ask, "Have you heard of company XYZ?" That could be Goldman Sachs or Morgan Stanley pitching your deal to Google. It is worth your time to keep these bankers up on your company.

When you are approached by corporate development from some big balance sheet buyer like Google or Yahoo!, respond professionally but don't drop your focus on sales, on keeping your customers happy, and keeping your business on track. Everyone has seen a company sign a letter of intent (LOI) with a big balance sheet buyer, only to see the due diligence (DD) process became so grueling that sales slip, causing the price the buyer is willing to pay drop as well.

Everyone will tell you that you should never negotiate with only one buyer or investor. Good advice of course, but not possible for everyone. If you can, of course, try to get as many buyers to the table as you can, hire a banker, and have the banker approach the full constellation of would-be buyers while you keep driving sales and your core business. Try to involve your lawyers, your investors, your whole network. Try to persuade them to do as much of this work as possible for you. Your number one BATNA (best alternative to the negotiated agreement) is to keep going and not sell. Be polite and professional, but remember your priorities: If you can't attend a meeting with a potential buyer because you need to see a customer or hire a crucial new employee, don't overstress; that's where you should be—running the business.

You should conduct DD on your buyer just as you should on your investors and suppliers. Once they start asking for more time and information, you should qualify how serious they are given where you are in the process. Some entrepreneurs think they are in play when they are not. Corporate development folks are doing their job to meet you for lunch, but there may be no momentum or rhythm of a deal that's going to happen anytime soon. I've seen some of my own CEOs defer raising their next financing round because they think they are in play—big mistake.

Feel free to ask the person you are dealing with whether the CEO and CFO have signed off on the deal. Do they even know about the discussion? Is there a group head or business division sponsoring this acquisition, or are you just a bright and shiny object the corp dev group thinks would be nice to have?

Every M&A discussion is like a job interview. You should figure out whether you really want to "work" at that company. Some deals are talent deals, just buying people with a quick tuck-in. Most deals are buying intellectual property (IP), strategic growth, or expansion of some kind; but *every* deal is a talent acquisition to some extent. Cultures should match. In an ideal world, you will have "violent likability" where the buyer thinks the personalities of the target company's senior management team are a perfect fit with the culture of the buying company.

On a legal and deal structure front, you should always ask for a non–disclosure agreement (NDA) before sharing too much info. Urge the buyer to sign a non-solicit agreement (NSA) preventing them from trying to hire your CTO and other members of your team who have the IP and know-how in their heads. Some acquisitions are about expanding their corporate DNA. Google was an algorithm place trying to become a Facebook and Groupon place.

Always get as much cash up front as you can. Often with acquisitions, part of the consideration is paid to the management team of the acquired company in the form of individual compensation referred to as *earn-outs*. Earn-outs are often tied to specific performance milestones defined in the M&A

agreement. Earn-outs come and go. I am basically against them at a high level for a variety of reasons. They can lead to misalignment of interests. They may result in messy legal disputes. If you are the company being purchased and a big slice of the exit is tied up in an earn-out, you may have little control over making that new business division perform. Most acquisitions are like scrambled eggs, where your company will be integrated into a bigger machine. Good luck driving the metrics that release your earn-out cash. You may have been purchased as a hot topical accessory that may become less relevant to the strategic direction of the acquirer over time. After the purchase, you may no longer be as relevant or the buyer may drop your business line altogether. You have no control over this. Your key employees may not dig working for the man and miss the good old days when you and your cofounder set the vibe in the office. On the flip side, if you see 50 percent of your exit tied up in the earn-out, you may become obsessed with hitting your numbers to see your cash. This may not be in the best interest of the overall company and may prevent you from moving up in the new organization. Bottom line, make these earn-out arguments and transform all that promise into cash today.

If you are dealing with a big balance sheet buyer like a Google, you will be forced to sign a no shop/no talk agreement that says you will not shop your company to other prospective buyers during the period of time that Google is engaged to consider buying you. Make sure none of your opportunistic friends are shopping your deal hoping for a referral fee. Keep control of the flow of information. Stay focused on your current business.

Big balance sheet buyers acquire companies for different reasons. There is a hierarchy in how much they value your company: revenue multiples, profit, IP, or employees. Understand the buyer's hierarchy and position your company to move from one category to another to increase what the buyer is willing to pay for your company. Here are the most common buyer's hierarchies:

1. Team hire ("acqui-hire")
2. Team buy
3. Technology buy
4. Business asset
5. Strategic asset

Team hire or *acqui-hire* is the lowest value the buyer will place on your company. The buyer is literally picking up some technical talent for specific industry segments like apps or mobile, or for segments with a different DNA like gaming, social, or Groupon-esque daily deals. The team may be dispersed once the acquisition is made.

Team buys can have larger ticket size and range between $1 to 5 million paid per manager or engineer. In this case the team will stay together working on the same product or service, but the buyer does not see any acquisition of intellectual property or major market share.

In a *technology buy*, the technology is integrated into the acquiring company, hence worth more. Deal size goes up, and the terms get better for the purchased company. With a technology buy there are likely to be more companies competing to acquire the prized technology. The buyer might even buy the technology and not use it, to ensure that its competitor does not acquire it to fill a product gap or move ahead of the buyer.

Business asset is the same as a technology buy, but with more revenue and customers. Unlike the previous categories, discounted cash flow (DCF) models are used to value the purchase, both for the stand-alone company as well as for the integrated post-acquisition company. The deal size can be significant for business asset purchases. Classic M&A value is calculated considering how the buyer can increase sales of the target, reduce costs with roll-up economics, consolidate payroll and human resources (HR), and so on. Specific customers, actual contracts, and operating in new geographies begin to add to the price tag, making these acquisitions more and more valuable.

Strategic assets are the truly unique buys. There was only one YouTube, and Google had to own it. Facebook could not allow Twitter or Google to buy Instagram. This is essentially like bidding for the Mona Lisa—only one company with that one technology and that real category-killer business. Discounted cash flow is considered, but the auction drives up the value and the world reels at the price.

Once you determine in which category the buyer slots you, your job is to convince them that, with time, they will benefit from elements in the hierarchy above you. Help the buyer justify a higher price and more upfront payment to their target: your company. Identifying the buyer that gains the most from acquiring the mix of what you bring will also move you up the buyer's hierarchy.

If you are within 6 to 18 months of selling your company, now is the time to contact a reputable wealth management group that can help put your family estate plan in place to optimize your benefit over time. Trying to do this just before an exit is not a good idea.

THREE KINDS OF BUSINESS BUYERS

Dave Berkus, author and business angel, describes three kinds of business buyers:

> This is one of my favorite insights, since I lived this one in a positive exit from my computer business. Most people will tell you that there are two kinds of eventual buyers for your business: financial and strategic. A *financial buyer* will analyze your numbers, past and forecast, to the nth degree and calculate the price based upon the result, after carefully comparing your numbers with those of others in the same and similar industries. The object of a financial purchase is to negotiate a bargain, capable of payoff through operating profits or growth over time, or even of immediate profit from arbitrage—knowing of a purchaser that is willing to pay more for your company if repackaged, or even with no changes at all.
>
> A *strategic purchaser* is one that understands what your company has to offer in its marketplace and how your company will add extra value to the purchaser's company. Strategic buyers look for managerial talent, intellectual property, geographic expansion, extension into adjacent markets, and more that will be achieved with the acquisition of your company. Such a purchaser usually is willing to pay more to secure this new leverage, understanding that the value of the acquisition is more than the mere financial value of your enterprise. Most investment bankers will coach you into

helping them find you a strategic buyer, knowing that such sales are quicker, often less focused upon the small warts of a business, and yield higher prices than financial sales.

There is a third class of buyer I discovered firsthand when selling my company—the *emotional buyer*. This rare buyer needs your company. He must have you or one of your competitors, and now. The buyer may be a public company attempting to defend decreasing market share and being overly punished by Wall Street. You may represent the only obvious way to protect against obsolescence from a buyer's declining marketplace or failure to compete against others with better, newer technologies. You may be a most successful direct competitor, one that the buyer's salespeople have observed jealously and nervously, sometimes even jumping over to your company as a result. No matter what the emotional focus, the buyer cannot continue to stand by and watch its business challenged so effectively. The price negotiated is not at all the critical factor in the emotional sale. It is the elimination of pain that drives the buyer to action.

I experienced just this phenomenon and profited by the added value in the transaction provided by an emotional public company buyer for my business. The potential buyer was a hardware company, well aware that margins were decreasing and that software companies, once considered mere vehicles to help sell hardware, were now becoming the central component in a sale, mostly because hardware was fast becoming a commodity as prices dropped. My buyer-candidate had previously licensed our firm as a distributor, a value-added reseller for its hardware. As we grew to capture 16 percent of the world market in our niche, we successfully migrated from the single platform of the buyer-candidate onto hardware from any of its competitors from IBM to NCR to HP and others. At the same time, the buyer-candidate realized that we had become its largest reseller. In one of many meetings with the buyer's CEO, I "accidentally" dropped the truthful fact that his hardware now accounted for only about a third of our hardware revenues, down from 100 percent several years earlier. It did not take but moments for him to realize that his largest reseller was giving his company only a third of its business, that his revenues were declining and ours increasing dramatically. Simple in-the-head math shocked him into the realization that if he could increase our use of his equipment in more sales, he could slow or stop the decline in his revenues and he could migrate into a more software-centric company, much more highly valued by Wall Street, which was punishing his company for its decline and coming obsolescence.

The resulting negotiation was rather quick and very lucrative for our side. It was the first time I had witnessed an emotional buyer, and I appreciated the difference between "strategic" and "emotional" immediately. Ever since, I have been urging my subsequent company CEOs and boards to perform an exercise at regular intervals to seek out and identify future strategic and emotional buyers.

How Instagram Secured a $1 Billion Valuation

Nic Brisbourne, partner at DFJ-Esprit, reviews the factors in Instagram's high valuation by Facebook:

Facebook's $1 billion acquisition of Instagram has triggered discussions about how and why such a young startup with no revenues could achieve such a high valuation. If the gossip and rumors are to be believed, Instagram employed two pretty standard tactics to maximize their valuation on exit. First they used a venture capital round to induce Twitter to make an offer; next they took that offer to Facebook and doubled their valuation.

There are elements of this that every startup can learn from. If you have M&A discussions that are not moving forward as fast as you would like, then raising a round of venture forces the potential acquirer into making a decision. They know that once a round is closed the valuation required to get a deal done will likely have to go up in order to satisfy the new investors; so if they want the company they will get off the pot and make an offer. According to Venturebeat, Instagram had been talking to Twitter for some time but didn't get an offer until their venture deal was about to close.

Fear and competition are important drivers in M&A. It is often the case that market leaders only become interested in buying startups when they learn that one of their competitors is close to making an acquisition; they start to fear for their market dominance. Photo sharing is at the heart of Facebook, and they are vulnerable on mobile. It is easy to see how the combination of Twitter's strength and Instagram's coolness might trouble them.

Obviously, these strategies only work if the startup is highly desirable. Instagram was hot enough to be wanted by Twitter, courted by venture capitalists, and scary to Facebook. Most startups aren't that lucky. It is important to be realistic about potential exit valuations and whether the company is special enough that acquirers will enter into a bidding war.

When I met Gary Johnson, director of corporate development at Facebook, I couldn't help but ask him about Instagram. He said, "Before talking price and terms when seeking to sell your company, you should first take the time to talk alignment, vision, product road map, cultural fit, etc. This is what happened with Instagram. We made sure that we agreed perfectly on the best way to share photos; the result is successful integration and retention of the team. Instagram went from 27 million to 100 million users in a matter of weeks. It was a $1 billion acquisition, now undoubtedly a huge success."

ADVICE ON THE $300 MILLION SALE OF ADIFY

When Yahoo! called Russ Fradin, CEO and cofounder of Dynamic Signal and former CEO and cofounder of Adify, saying they wanted to buy his company, he was professional and took the position of, "Sure, I'm happy to tell you what we do . . . we'd be happy to sell our company to you, but we are in no rush, we are focused on our business and, oh, by the way, we are getting more valuable every day." Be professional and share information, but don't be or appear to be too eager.

How Liquidation Preferences and Carve Outs Play in Exit Scenarios

Antoine Papiernik, partner at Sofinnova Partners, gives this insight:

> The more VCs involved with a company, the harder it becomes to bring the company to an exit. With many VCs in the cap table, you get many differing point of views and motivations around each financing, staffing, and exit decision. Some of the VCs may be limited on cash to continue to invest in that company the reserves of their fund, the timing of their fund, loss of belief in the company, and many other factors. Management needs to lead a company to an exit with the support of a subset of the board. If management does not get paid, the exit will not happen. Liquidation preferences dictate how much of the exit price goes to pay back VCs before management gets any money from the exit proceeds. The result is that companies have a specific liquidation preference hurdle to clear before management sees any cash. Often in the capital-intensive deals the liquidation preference may be $150 million to $250 million.
>
> As a result, if an opportunity comes along to sell the company for $250 million rather than $1 billion, the VCs may not see that opportunity. Management simply would not inform the VCs of this. This is bad. So VCs need to provide management with an incentive. This is done with a management incentive plan known as a carve out. We at Sofinnova make sure our managers have carve outs so they know they will benefit from a sale. This is not the VC

"being nice." VCs will regret it if you don't put these in place. We once had a deal where we invested in the series A alone and then carried the company through series B and C. We could have sold the company after series A and gotten our money back; but instead we replaced the CEO, recapped, and kept fighting on. We then ended up with a third CEO before getting to the exit with a 3-times liquidation pref. These nightmares and recaps could have been avoided had we exited after series A and rewarded the founding CEO. This is a mistake we would not make again. In the end, management needs to lead the company to an exit with the support of at least a subsection of the board.

Antoine Papiernik at Sofinnova is right. Always put a carve out in place. Do not wait until you think you need one to keep management around for a sale that returns 1 times your cash back or most of your cash back. Put a carve out in place for 100 percent of your deals so you get the information. You can always block the sale.

How to Smoke Out the Serious VCs in Your Syndicate

Antoine Papiernik had this to say about working with VCs:

> Sometimes a CEO or leading VC needs to smoke out the VCs that are not serious about supporting and building the company. One option at your disposal is to put in place a bridge financing with a 20-times liquidation preference plus a new option plan for management. This is a pay to play, and you find out pretty quickly who wants to play. If investors do not invest, they get washed out. You can't accept free riders who want to find reasons to look for the future. Only soldiers that can fight should be in the battle. If you lose belief, sell for one dollar. Toxic prefs protect against a dead syndicate.

LARGE TRADE SALES OF PRIVATE, VENTURE-BACKED MEDICAL DEVICE COMPANIES

Antoine Papiernik, partner at Sofinnova Partners, reviewed a few of the largest trade sales of a private, venture-backed medical device company in history:

> We put €49 million into Movetis and three years later sold the company for $428 million. This was a triple-digit exit for the founder, Dirk Reyn. We invested €4.5 into CoreValve, beating out two U.S. competing VCs, then followed 18 months later with a $33 million round, syndicating with Apex and Maverick; then sold to Medtronic for a $700 million up-front payment with 2 times $700 million in earn-outs, one of the largest trade sales of a private, venture-backed medical device company in history. This surgeon entrepreneur started with no money and personally reached a triple-digit exit in five years.

ACQUI-HIRE EARLY EXITS: VCS VERSUS FOUNDERS

Benjamin D. Kern, partner at McGuireWoods, discusses early exit scenarios where investors' and founders' interests conflict:

> During periods following spikes or rapid growth of seed stage or series A and B–round funding, it becomes more common to see companies acquired in their early stages, sometimes pre-revenue and before their products or approaches have matured. Established businesses who seek to grow their teams or technology platforms may make strategic purchases of startup companies because the valuations can be relatively low, and because the founding management team may have entrepreneurial energy to add to the acquirer's team. For investors, these "early" exits rarely represent a significant

ROI. This type of deal may be structured to provide a minimum positive return to investors, while the purchaser dangles contingent compensation packages potentially worth several million dollars over time in front of the young management team. Most standard investment documents do not anticipate these types of exits or provide investors with more than basic tools to leverage in the discussions with the founders or acquirer.

These early exits may invoke a discussion parallel to investors' "jockey versus horse" debate. While the quality of a company's management team is generally considered an important factor in making an investment decision, "horse" investors approach portfolio companies with the assumption that a management team may be reconfigured over several years. "Jockey" investors, however, cite the management team as the primary factor in choosing investments. When early-stage activity spikes, demand for enthusiastic technology talent can result in competition among investors, as well as a type of competition between early-stage investors and the strategic acquirers that investors seek to work with at later stages.

In describing the value of the target, a strategic acquirer may point to the young but aggressive team (especially when talking to the team) and praise their energy and accomplishments. Whether or not the acquirer is confident in the team, using a "jockey" approach to acquiring a company results in acquisition terms that can have very favorable characteristics to the acquirer: e.g., low purchase price for the technology and comparatively high, but contingent, compensation to the founding team, often in the form of restricted stock. Once the founding team has been sold on the deal, the discussion turns to the boardroom.

Selling a deal with a minimal return to investors would ordinarily be all but impossible. An investor who doesn't like the proposed return will almost always have a blocking right that can be used to stop it. However, a blocking right can be a blunt tool, and may not lead to a better result for the investor. Early in the company's life cycle, the investor may not have deployed significant funds into the company. The management team may be lean, and after the acquirer's pitch, is often highly motivated to do the deal. Unlike later-stage companies, where the investor may have deep relationships with other board members and relationships in the company's industry, an early-stage investor new to an investment may not have a large array of alternatives. Early in these deals, the investor may still be building relationships and may need to consider carefully the impact of blocking a deal on reputation, particularly when the proposed price cannot be disclosed. It is sometimes easier to take the low, but positive, return and move on.

I first saw this deal structure and dynamic several years ago in a healthcare technology company. That structure seems to have become the default for early-stage acquisitions since the public offering and acquisition markets have again become more active.

For illustration, let's say that a group of young entrepreneurs develop "CatBox.me," a social media business that revolutionizes the sharing, tagging, and curation of adorable cat videos, with robust cross-platform integration capabilities. The business thrives on the founders' viral and enthusiastic social media following; with sponsorship deals and an advertising gold mine just over the horizon, the company raises $1.5 million in series A funding on a $3 million pre-money valuation, contingent on the founders quitting college and on conversion of the business to a C-corp.

The company uses the growth capital to expand its outreach team by hiring bloggers, and engages Ruby developers to do product development, adding a clean mobile interface, real-time geo-tagged uploading, and fault-tolerant, high-volume cat video streaming.

The founders work hard for a year, but fund-raising and corporate management require significant time from the founders. On a visit to a prospective corporate partner, a large online pet food business, the pet food business presents an acquisition offer to the founders.

The offer details $10 million in total consideration. The term sheet refers to an asset sale for $5 million, with $2.5 million stock retention packages for each of the two founders. All consideration payable to the founders, in both the asset purchase and the retention packages, would take the form of restricted stock, vesting over four years based on continued employment. The pet food company explains to the founders that it is building its own cat video distribution network, which will soon result in a well-funded competitor to CatBox.me. Acquiring CatBox.me will give the pet food company an advantage of several months in its development efforts, but only if the offer can be accepted within a day and completed within a matter of weeks. The pet food company goes on to say that while the CatBox product is of only marginal value, it sees the founders as exactly the kind of go-getters it needs on the pet food company's new social media team.

The founders do some back-of-the envelope math and think the numbers look good. The total consideration seems like it's about 3 times their last pre-money. When the founders look at how the consideration is allocated among all the stakeholders, they estimate that the investors would get about $1.7 million—more than the original investment, and that the founders would split the remaining $8.3 million. By the time the founders leave the meeting, each has already mentally spent the acquisition proceeds.

But the frantically called board meeting does not go well. The investor directors call the offer a nonstarter, pointing out that the asset purchase structure in a C-corporation could result in high tax costs, most of which may not be offset by net operating losses (NOLs). The return to the investors would be negligible, and the founders may be saddled with huge tax bills for the present year, without any cash proceeds to pay the taxes. The investors suggest that the founders ask for a much higher purchase price, without the compensatory elements, and that the deal be structured in a way that reduces the tax cost.

When the founders go back to the pet food company, it acknowledges some of the deficiencies in the tax structure, but indicates that without some of the tax characteristics it wanted, it will not be willing to offer as much for the company. The founders are given a new term sheet that suggests that the documentation will reflect a tax-free reorg structure, keeps the price to be paid in the merger at $5 million, and reduces the founders' compensation package offer from $2.5 million each to $2 million.

The founders have a difficult conversation with the board, in which the founders express their fatigue, suggest that the pet food company is losing interest, begin to question their ability to continue CatBox.me as a separate business, and point to new competition in the market and increased capital needs if they are to continue. For the first time, the founders become extremely bearish on the prospects for their company and suggest that accepting this offer may be the only hope the investors will ever have to recoup their investment.

Now the investors are faced with few attractive prospects. The founders have suggested that there is no possibility to ask again for a higher valuation. They have further suggested that any restructuring of the consideration package will be unacceptable for the pet food company, as a critical driver of the deal structure is to reward and motivate the "jockeys," rather than to pay for a "horse" near the end of its racing career.

The investors can block the deal through exercise of their negative covenants, leaving them with an investment in a company with damaged founder relationships and with an unmotivated management team. Or the investors can accept an extremely small return from several years' worth of work for the company, while the founders take rich compensation packages. The investors grudgingly decide to approve the acquisition.

Only after the difficult interactions with the board, and after negotiations have progressed, do the founders begin to understand more about the deal they've accepted. The restrictions on the stock they will be receiving present some risk that the transaction will be taxable to the founders, despite the term sheet's recitation of an intent to structure a tax-free reorganization. The restrictions also provide little comfort that the founders will actually receive value for the sale of the company, or receive the full compensation packages they've been banking on. There is no guarantee that the $7.3 million portion of the consideration that will take the form of restricted stock will be received, or will be worth the value recited for the stock at closing.

It is not clear whether the acquirer really believes that the founders are prodigies, worth multimillion-dollar, multiyear compensation offers. The founders momentarily wonder whether the acquirer really plans to pay out these packages, or whether it has used a strategic approach to gain access to a network of cat lovers, and a platform built over several years and with investor money, for as little as $1.7 million plus transaction costs. If the founders turn out not to be prodigies, or can be replaced within the pet food organization, the company can easily transition them out and hold onto large portions of the consideration.

This story, despite its gritty feline realism, is an amalgam of four or five formation-to-exit deals we've recently done on the company side or investor side. None of the details are real, but examples of deals like this can be found in numerous securities filings, typically without disclosure of any numbers.

A quick search of publicly disclosed information about similar deals produces comments like the following from companies embarking on acquisition sprees: "The [acquired company's] team [members] have already become valuable contributors to [the acquirer's] social media capabilities. We're thrilled to have them aboard and excited to see what we can create in 2013 and beyond.... The company has a who's-who list of investors." And the following, regarding what may happen after an acquisition: "Within a year of [acquirer's] acquisition of [acquired company], a daily deals site, the founders of [acquired company] have left the company for other entrepreneurial ventures."

Investors shake their heads at these deals, and examine their portfolios for others where the outcome can be prevented. Founders approach them with optimism that they will secure a nice nest egg, but an understanding that, at worst, they will have achieved a résumé-builder and a good learning experience. Acquirers look at these deals with interest, seeing them as an attractive way to mitigate risk and take advantage of the proliferation of early-stage funding.

In a postmortem on these deals, the investors and their lawyers may look at ways that the outcome may have been influenced. Here are some of the candidates for approaches more nuanced than the exercise of a negative covenant.

Treat a Management-Focused Acquisition as an Employment Deal

When an acquisition offer is heavily focused on compensation, the deal starts to look more like an employment offer than an acquisition. A heavy focus on compensation can take the form of management compensation well in excess of market compensation or the acquirer's payment of a significant portion of the purchase price in restricted stock that is contingent on continued employment.

Few investors would be comfortable knowing that their investment money was going to be used more for the purpose of building the founders' résumés for future employment than for the purpose of building the company's technology or market position. Investment documents typically include tools for dealing with the departure of a founder who wishes to seek other employment.

There are a number of implications to treating a term sheet as primarily an employment offer rather than an offer for enterprise acquisition. Among other things: (1) a founder who accepts other employment may not be able to retain his or her stock in the company; (2) for a company where replacing the founding management is an alternative, the investor's investment in the company and its technology may be able to continue, despite the founder's departure; and (3) the company may be able to constrain the departing founder from competing.

The first of these, related to the founder's stock, may require additional thought in the drafting of standard investment-related documents, and the restricted stock agreement in particular. A standard restricted stock agreement may provide that a founder's stock may be forfeited or repurchased at cost if the founder leaves the company prematurely (before the stock has vested). However, founders often negotiate change of control vesting, which would accelerate vesting of the stock on an acquisition transaction. These change of control vesting provisions typically do not set requirements for the type of acquisition that will trigger the vesting, but they can be drafted this way. For example, change of control vesting could require that a certain return be achieved for investors or could require that the proceeds of the transaction, defined broadly, be allocated in accordance with the provisions of the company's charter.

Say No before the Founders Are Shown the Money

In the fictitious CatBox.me, the founders were seduced by the numbers presented by the acquirer in the initial meeting and probably effectively made the decision to sell the company before the investors were consulted. In some circumstances, better results could have been achieved if the investors had dealt directly with the possibility of this type of acquisition before the founders are confronted with the acquirer's sales pitch. This can be signaled by provisions in a company charter or stockholders' agreement that establish definitions for a category of compensation-based transactions and treat approvals, redemption rights, or control provisions differently in the context of these transactions. For example, the company's documents could make clear that a transaction with a disproportionate portion of the total consideration going to the company's founders will invoke the founder's fiduciary duty to avoid self-dealing and require involvement in negotiations and approvals by disinterested directors.

Less formally, an investor could simply start a dialogue with the founders early on, in which the investor describes a compensatory transaction and signals to the company that these types of transactions will not be approved. If a founder knows the investor's ultimate position before being presented with this kind of opportunity, it is more likely that negotiation for a less compensatory deal will begin earlier, before the founder has become enamored of the idea of the compensatory transaction.

Define Liquidation Consideration Broadly to Include Excess Comp Paid to Founders

A rigid approach, giving an investor a better starting point in negotiations, would be one that defines acquisition sale proceeds broadly enough to include some portion of founder compensation as proceeds that must be split according to the liquidation waterfall. For example, if an acquisition offer purports to provide the founders with compensation valued at more than a threshold percentage (50 percent, for example) above what they are currently receiving, the amount of that compensation must be included in the funds to be split among all investors. This is an approach that is not often proposed, and when proposed, does not often survive the initial round of negotiations.

None of these alternatives is foolproof for an investor, and an acquirer may be firm and uncompromising in the way that proceeds are allocated. However, in heady early-stage investment times, investors are becoming increasingly conscious of the pitfalls of these early acquisitions and are seeking to find tools beyond traditional veto rights as a means to improve their ability to negotiate with a seductive acquirer who seeks to win over a management team.

SEVERAL PERSPECTIVES ON ACQUI-HIRES

I recently asked the head of corporate development and senior corp dev execs at Facebook, Yahoo!, and another large Internet company (let's call that exec "Anon") about their perspectives on acqui-hires where much of the economics flow to the team and not the investors. This is what they said:

"Anon" found the question to be of paramount interest. He advises entrepreneurial teams to discuss this openly with their VCs rather than try to push it past them without transparency.

Gary Johnson, director of corporate development at Facebook, responded, "When you are at the inflexion point of taking first investment from VCs after angels or taking more cash from your VCs, that is a good time to come and talk to us."

Jackie Reses, executive vice president of people and development at Yahoo! (interestingly in charge of both M&A and HR), said, "If you see your startup is not working, you should come to us and let us get you working on something with a higher purpose. If you are a VC you should view this as a good alternative to losing more money and refocus your finite time on your upward moving portfolio companies.

Rob McIntosh, head of corporate development at Autodesk, said, "I don't know if they teach this to budding investment bankers at Harvard Business School, but often in the Valley and around the world companies are acquired not for lowering costs, increasing revenues, product, or geographical reach, but to increase 'coolness.' This app we acquired may not make money for us, but it's 'cool' so it has marketing value and makes recruiting easier; therefore, we view it as a very successful acquisition."

I've heard people say that Silicon Valley outpaced Route 128, Boston's tech corridor, in the 1980s and 1990s because everyone in the Valley's ecosystem is open, whereas East Coast people are too protective of information and less likely to help each other before being helped. On the topic of M&A, Gordon Payne, SVP, general manager of desktop and cloud divisions at Citrix, said, "Openness and transparency benefits a startup. If we know the direction a startup is heading with their product, we are likely to stay out of that area to avoid overlap; so when we buy them it's a better fit. This kind of openness goes against the nature of many folks, but fits with my motto of 'no secrets in the fast lane.'"

Our friend "Anon" had some advice on how to get on the radar of the big balance sheet buyers: "If M&A supports an acquisition and our CEO wants the company and we buy it, but the product group does not like it, the body will reject the organ. The best way to get on our radar is to get a product group to champion the buy."

Parag Patel, VP of global strategic alliances at VMware, said, "VMware is always seeking out new technologies with which to differentiate ourselves and serve our customers better. To that end, one of the best ways to get on our radar for an acquisition is when we hear from our customers that they are using your product. Another very good way is to capture the interest of our senior technical people, who are always interested in technologies that can be disruptive or augment our products."

Back in the 1990s, I heard it said that the best way to get the attention of Chambers, CEO of Cisco, was to steal a customer.

SEEK TRUTH IN FACTS: STATISTICS ON VENTURE EXITS

I crunched some numbers when thinking of starting The Founders Club equity exchange fund. I wanted to see what percentage of entrepreneurs were making nothing and what the distribution curve looked like for entrepreneurs making different-sized exits. This research helped drive my decision to create equity exchange pools and create a sensible solution for venture-backed entrepreneurs to smooth out the extreme variance in financial outcomes. I shared my research with Nic Brisbourne, partner at DFJ-Esprit, whose blog on the subject follows:

The Relationship Between Exit Value, Money Invested, and How Well the Founders Make Out

The following stats show exit values as a multiple of the amount of venture capital invested. I got the data from Andrew Romans of

The Founders Club. Due to liquidation preferences you can expect that, if the exit is less than or equal to the amount of capital invested, the founders won't have made much money. It is common practice in these downside scenarios to do a deal that provides management incentives to execute on a low-value exit, so the founders will typically get something, but it will certainly be below early expectations. Clearly the VC hasn't done very well here either.

If the exit is in the 1- to 4-times capital invested range, then the founders can expect to receive cash in the neighborhood of the paper value of their shares when the VC invested. This follows from the very rough rule of thumb that, in a typical VC round, the investor gets one third of the company for his or her money. In this scenario the VC has probably made a small profit, but not enough to get very excited.

When the exits get to be more than 4 times the money invested, the founders start to do very nicely.

If you take the standard venture capital model that looks for one third of the portfolio to be winners, and you factor in the fact that a good portion of companies never really exit, this figure feels about right. Much higher would suggest that VCs weren't taking enough risk; much lower would raise legitimate questions as to whether the venture capital industry was delivering any benefit to entrepreneurs, and we probably wouldn't be making acceptable returns for our investors.

Table 8.1 shows some of my research that Nic examined. The takeaway is that this is a game of extreme winners and losers, leading me to conclude that it makes business sense for entrepreneurs to invest 2 to 10 percent of their founder stock into an equity exchange fund managed by professional VCs like The Founders Club. The numbers in Table 8.1 are only for "disclosed" M&A transactions. Only a third to a half of M&A transactions disclose the numbers.

Table 8.1 Relationship Between Transaction Value and Investment

	2007		2008	
	M&A	Percentage of Total	M&A	Percentage of Total
Deals where transaction value is less than total venture investment	34	22.67%	24	27.59%
Deals where transaction value is 1 to 4 times total venture investment	55	36.67%	23	26.44%
Deals where transaction value is 4 to 10 times total venture investment	32	21.33%	26	29.89%
Deals where transaction value is greater than 10 times total venture investment	29	19.33%	14	16.09%
Total disclosed deals	**150**	**100.00%**	**87**	**100.00%**

FUND PHYSICS: EXPECT IMPROVED IRRS FROM SMALLER FUNDS

The IPO market has reopened in the United States, but for most companies that fail to build sales above $100 million, M&A will remain the preferred form of exit. VCs are failing to react to this. A key driver for this is "fund physics." With the volume of companies and grouping of big balance sheet buyers, we will see many $30 million, $50 million, and $100 million size M&A exits. Driven by an increase in angels, accelerators, and crowdfunding, combined with the lower cost of starting companies, we will see an increase in smaller exits. In this new world, a smaller VC fund can achieve better returns than a mega-fund. Managers of a billion-dollar fund, or even a $200 million fund, cannot take the time to make a $100,000, $500,000, or $1 million investment. Selling a portfolio company for $50 million with a 10-times cash on cash return has no meaningful impact on the mega-fund's IRR. The days of Cisco and Lucent paying $2 billion to $7 billion to acquire a venture-backed startup seem to be in the past. Most of the acquisitions made by the big acquisitive technology companies are under $50 million.

Despite these combined changes, VCs are accustomed to management fees on $200 million-plus sized funds. Fund physics now makes it hard for them to make angel investments or benefit from small exits, particularly exits where much of the value is in employment agreements for the founders. Some VCs have launched seed funds to address this market. The seed fund acts like a micro-VC, making many small bets on raw startups. The main $200 million–plus funds can still make $2.5 million to $10 million size investments into a small subset of the seed portfolio, those that progress to the venture stage of development.

The problem that emerges is negative signaling, when a startup raises seed funding from the branded seed fund of a known VC, but then pitches that VC's main fund to invest in a series A financing. If the answer is no, when that startup pitches another VC, the first question the new VC will ask is, "Is the main fund of your existing VC going to invest in this series A round?" Taking seed funding from a branded VC without the support of the main fund is poison for the operating company. Some of the large funds are now deploying seed funding via scouts, typically successful entrepreneurs they trust to go out and make small angel investments without bringing the negative signaling associated with investing from a seed micro-VC branded with the same name as the main VC. Net net, expect to see the launch of many smaller funds that are free of "big fund physics."

9

Do We Need All
These Lawyers?

Antoine Papiernik, partner with Sofinnova, referred to the "nightmare" of legal documents with series A, B, C, and D:

> Living with a legacy of legal documents from series A, B, C, D, and often E and beyond becomes a nightmare to keep track of. Inevitably, some legal term or clause you thought was insignificant can become extremely important. The more VCs involved, the harder it becomes to get clarity on the legal aspects.

At The Founders Club we often find mistakes in the cap tables of VC-backed companies. Friends of mine run a cool company that fixes this. All-Rounds (http://allrounds.com) enables CFOs, VCs, lawyers, and accountants to input cap table info into something like TurboTax. The program just spits out the correct information, evaluates proposed financings, K-1s, removing the mistakes Antoine refers to, saving time, automating private capital management, as well as workflows and data flows that exist among all parties.

WHAT ARE THE KEY TERMS IN A TERM SHEET?

Nic Brisbourne, partner at DFJ-Esprit, has this to say about a term sheet:

> A lot of what you read below is drawn from the excellent *Venture Deals: Be Smarter Than Your Lawyer and Venture Capitalist*, by Brad Feld and Jason Mendelson, which I thoroughly recommend to anyone thinking of doing a venture deal.
>
> First up, some categorization. The "terms" in "term sheet" can be put into four buckets:
>
> - Terms that drive the economics of the deal—the most important of which are *valuation, liquidation preference*, and *anti-dilution*
> - Terms that pertain to control of the company post investment—the most important of which are *board structure* and *protective provisions*
> - Clauses that are legally binding on signature of the term sheet—the most important of which are *exclusivity and costs*
> - Everything else . . . which usually doesn't matter much.

Valuation

There are five numbers associated with the valuation: pre-money valuation, amount raised, post-money valuation, share price, and dilution. They are linked by the following equations:

- Pre-money valuation + Amount raised = Post-money valuation
- Share price = Pre-money valuation / Number of shares in issue pre the round
- Dilution = Amount raised / Post-money valuation

So, if a company is raising $5 million series A round at a $10 million pre-money valuation (sometimes shortened to "$10 million pre-money" or even "$10 million pre") then the post-money valuation will be $10 million + $5 million = $15 million and the dilution will be $5 million/$15 million = 33 percent. If our hypothetical company had 1 million shares in issue before the round, then the share price will be $10 million/1 million = $10.

The dilution, also equal to the new investors' stake, is the amount by which the existing shareholders see their percentage stake fall—so if prior to the deal our hypothetical company had four founders, each with a 25 percent stake, then their percentage holdings would all fall by 33 percent to 17 percent. However, even though the percentage stake held by each of the shareholders would drop, the cash value of their holding may well have risen, as the value of the holding equals the number of shares they own multiplied by the share price.

In this example, each of the founders owns 250,000 shares (one quarter of the shares in issue before the round); at a share price of $10 their stake is worth $2.5 million. After the round, when their percentage holding has dropped to 17 percent, they still own 250,000 shares that are still worth $10 each and $2.5 million in total. At least on paper.

Moreover, if the share price of the investment round is higher than a previous round, the value of each shareholder's stake will have increased despite the fact that the percentage stake has dropped.

The important thing is that during a VC round new shares are issued and, because the value of a stake is a function of the number of shares held and the share price, that value may have increased even though the percentage stake has dropped. The percentage stake remains an important way to quickly estimate the value of a holding in an exit scenario when the number of shares in issue remains constant, although any liquidation preference will have to be taken into account.

This decoupling of value and percentage stake is very important but a somewhat counterintuitive point for many, but it is a crucial one to understand for anyone who aspires to raise VC.

Many term sheets will include a *cap table*, which describes the share structure after the round, capturing much of the information and logic described above. The post-investment cap table in our hypothetical example would look like Table 9.1.

Table 9.1 Post-Investment Cap Table

	Common Shares	series A Shares	Total	Stake
Founder 1	250,000		250,000	16.7%
Founder 2	250,000		250,000	16.7%
Founder 3	250,000		250,000	16.7%
Founder 4	250,000		250,000	16.7%
New investor		500,000	500,000	33.3%
Total	1,000,000	500,000	1,500,000	100.0%

Other key economic terms include liquidation preference and anti-dilution, the most important control terms; board structure and protective provisions; and exclusivity and cost. With these terms understood you should be able to tell whether a term sheet is attractive or not, but there is a lot that isn't covered here and there is no substitute for a good lawyer.

Liquidation Preference

Most venture capital investments come with a *liquidation preference*, which means that on exit the investor gets her money back before the other shareholders get anything. Liquidation preferences come in two flavors, participating and non-participating. If the investor has a participating liquidation preference, she gets her money back first and then shares in any remaining proceeds according to her equity percentage. If she has a non-participating liquidation preference, then she has to choose between getting her money back or getting a proportion of proceeds equivalent to her equity percentage.

Anti-Dilution

Anti-dilution terms compensate the investor if there is a subsequent round of investment done at a lower share price, often called a *down round*. The mechanism by which anti-dilution works is a retrospective adjustment of the share price so that the investor gets more shares, as if she had originally invested at a lower share price. There are three flavors of anti-dilution to be aware of:

- *Full ratchet anti-dilution*, in which the investor's share price is adjusted all the way down to the share price of the new round
- *Narrow-based weighted average anti-dilution*, in which the investor's share price is adjusted partway down to the share price of the new round, depending on a formula that considers the amounts invested
- *Broad-based weighted average anti-dilution*, similar to narrow-based, but reduces the share price slightly less, thus favoring the entrepreneur

Full ratchet anti-dilution is very favorable to the investor. Most term sheets have one of the two weighted average formulas, with broad-based being the most common.

Board Structure

Most term sheets stipulate the structure of the board post investment. Most good investors want to ensure a well-functioning board, which is small enough to act quickly and where every member will make a meaningful contribution. Four to seven people is a good size for a board, and generally speaking, the smaller the better.

Voting control of the board, and who has it, is important. Voting control can come either from having the right to appoint directors who will presumably vote as directed by their appointer, or by giving multiple votes to a single person. Mark Zuckerberg famously controlled the Facebook board by insisting that he be given three votes. Typically, each major VC will want a vote, the CEO will have one, the chairman will have one, and the founders will have one or two (some of these could be the same person). As the company grows and raises more money, the number of VCs on the board typically rises and the number of founder votes typically declines, so at the early stages the founders will control the board but at later stages that control will pass to the investors.

Whether the investors or the founders have the right to appoint the chairperson can be a swing factor in who has de facto control of the board.

Protective Provisions

Most term sheets have a list of 10 to 15 actions that the company will only be allowed to complete with the explicit approval of the investor. These terms are designed to make it impossible for the management of a company to go off-piste and neglect or ignore the agreements they have made with their investors. Typically you would expect to see operational provisions like "approval of the annual budget," "material expenditure outside of plan,""sale or disposal of all or part of the business" on the list. Often, just a signature or e-mail approval from the investor director is sufficient to cover management's actions.

You would also expect to see shareholder-related provisions including "change of the company's articles of association" and "issue of new securities with superior rights" on the list. These are more important as they mean that the company won't be able to raise more money without the consent of the investor.

All the protective provisions listed above are pretty standard, and I don't know many VCs who would invest without them.

Exclusivity and Costs

Every term sheet that I can remember, and certainly every term sheet I have ever issued, contained a paragraph at the top saying it was not legally binding except for the clauses relating to exclusivity and costs (and sometimes confidentiality). Exclusivity and costs are important to the investors because they are about to start spending significant sums on legal fees and maybe other advisors, and they want to know that the company is serious about taking their money.

By agreeing to the exclusivity clause, the company shows it is serious enough to forgo conversations with other VCs, typically for an initial four- to eight-week period, which can be extended.

The cost clause is more evidence that the company is serious about taking investment. It usually stipulates that if the company pulls out of the investment it will cover the VC's costs up to an agreed cap, usually of $30,000 to $70,000 for a venture investment, depending on the legal complexity and the advisors the VC intends to use.

The company and entrepreneur should also expect that the VC is serious, and shouldn't be shy in seeking to understand how far through their due diligence process the investors are, what extra work they need to do (beyond legals), and whether they see any reason why the deal shouldn't complete. Some investors list out the extra work they need to do as "conditions precedent" to completion. If there are any material doubts on behalf of the investors, then it is probably better to get them resolved before signing the term sheet.

Here are some very basic fund-raising concepts that entrepreneurs should master:

- Pre-money valuation (pre)
- Round size (round)
- Post-money valuation (post)
- Percentage to the new investors
- Liquidation preferences

Add the round to the pre-money to get the post-money. Calculate the percentage of the company sold to the new investors by dividing the size of the round by the post, or by dividing the small number by the big number (most cases). When fund-raising, keep an Excel spreadsheet open all day showing this small calculation; that will help you see what percentage of the company would go to investors at different size rounds and at different pre's.

If the company sells 33 percent of the share capital to new investors, then the pre is exactly twice the size of the round. So if the round were $2.5 million and the company sells a third of the company, the pre would be $5 million and the post would be $7.5 million. For quick "in your head" math you can just double the size of the round to calculate the pre, assuming 33 percent dilution. For IT deals, dilution on a series A is typically 20 to 40 percent, the amount of the share capital (equity in the company) that has been sold to the new investors.

When things are going well, the series B (or next round) is raised at a higher valuation, the size of the round is larger, and new investors join the syndicate. Same for series C and D. Life is not always ideal, so one sees flat and down rounds as well as up rounds.

Other legal terms are important, but every entrepreneur should understand liquidation preferences. This is the money you must repay the investor from the liquidation (sale or IPO) of the company before the entrepreneur gets his or her pro rata ownership share.

No Time Like Right Now to Settle a Legal Dispute

Richard Kimball, cochair of the technology practice Edwards Wildman Palmer, has represented more than 40 venture capital firms and dozens of technology and life sciences companies over the course of his career. Here is his story about settling a legal dispute:

I have a story that I tell to entrepreneurs which is my way of demonstrating how important it is to settle disputes and codify relationships before a lot of value is built. On the eve of an IPO being declared effective, a lawsuit was filed for $1 million by two software developers who had allegedly developed some of the company's code. The founder and CEO said that he would never pay them $1 million, that the code they developed was crap, and he didn't use it. Years before when the company was just starting out, the founder hired these guys to develop some code. He had promised them some shares but never gave them to them because he said their code was useless. At the time, they offered to settle their claim for $7,500. He refused. When you looked at the facts, at the time of the offer of shares, the company only had about 50,000 shares authorized and the number of the shares that were being offered to the developers was a fairly significant portion of that amount. The founder said that he had planned on authorizing more shares and doing a split and then issuing them shares. He did all that, but months later. So, in retrospect, the facts were quite unfavorable, and of course the developers had leverage since the company could not go public with such a potentially big cloud over its capital ownership. The case did get settled, but not for $1 million as the founder said that he would never pay them that much. He didn't. The settlement amount was $999,999.99.

Here's a memorable quote from a lawyer in the context of a legal dispute, "You don't have a monopoly on the truth." This means that you may think $2 + 2 = 4$ and your opponent claims $2 + 2 = 5$. Don't get red in the face about a lawsuit you can't afford to fight against a larger company with money to go the distance. The point is that the truth is very selective and our own perception is distorted. If you are in a legal dispute, your company probably played a hand in getting there; what may be in your best interest is to agree that $2 + 2 = 4.5$, to make a compromise and to get out of there. A legal dispute for an early stage company can be toxic. Keep your eye on the big points like your equity, intellectual property (IP), and any kind of revenue share. Put new options on the table like a first right of refusal or other concessions you can live with. Try to find a win-win where you can help the other party, put that new idea on the table and make it positive. As always, be Mr. Spock, completely unemotional. This is one area where passion is not a plus.

DUMB LICENSING

Ben Goodger, partner at Edwards Wildman Palmer, has this to say about dumb licensing:

> We were advising a potential purchaser of a well-known bread and bakery brand, backed by (I think) private equity. The transaction was going very well, but one of our junior lawyers, representing the buyer and investor, reviewed the licenses which the business had already entered into. She spotted that the whole territory of Ireland had been licensed to a third party for 10 years without any kind of break clause, and thus could not be terminated during that period absent breach or insolvency. She mentioned this to the supervising partner, whose initial reaction was that this couldn't be that significant and was just a detail which could easily be overcome. However, he did mention it as a footnote in the due diligence report.
>
> The purchaser in fact had very big plans strategically for the territory of Ireland and seized upon this fact. He telephoned the partner and demanded to know if this was a real issue or not. The partner, not actually having read the license, passed the buck entirely to the junior lawyer. The upshot was that the CEO of the purchaser and its venture backers telephoned the junior lawyer to ask her directly if this license was a commitment which could not be undone without breaching the contract or paying a large amount of compensation. The junior lawyer took a deep breath and stood her ground: Yes, that was correct: under the terms of the license, if they bought this business, they would be committed to that exclusive license for the territory of Ireland for 10 years and would not be able to get out of it unless there was a breach for insolvency. The

purchaser and its investor thanked her politely for her diligent work. They then called the deal off. It was that important to them. If the senior partner had not mentioned it to them (although he himself thought it was an unimportant detail) and the transaction had proceeded, then his law firm would have no doubt wound up with a negligence suit!

LETTING A LICENSEE GET OUT OF CONTROL

Ben Goodger, partner at Edwards Wildman Palmer, has this to say about an out-of-control licensee:

> In another situation I recall, a well-known international book publisher wanted to sell off its children's book division to a purchaser backed by a VC. The "jewel in the crown" was a children's book which had been written in the 1950s, and which had been languishing as a very underperforming asset until they had been approached some years earlier by the maker of TV animation programs. A license deal had been done, which enabled the TV company to create an animated TV series which had been very successful, and which had spawned a huge merchandising operation. The book publisher thought that a lot of the value of this character was still owned by it. However, over the years it had entirely overlooked the fact that the licensee, the TV production company, had filed trademarks for all the business operations except books. The TV production company controlled films, DVDs, toys, games, clothing, confectionery, etc. The licensee's business in this children's book character was in fact hugely more valuable than the original books. The fatal problem when this was examined from a legal perspective was that the book publisher had sat back and received royalty income from this operation without thinking about it, and it was therefore impossible, or very difficult, for it to argue that it had not consented to the licensee going off and registering the charac-

ter as a trademark in its own name, in all these many classes of business. It had effectively, therefore, "lost control" of its main asset. The deal proceeded, but the purchaser said, "I am buying a piece of litigation," and discounted the price by approximately 50 percent.

SOMETIMES YOU HAVE TO GO DOWNHILL TO GET TO THE TOP OF THE NEXT HILL

Charles Cella, founder and partner of GTC Law Group, tells this story:

This story is about a company trying to disrupt an industry that was dominated by three sleeping giant companies that had almost complete oligopoly position over a $5 billion industry. Very early on, the client identified a long-term technology trend that would likely play out in the industry, using basic principles like Moore's law to predict an eventual shift in the costs. The company set out to patent everything around that long-term technology, including an "IP stack" that covered not only the supporting technologies, but applications of the technologies in more than 40 specific submarkets within the industry. Once the giants realized that the company was building a formidable IP portfolio, one of them approached the company in 2002, during an abysmal capital market and at a time when the company was desperate for a capital infusion, and offered an eight-figure price for a perpetual nonexclusive license to the IP. The license would leave the company free to tackle the market and license other players, and would provide more capital than it was trying to raise in its venture round, on a completely non-dilutive basis. Despite its desperation and the sweet nature of the deal, the company said no. Why? Because it believed the long-term value of the technology and IP should be in the high 10 figures and that the prospective giant was one of only three parties who could pay that much. So, to preserve the possibility of an exit, the company went through a down round, accepted some dilution, and continued on its path. Several years later, the company was acquired by that same prospective licensee for just under six figures. Lesson learned: The path isn't always a hockey stick. Sometimes you have to go downhill to get to the top of the next hill, but it takes a special CEO to take that trip.

It Is Better to Be Lucky than Good

Charles Cella, founder and partner of GTC Law Group, describes a "lucky" outcome involving exclusive licenses:

A target company (no names on this one) granted an exclusive license to one party in the field of "financial services" and an exclusive license to another party in the field of "banking." Needless to say, we thought the separation between "financial services" and "banking" was somewhat less than complete. In fact, if you draw a Venn diagram, the overlap might put the entire "banking" field inside the "financial services" field. Both licenses were to prominent industry players, each of them with enough clout to cause a lot of damage in litigation or in the marketplace. The legal effect was that the second agreement was a breach of the first agreement (violating the exclusivity provisions) and the existence of the first agreement implied a breach of the representations and warranties in the second agreement. The broad nature of the fields probably would have rendered the company dead in the water from the point of view of financing (more on that later). The simple lesson is that exclusive licenses need to be granted with great care. This one was easy to spot, but we have seen many examples where one exclusive is granted at the level of technology and another is granted at the level of channel or market, such that it is very difficult to tell whether there is overlap or not. Back to our "dueling exclusives" company: How do you solve the problem of having granted two clearly overlapping exclusive licenses for the same technology and IP, one of those rare "legal due diligence" items that would actually be fatal to a deal? Answer: have one of the licensees acquire the other one, so that neither of them cares about the breach! This actually happened, the company raised financing, and was eventually acquired by one of the licensees. Lesson: It is better to be lucky than good.

10

Ladder to Liquidity: The Secondary Market

There has been a transformational culture shift in the Silicon Valley that is now spreading across the globe. In the past, if a founder or even an early investor sold any stock before the IPO or definitive M&A liquidity event, the market considered that a negative signal. If Bill Gates is selling any of his stock in Microsoft, then he must know something we don't and MSFT is overvalued. Everyone sell in a panic! But maybe Bill Gates just wants to buy a boat or donate some cash to charity. Secondary transactions are here to stay. This is another part of the game everyone should understand. A secondary market has emerged for entrepreneurs and investors to sell some or all of their equity in advance of a classic liquidity event. It's a win-win-win for all parties.

HOW EARLY-STAGE ANGELS AND VCs CAN GET THEIR CASH BACK PRIOR TO AN EXIT

Angels invest before VCs, but they are often crushed in the cap table as VCs pour large amounts of capital into investment rounds. If the angels do not have sufficient funds to follow their investment, they cannot avoid dilution. When trying to raise angel funding, I have often heard angels say they need to wait for an exit to get more cash to put to work on a new investment. Angels in the past have not sold shares until the final liquidity event of the company, whether an IPO or M&A transaction. This should change.

Angels should be able to invest before VCs. As the valuations grow along with these larger investment rounds, the angels should be allowed to sell some of their shares and begin to make a gain from the uptick in valuation. This might be in the series A, B, or C investment round or in all three rounds. An angel might invest $50,000 in an angel round and then, when the series B has a pre-money valuation of $25 million, the angel might sell at least $50,000 worth of shares while still keeping some shares in the company to be sold at a higher valuation or the final exit.

That cash flow to the angel can be used to seed finance the ecosystem, bringing more and more high-quality deals to the VCs. VCs should view this as a positive, a simple opportunity to buy shares from the angel at a low price and sell them higher at the final exit, making returns for the VC's LPs. Done properly, the angel should be able to net a return, keep some shares in the company, and bring its cost of the investment to zero, making up for losing investments. Seed stage VCs should do the same: sell shares in single secondary transactions to larger or later-stage VCs or private equity funds. Eventually we Silicon Valley people hand the private deal over to Wall Street where it gets sold or goes public; but in our angel to VC food chain, we should be able to get off the escalator at any time. This enables VCs to raise small funds, show some early returns, and raise more funds. It enables VCs to take some risk out of their model and take credit for accretion of value. It solves part of the problem that has historically plagued markets like Israel where VCs sell their portfolio companies too early, desperate to put some points on the board. In the real world we see companies become "very hot" with soaring valuations and then, before crystalizing a definitive liquidity event from an IPO (surviving the lock-up period following the IPO) or M&A transaction, the stock crashes to zero or takes a massive hit in valuation from a peak-hyped financing round. In the technology world things change quickly; Friendster can lose to MySpace and MySpace can lose to Facebook. This is another reason it makes sense to take some chips off the table when the valuation is attractive.

A great example illustrating this vision for the future, where investors can get on or off the escalator at any time, is Poggled. Founded in Chicago, Poggled is basically Groupon for alcohol. Poggled contacts a bunch of women and sells the first 50 tickets to a nightclub or party, with all you can drink booze included for $1 per woman. The women are required to sync to their Facebook accounts so men can see the photos of the women that will go to the party. Poggled then markets this party to men at a much higher price point, all at a Groupon-type discount where guys are able to go to an all-you-can-drink event with a bunch of women, benefiting from seeing the photos of the women before buying their tickets.

Poggled's founders managed to bootstrap through a sponsorship revenue deal with Diageo, a large alcohol company that owns Smirnoff and many other name brands. They then raised $500,000 from the founders and investors in Groupon. Even today Poggled is subletting office space inside Groupon's offices in Chicago. What's interesting is that Groupon incubated this company with cash and mentorship. Groupon founders took the deal up and down Sand Hill Road, meeting all the big VCs about investing in the series A round. They struck a deal with NEA who also led the series A for Groupon and agreed to interesting terms. The series A was for $5.6 million. Of this, $500,000 went straight back to the seed investors; they made all of their money back in less than a year. Another $50,000 went to each of the two cofounders of Poggled. One of them, Joe Matthews, told me the details, saying that he and his cofounder didn't even want to sell shares at that valuation, but the Groupon guys pushed them to take it. The remaining $5 million was injected into the venture for growth. I think this is a model transaction: someone can invest in the seed round, add huge value and then get his cash out so he can do it again and perpetuate the ecosystem. Going a step farther, early-stage VCs should do the same thing.

As always, a seller gets better pricing and terms when he or she pulls more buyers to the table for the same transaction. We encourage any seller to come to The Founders Club and see if we can buy the shares from a founder or early stage investor or provide a loan to the shareholder to minimize her tax burden and simplify the transaction. See below to find out more about how we can creatively structure secondary transactions and provide capital for employees in need of capital to exercise their stock options. I am told that the biggest salary at Palantir Technologies is $130,000, yet the valuation of the company surpassed $4 billion in 2012. We provided some liquidity to a former C-level executive who was quite pleased with the $4 billion-plus valuation, and we got into a deal that is nearly impossible to access. We are doing the same with Twitter and many less-known later-stage deals where these expansion stage companies are within 1 to 3 years of a definitive liquidity event. It makes sense for the founders and early investors to take some chips off the table now for liquidity, and it is attractive to investors to invest in real companies that will return cash quickly rather than tying up money for a decade in classic venture.

To Sell or Not to Sell: The Secondary Market for Startups

Many special purpose funds have been raised to buy shares from founders and even from low-level employees with stock options at Facebook, Twitter, Groupon, Zynga, LinkedIn, Pandora, and many others. The founders of Groupon took this to an extreme and took out over $500 million in advance of their IPO, sparking discussion of the long-term viability of that company.

At the same time, mature VCs have learned from experience that providing some liquidity for their founders makes sense, not only for the entrepreneur but also for the VC. Joerg Ueberla, member of the advisory board of The Founders Club and a general partner for 10 years at Wellington Partners, one of Germany's largest VC funds, told me that it was only after three years of investing that he realized that, without any liquidity, some founders were jumping at the first opportunity to sell their companies rather than hold out for the optimal price or an IPO. The IPO market has been closed for much of the past 10 years, really only available to companies with the ability to reach a $250 million exit. Between 2002 and 2010, only 80 companies per year on average had exits in excess of $50 million. Consider that number 80 in the context of 1,500 venture-backed companies being financed during each of those years in the United States.

Zohar Levkovitz, a local friend of mine and founder and CEO of Amobee, which was like a double click advertising network on mobile phones, had an opportunity to sell the company for a few $100 million to Yahoo! Within a few days of Google's acquisition of AdMob, Yahoo! submitted a term sheet to buy Amobee. Zohar owned a very large slice of the equity and was keen on taking the deal. Sequoia, one of his VCs, paid him $5 million buying some of his shares for cash. He then voted to decline the acquisition offer and soldier on, and the board was aligned between VC and CEO. Singtel later paid $321 million buying the company two and a half years later—a great outcome for Sequoia and founders. Zohar told me he left $15 million on the table, meaning that is what Sequoia made on the direct secondary purchase of Zohar's founder shares. However, Zohar continued that he is today very happy with his decision to take the $5 million because it de-risked his family situation; he bought a house and became an active angel investor again. Zohar is forming his own VC fund now with a very differentiated strategy; I have committed to invest in his fund personally.

Another great example, which also reveals a typical deal structure, is Rebate Networks. The company was founded by two successful serial entrepreneurs. Michael Brehm, Rebate's COO, sold studiVZ.net, the largest social network in Germany, for €85 million. Stefan Glänzer, cofounder of Last.fm, enjoyed Last.fm being sold to CBS for $280 million. Both cashed out nicely at their previous ventures, so they were not in any need of liquidity. Michael contacted me to inquire about selling some Rebate Networks shares via The Founders Club. At that time his company had raised €34 million with a sizable post-money valuation. He owned a sizable slug of the share capital, and the liquidation preference was greater than the amount of funding raised. If the company were sold above a specified amount, then the liquidation preference would disappear and everyone would be paid pro rata. At the time Michael contacted me, he felt he was getting close to the specified target amount to remove the liquidation preference, but he did not want to pay any dividends to shareholders, which would slow down their approach to the target. Selling some equity for cash made sense to him as the preferred way to gain liquidity without slowing down the growth of the company to remove the big liquidation stack.

To understand the evolution of the secondary market and new deal structures, it is worth looking at the past. Many VCs and entrepreneurs go on about the good old days of the "Four Horsemen," four investment banks that covered the VC's portfolio investments, fit into the culture of the Valley, and IPO'd and sold these companies to big balance sheet buyers. They rode high from the 1960s to the late 1990s. The big boys on Wall Street referred to these San Francisco competitors as the HARM group, but Hambrecht & Quist, Alex Brown & Sons, Robertson-Stephens, and Montgomery Securities preferred to be called the Four Horsemen. In those days, VCs benefited not only from early stage coverage of their portfolio companies by the Four Horsemen, but also from the Horsemen's advice on how long to hold onto any stock they received in M&A transactions when the VC suddenly held publicly traded stock in the acquiring or merged company. The world has changed radically in the last 10 years, particularly when it comes to secondary markets and how entrepreneurs and investors can gain some liquidity. Let's take a look at today's emerging secondary markets. The Four Horseman were all acquired by larger banks, and liquidity for VC-backed startups began to dry up.

THE DIRECT SECONDARY MARKET: SELLING SOME SHARES FOR CASH BEFORE A LIQUIDITY EVENT

In 2002, the average time between series A and exit was two years for a U.S. Venture-backed company. By 2008, that had grown to seven to nine years. If VCs were hoping to close their funds within a 10- to 12-year time frame, and the IPO market was closed to most companies with revenues under $100 million, we were clearly in a liquidity crisis for entrepreneurs and VCs.

Next time your investors are trying to sell you on the glory of being a cash-strapped entrepreneur and not taking a salary, taking a lower salary, or holding out for a bigger exit, tell them that you plan to keep your marriage together and you want to pull $250,000 to $500,000 out of your next funding round. If you are in my club, I would be happy to call or meet with your VC to drag him or her out of the cave and into the light of reality and support your wish to get some early liquidity. Far from injecting lazy juice into an entrepreneur, a modest injection of personal capital builds personal stability and aligns the entrepreneur with the investors to hold out for the optimal exit—good for all stakeholders.

FOUNDERS' PREFERRED: BEST STRUCTURE FOR FOUNDER EARLY LIQUIDITY

John Bautista, partner at Orrick, has this advice about early founders' stock:

> At the time of company formation, founders should consider setting up their capital structure so that a portion of their holdings are in the form of founders' preferred stock. Orrick invented this structure a couple of years ago, and I am putting it in place with most of my new companies.
>
> Specifically, founders' preferred gives the founders the right to convert a portion of their founders' stock (up to 20 percent) into a future series of preferred stock in order to sell it to future investors. This benefits the founders because they can sell stock at the preferred stock price. This benefits investors because they can buy from the founders exactly the same series of preferred stock as the company is selling in a venture financing. And this benefits the company because preferred stock is being sold, avoiding 409A problems on employee common stock; the company keeps the employee common stock at a discount to the last preferred stock price.
>
> As part of this structure, please note the following:

- Most VCs are OK with this structure if the founders' preferred stock portion is kept to no more than 20 percent of a founder's holdings.
- The founders' preferred stock portion needs to be fully vested. The founder's remaining common stock holdings can still vest over the usual 48 months.
- Founders' liquidity happens in connection with a future financing event. Based on empirical data, it is usually in connection with a future VC or strategic financing where the investor is also buying preferred stock from the company.
- The founders' preferred structure needs to be put in place at the time of company formation. There are potentially income tax problems if it occurs later.
- The founders' preferred has the same voting rights as the founders' common stock and is junior to the preferred stock purchased by investors.

Here are the main ways you can get cash in your pocket before selling or listing your company on the stock exchange:

- Sell shares via an auction website or broker.
- Sell shares to your existing VCs.
- Sell shares to direct secondary funds.
- Swap shares for ownership in an equity exchange fund.

The best-known auction website brokers are SecondMarket and Shares-Post. The advantage of selling via these guys is that they contact many prospective buyers for their auctions, thereby increasing demand for your finite supply of stock. It is important for a company and its investors to control who is selling what on these exchanges and the flow of information. You can imagine that a CEO might not want private information like his cash position and burn rate showing up on an online due diligence room for all to see or that a newly hired executive spends the first two weeks on the job selling equity. This is a very dynamic space, but it would appear that much of SecondMarket's revenue came from doing Facebook trades and they needed to pivot once that window closed to find new revenue streams. Much of the activity on SharesPost has been for small amounts and not big blocks of founder stock being traded.

DIRECT SECONDARY FUNDS

The next option for entrepreneurs seeking early liquidity is to sell some shares to direct secondary funds. These funds buy shares from founders, early employees, angels, VCs, and corporates one company at a time. Most of the big direct secondary funds contacted The Founders Club seeking deal flow for their funds, and we began to work with them to provide liquidity to our members. Then we began to raise funds ourselves to make direct secondary investments.

Globally, there are a number of direct secondary funds with a high degree of variance in how they operate. Some will buy as little as $50,000 from a venture-backed entrepreneur with strong revenue traction. Others might represent very wealthy family offices seeking to buy $50 million strips of Twitter shares. Many direct secondary funds are first class, but others can be bottom feeders looking for a bargain rather than adding value or buying shares at a fair price.

We found that this made so much sense that we decided to raise our own direct secondary fund. We could see there was a need for a new direct secondary fund that understood founders, angels, and VCs, and could be a value-added investor rather than a simple arbitrageur. I discuss this below when explaining The Founders Club model.

WHEN TO TAKE YOUR CHIPS OFF THE TABLE

If you gambled $200 playing poker and grew your $200 to $5,000, would it be logical to bet 100 percent of your winnings on the next hand? Absolutely not! You would put $4,800 in your pocket to take home, and then keep gambling with the initial $200. Maybe blow another $200 after you lose the first $200. The moral of the story is that it is almost sick and twisted that VCs encourage wild risk taking when the value of their companies goes up. The strange culture in the Silicon Valley applauds the stupidity of betting the full five grand that you grew from $200, even when it may have taken five years of your life to get from starting the company to the point where your stock is nominally worth $4.5 million. Someone is trying to talk you into keeping all of your chips on the table and putting not even 2 percent into your pocket to take home now. My advice to entrepreneurs: Carefully diversify some of your equity into cash or an equity exchange fund. Again, that's the objective of The Founders Club. The win-win-win is to create a marketplace for private stock along the way. That is also why I joined the board of Howard Leonhardt's The California Stock Exchange.

THE FOUNDERS CLUB EQUITY EXCHANGE FUND MODEL

A new and innovative way for founders and early investors to achieve some liquidity from their otherwise illiquid founder or preferred stock is to invest some of their stock into an equity exchange fund. The way this works is that founders or angels transfer ownership of some of their stock into a limited partnership in return for ownership units in the limited partnership that owns stock in many companies. The limited partnership can collect stock positions in 15 to 100 or more companies. Each time there is an exit everyone gets paid. The Founders Club manages a family of equity exchange funds where entrepreneurs agree to pool a portion of their equity into a VC-style fund composed of stock in venture-backed startups. Founders typically invest between 1 and 10 percent of their personal founder stock, achieving diversification and becoming prolific angel investors. Each fund comprises a portfolio of high-potential companies, thereby affording any single entrepreneur a strategy to create wealth, achieving venture returns while accomplishing portfolio diversification. They achieve this without waiting years for their own personal exits and without the hard vetting work required for smart angel or VC investing. For some founders, investing equity is a hedge; for all, it is an investment and membership in a highly beneficial club.

Beyond using their stock to become the equivalent of a cash investor in a VC fund, once companies join The Founders Club, we put them into our funding machine and introduce them to angel and VC investors, mentors, and key ecosystem contacts that can help these companies become successful and ultimately to buyers to impact the exit.

The unique exchange fund model provides us with some of the highest volume and quality deal flow of any VC firm. We receive well over 4,000 investment opportunities each year. Deal flow is the lifeblood of VC fund performance. The Founders Club also has a unique deal selection machine in place. Deals are sent to us from people that we already know. If a subject matter expert that we know and trust sends us a deal in a sector he or she knows, that is a good starting point. If the deal is vetted by our selection committees and voted in by existing CEOs and founders, that is an added layer of due diligence and vetting. We actively triangulate information from over 40 VCs on The Founders Club advisory board as well as among our CEOs, founders, and angels.

Each time one of our portfolio companies realizes a liquidity event via an IPO or M&A transaction, The Founders Club sells the percentage of the company we own, returning cash to our fund. We do not invest that cash into any companies; instead we pay a classic 80/20 split: our LPs (you founders, CEOs, and angels) are paid 80 percent of the cash, while 20 percent is paid to The Founders Club management company to take care of operating expenses, our cash investors, and some retained profit.

By joining The Founders Club, you have invested thousands or millions of dollars into a VC fund where all of the companies are already VC backed with the ability to exit within one to three years. If there are at least 15 companies in your exchange fund, there is a statistical probability that you will receive cash before your own exit. This is the early liquidity. The Founders Club does not charge the 2.5 percent annual management fee you would pay to a classic VC fund over 10 years, removing at least 15 percent pressure from the internal rate of return (IRR) of your investment. This means that the 15 percent IRR you might receive from investing in a VC fund would look more like 30 percent IRR from your Founders Club investment.

We operate different equity exchange funds, but the focus is on our Growth Fund, which is exclusively available to founders or other shareholders in companies that have minimum revenue of $10 million for the last 12 months and year-on-year revenue growth of 25 percent. I also teamed up with a former classmate from Georgetown University to launch Georgetown Angels, where we are growing our base of serious angel investors. You don't need to be a Georgetown alum to invest with us. What is interesting about how we structure our angel deals is that we can take a $50k investment from an accredited angel investor and put it not just into one deal, but spread it across 10 different angel deals providing meaningful portfolio diversification while getting cash into the best angel investment opportunities. Beyond access to capital, we provide our portfolio companies with an ecosystem to make their companies more successful.

We assemble our network of entrepreneurs, angels, VCs, and big balance sheet buyers through an exclusive calendar of events every year where we provide fun and casual networking opportunities such as portfolio demo days, skiing, snowboarding, and wine tasting. Our demo days typically attract a few hundred angels, VCs, and corporate development execs. We know that when you put great people in a room together amazing things happen. This relaxed networking creates relationships that often prompt our members to work collaboratively throughout the year. The events and trips to Europe or the States facilitate this cross-pollination. We believe that not everyone needs to move to the Silicon Valley to access a global network, one that makes all parties more successful.

Lastly, I recruited a few former VCs and a broker dealer FINRA member investment bank to focus on liquidity and later-stage transactions. If you have a company with $25 million in revenue and good growth and are seeking liquidity or to raise more funding, please get in touch. If the equity exchange fund is too exotic for you, let's keep it simple and sell stock for cash. We believe investing in a later-stage company within one to three years of a liquidity event makes sense. This liquidity in turn provides cash to founders and early investors to become angel investors and complete the seed rounds for new companies or invest in our other later-stage deals. You can now imagine how some companies are backed by some very powerful people. It's all connected!

Afterword

Whether you think you can or can't either way you are right.
HENRY FORD

This book is version 1.0, a first crack at capturing the passion, the techniques, the triumphs and failures of the innovation world and of those who make it live and breathe. I am lucky enough to remain in daily contact with members of this ecosystem: CEOs, founders, angels, lawyers, VCs, and big balance sheet buyers. Every day brings new stories, so I will keep curating content from the practitioners. If you are learning lessons from real venture-related experiences or have an entertaining story to tell, please write them down and e-mail them to me to be included in the next release of the book, v.2.0. The editors at McGraw-Hill knew that this book needed to be reduced in scope by over 50 percent to be readable, so they cut the international sections covering Israel and Europe. My next book will focus on the international non-U.S. Venture scene. Please send me your story if you have a good one with a lesson learned. I can always add it to my blog—*The Hitchhiker's Guide to Venture Capital* (www.founders-club.com/blog). Subscribe to it to get my latest stories and musings via e-mail alerts.

I am always looking for new deals seeking liquidity, funding, or seeking to join our exchange funds, more angel investors, and more investors interested in VC funds. If you want to invest, or if you are seeking investors, please get in touch. I can be reached any time at info@founders-club.com or www.founders-club.com. Because of the subjects covered, please refer to the legal disclaimer on the copyright page.

Operate in a team, give to and draw from the ecosystem, maintain absolute belief and confidence in yourself and your colleagues, and be fearless.

Wishing you good luck and happiness!

Andrew

July 2013

Acknowledgments

I would like to thank everyone who helped to make this book possible. I am thankful and inspired by all the coauthors, contributors, interviewees, and all of my "expert readers" and editors. A special thanks to Elton Santusky and the team at law firm Wilson Sonsini Goodrich & Rosetti (WSGR). Thank you to the 200-plus VCs, entrepreneurs, and service providers who suggested book titles as part of my crowdsourcing of the title and the book cover art. Thanks also to Bill Harris, founder and CEO of Personal Capital, a Venrock-backed company in the Valley, and the first CEO of PayPal and former CEO of Intuit, for taking the time one late night to design a possible book cover and come up with a cool title for the book "Tales from The Silicon Valley." This is a great example of the Silicon Valley culture of helping the other without asking for anything. In the end, this behavior turns water into wine. Thank you everyone who played a role in helping me find the best literary agent and publisher. Thanks to Bill Draper (author of a bestselling book on VC, *The Startup Game: Inside the Partnership Between Venture Capitalists and Entrepreneurs*, which every entrepreneur, VC, and service provider should read) for being kind enough to introduce me to his literary agent. Thanks to Glenn Reid, who spent many hours in front of the whiteboard creating products with Steve Jobs at Apple before founding Inventor Labs (what a cool guy!), for introducing me to his literary agent who got me offers from the big five publishing houses and McGraw-Hill. Thank you to McGraw-Hill for being so great to work with. Thank you, Pitch Johnson, for your time and the introductions to professors at Stanford. Thanks to all of you who contributed stories to this book that did not make it into the 220-page limit. We edited out more than 50 percent of the content to get to this target size. All of these contributions will come out in my second book or my blog! Importantly I must thank my mother, Lyn Adams, and stepfather, John Cusick, who first edited the book for hundreds of hours in Maine and then flew to California on angel's wings and edited the book for another few hundred hours to meet McGraw-Hill's requirements. My living room table looked like a startup, covered in printouts with the three of us discussing the importance of each section that we cut from the book and then returning to type away at our Macs . . . Thank you, Mom and John!

First, last, and always, thank you to my wife, Pavlina Romans, for her constant support, even with the laptop on in bed at 5 a.m., and to our twin boys, Max and James, for putting up with me working when I should have been playing with you on the beach.

To me, this book has become much like the global Silicon Valley eco-system itself. The magic is that it's all connected, and I'm just thankful to put these many bits into one book. Finally, thanks to all of you who have left and will write positive reviews on Amazon, blogged and Tweeted about the book, and helped promote the spread of this first edition. Those reviews and Tweets are all good karma. Thank you.

Index

A round, 19
Accel Partners, 9, 10, 65, 114
Accelerators, 6, 22–27
Accenture, 82
Accredited investors, 34
ACE (Asia Capacity Exchange), 161
Acqui-hires, 169
Adify, 12, 173–174
AdMob, 209
Adveq, 96–99
Advisors, boards of, 37
Airbnb, 117
Alex Brown & Sons, 210
Alien (film), 117
Alignment, 98–99
All Rounds, 191
Almeida, Paul, 14
Alternative assets, 70
Amazon, 11
Amgen, 72–74, 76
Amobee, 209
Amortization period (venture debt), 93
Amount (venture debt), 92
AMV (Asset Management Ventures), 73, 76
Anderson, Phil, 15, 51
Angel, Jim, 14
Angel equity financing, 55
Angel groups, 57–58
Angel investing, 6
AngelList, 10, 28, 116

Angels (angel investors), 6, 17–28, 35–43
and accelerators, 22–27
and convertible note vs. priced round, 37–40
Ron Conway, 20–21
founder-friendly, 57
legal factors when choosing, 56–57
networking by, 58–59
origin of term, 17
pitching lawyers before pitching, 53–54
procuring funding from, 28, 35–37, 41–43
and secondary market, 205–208
and start-up "Cambrian explosion," 18–20
and valuation level, 41
Apax, 70, 160
Apex, 176
Apple, 2, 43, 47, 162
Arbinet, 18
Archetypes, 45–46
Arrington, Michael, 8
Asia Capacity Exchange (ACE), 161
Asset gatherers, 98
Asset Management Company, 73
Asset Management Ventures (AMV), 73, 76
Assets:
business, 169
strategic, 169
venture debt as class of, 95–96

Associates, 66
Atria Software, 104
AT&T Systems & Billing, 15
August Capital, 13, 119
Autodesk, 185
Available amount (venture debt), 92

Backend fee (venture debt), 94
Balance sheet, 106
Bank of America, 152
Banks, 5, 87–88
Barbell strategy, 65–66
Barr, Katherine, 124–127
BATNA (Best Alternative to The
    Negotiated Agreement), 128
Bautista, John, 55–57, 211–212
Bebo, 10
Bell Labs, 79
Berkus, David, 170
Best Alternative to The Negotiated
    Agreement (BATNA), 128,
    166
BioCision, 117
Biotechnology, 76
Birch, Michael, 10
Bivens, Mark, 146–147
Blazensky, Derek, 142
BlueMountain, 25
BlueRun Ventures, 36
BMC, 75
Board meetings, 143–144
Boardroom dynamics, 140
Boards of advisors, 37
Boards of directors:
    responsibilities of, 144–146
    working with, 146–147
Boole & Babbage, 75
Boulder Ventures, 86
Bowes, Bill, 74
Boyatzis, Richard, 49
BranchOut, 7–10, 156
The Brandery, 27
Braniff, Ed, 15
Brehm, Michael, 209
Brevity (of pitches), 118

Bridge financing:
    fees for, 55
    and venture capital, 129
Brillson, Paula, 161–162
Brisbourne, Nic, 69–71, 117, 123, 186–
    187, 192–197
Broadsoft, 131
Brown, David, 25
The Buddha, 162
Bufferd, Allan, 97
Business assets, 169
Business buyers, exit of, 170–172
Business Insider SAI, 118
Business plans, 103
Business Week, 73
Buyers' hierarchies, 168–170
Buzzwords, 119
Byers, Brook, 74

California Stock Exchange, 29, 214
CalXstars, 23, 29
Campbell, Gordon, 45, 46, 48–51
Cap table, 194
Capital, August, 132–133
Capital providers, venture capitalists
    and, 87
Cardinal Venture Capital, 142
Carve outs, 174–175
Cash, 70
Cash flow, 129–130
CBS, 8
Cella, Charles, 202–204
Chambers, John, 79
Chang, Tim, 9–10
Chips and Technologies, 48
Chrysallis, 44
Churchill, Winston, 12
Cisco, 79
Citrix, 185
Classical funds of funds, 101
Cloud computing, 13
Cobalt Networks, 45–47, 49, 144
Cohen, David, 24
Collaboration, 50
ComedyBlaze.tv, 155

Communication, with VCs, 126
Communications Week, 14
Company building, 149–164
  and blackmail business model, 159
  Facebook, 151–153
  innovation and, 162–163
  Kazaa, 150–151
  and marketing, 157–159
  MySpace, 153–156
  and naming, 163–164
  realistic expectations in, 161–162
  Skype, 150–151
Competitive advantage, 113
Confidentiality, 127
The Container Store, 45
Convertible debt, 56–57
Convertible notes, 21, 37–40
Conway, Ron, 20–21, 24, 39, 42, 54, 56
Conway, Topher, 21
Core Capital, 2
Corporate governance, 135–147
  and board composition, 142–143
  and board process, 142–146
  and board seats, 136–140
  and boards of directors, 140–146
  and whole-brain thinking in the boardroom, 141–142
Corporate venture capitalists, 79–80
Covenants (venture debt), 95
Cox Enterprises, 12
Creativity, 50
CRM (customer relations management), 42
Crowdfunder, 33
Crowdfunding, 28–35
CrunchBase, 116
Currier, James, 9, 10
Customer financing, 130–132
Customer relations management (CRM), 42
Customers 1st (bank name), 164

Database Inc., 14
DD (due diligence), 57

Debt:
  convertible, 56–57
  venture (*see* Venture debt)
Dell, Adam, 157–158
Demos, 115–116
Deutsche Bank, 151
DFJ (Draper Fisher Jurvetson), 3
DFJ-Esprit, 69, 123, 186, 192
Diageo, 207
Dilution, 78
Direct secondary market, 210–211
Discount rates, 39
Distribution, product vs., 149–150
DN Capital, 159
Domino's Pizza, 152
Donation-based crowdfunding, 30–32
Dot-com bubble (2000), 3, 5, 19
Down round, 78
Draper, Bill, 74
Draper, Gaither and Anderson, 72
Draper, Tim, 3–7, 12, 68
Draper, William Henry, III, 72
Draper, William Henry, Jr., 72
Draper and Johnson Investment Company, 72, 73, 75
Draper Fisher Jurvetson (DFJ), 3
"Draper Wave," 3–4
Drawdown period, 92–93
Dual tracking, 132
Due diligence (DD), 57
Dynamic Signal, 12, 173

Early exits, 176–186
East Africa, 6
EBay, 19
Economic drivers, in spreadsheet models, 111
Edwards Wildman Palmer, 198, 200
Efrusy, Kevin, 9, 10
Ehrhardt, Rolf, 117
Einstein, Albert, 7
EIRs (entrepreneurs-in-residence), 67
Emotional buyers, 171
Emotions, 100
Endowments, 69

Entrepreneurship, 11–13, 26
Entrepreneurs-in-residence (EIRs), 67
Equities, 70
Equity rights (venture debt), 95
Equity round, 40
Equity term sheets, 91
Equity-based crowdfunding, 30–32
Escrow letters, 38
Excite, 165
Exclusive licenses, 203–204
Executive summaries, 105
Exit, 165–189
Exit value, 107, 186–188
Extend companies (extensible companies),
    156

Facebook:
    and aqui-hires, 185
    balance among product, user
        experience and advertising,
        151–153
    and BranchOut, 7–9
    contacts on, 42
    Ron Conway and, 20
    friend, 155
    and Instagram, 172, 173
    and investment percentage, 18, 21
    Pitch Johnson on, 73
    and King.com, 160
    and marketing, 157–158
    origins, 15
    and special-purpose funds, 208
    and the start-up Cambrian explosion,
        18
    as symbol of success, 39
    and voting control of board, 196
Facility fee (venture debt), 94
Family offices, 80–81
Fanning, Shawn, 10
Fee(s):
    backend, 94
    facility, 94
    formation, 55
    legal, 55–56
    management, 64

Feld, Brad, 24–25, 192
Financial buyers, 170
Financial information (for pitches), 119
Financial models, 106–114
FINRA, 30
First Round Capital, 118
Fish, Tony, 34
506 offerings, 33–34
Fixed income, 70
Flarion, 60
Flat round, 78
Flexible terms, 57
Floodgate Fund, 10
Formation fees, 55
Founder-friendly angels, 57
Founders, dealing with, when selling,
        178–183
The Founders Club, 129
    Nic Brisbourne and, 69
    and cap tables, 191
    Ron Conway and, 21
    and crowdfunding, 34–35
    and deal flow, 59
    and direct secondary funds, 213–216
    equity exchange fund of, 186
    André Jaeggi and, 97
    Pitch Johnson and, 73
    Alex Mashinsky and, 18
    and Rebate Networks, 209
    Andrew Romans and, 186–187
    and shareholders, 208
    Jörg Sperling and, 83
    and VCs, 10
The Founders Club Fund, 44
Four Horsemen, 210
Fradin, Russ, 12, 173–174
Freivald, Matt, 47
Friendster, 153
Fund physics, 188–189
Funding:
    angel, 35–37
    crowd-, 28–35
    online, 28
Funds of funds, 96–101
    and alignment, 98–99

and emotions, 100
managers of, 99–100
and segregated accounts, 101
and service agreements, 101
services, 100

GAAP accounting rules, 80
Gates Foundation, 119
Genentech, 74
General partners, 66–67
Georgetown Angels, 57, 216
Georgetown University, 14, 57
Glänzer, Stefan, 209
Global TeleExchange (GTX), 14, 15, 51
Goldman Sachs, 166
Goleman, Daniel, 49
Goodger, Ben, 200–202
Google, 20, 21, 155, 165
Google Ventures, 118
Google.org, 119
Governing Dynamics, 18
Great from the Start (Montgomery), 44
Greylock, 122
GroundLink, 18
Groupon, 9, 19, 21, 207, 208
Growth stage investments, 84
GTC Law Group, 202
GTX (Global TeleExchange), 14, 15, 51
Gust, 28, 116

Half.com, 118
Hambrecht & Quist, 210
Hannibal, 1
Hartenbaum, Howard, 13, 119, 132
Harvard, 74
Harvard Business School, 185
Hasso Plattner Ventures, 130
Hawk, Ken, 59–60
Hercules Technology Growth Capital, 86
Horowitz, Andreessen, 108

IBM Global Services, 82
Income statements, 106
Incubators, 22
Index Ventures, 160

Indiegogo, 33
iNeed, 34
Innovation, Steve Jobs on, 19
Innovation Warehouse, 34
Insight Venture Partners, 109
Instagram, 172–173
Institutional fund managers, 81
Institutional investors, 69, 70
Insurance companies, 69
Intel, 2
Interest rate (venture debt), 94
Interest-only period (I/O), 93–94
Internal rate of return (IRR), 21, 65, 107
Interns, employing, 130
Introductions (in pitches), 118
Intuition, 50
Investment(s):
  core economics vs., in spreadsheet models, 112
  minimum, 38
Investment materials, 103–119
  business plans vs., 103–104
  demo as, 115–116
  executive summaries as, 105
  financial models as, 106–114
  investor control schedule as, 113
  investor slide decks as, 105–106
  pitch as, 116–119
  video as, 115–116
Investor control schedule, 113
Investor slide decks, 105–106
Investors:
  accredited, 34
  choosing your, 52–53
  corporate, 71
  government, 71
I/O (interest-only period), 93–94
IRR (internal rate of return), 21, 65, 107

Jaeggi, André, 96–101
James, Josh, 163
Jamieson, Burge, 97
Jaquez-Fissori, Todd M., 86

Jaws, 117
Jobs, Steve:
   focus of, 149
   and innovation, 19, 163
   as rated by his VC, 43
   on *Time* magazine, 5
JOBS Act, 29–30, 33
Johnson, Franklin Pitcher "Pitch," 72–76
Johnson, Gary, 173, 185
Johnson & Johnson, 75

Kaiser, Bill, 122
Keilhacker, Kurt, 48
Kern, Benjamin D., 163–164, 176–186
Key terms (venture capital funding
   negotiation), 123–124
Khasanshyn, Renat, 51
Kickstarter, 31, 33
Kimball, Richard, 198–199
King.com, 160
Kleiner, 114
Knox, Dave, 27
Kopelman, Jack, 118–119

Last.fm, 152, 209
Later stage venture rounds, 84
Lawyers, pitching to, 53–54
LBOs (leveraged buyouts), 5
Lead investor, credibility of, 56
Legal fees, 55–56
Legal issues, 191–204
   and angel investor selection, 56–57
   anti-dilution terms, 195
   board control, 195–196
   disputes, 198–200
   exclusivity and costs, 197–198
   liquidation preference, 194–195
   protective provisions, 196
   valuation, 192–194
Lehman Brothers, 109
Lending, venture (*see* Venture debt)
Lending-based crowdfunding, 30–32
Leonhardt, Howard, 23, 29, 214
Leonhardt Ventures, 29
Letters of Intent (LOIs), 51

Leveraged buyouts (LBOs), 5
Levine, Paul, 103–104
Levkovitz, Zohar, 209
Licensees, out-of-control, 201–202
Licenses, exclusive, 203–204
Licensing issues, 200–201
Limited liability corporations (LLCs),
   57–58
Limited partners (LPs), 70
LinkedIn, 20, 21, 42, 163, 208
Liquidation consideration, 184
Liquidation preferences, 174–175, 197
LiquidSpace, 117
Ljubljana, Slovenia, 122
LLCs (limited liability corporations),
   57–58
LOIs (Letters of Intent), 51
Longstop dates, 38
LPs (limited partners), 70
LSE, 70
Lucent Technologies, 51, 79

Management fees, 64
Management incentives (boards of
   directors), 145–146
Management teams, 44–52
   archetypes in, 45–48
   collective intelligence of, 48–49
   recruiting, 51–52
   and social intelligence, 49–51
   and trust, 48
Management-focused acquisitions,
   178–183
Managers:
   of funds of funds, 99–100
   institutional fund, 81
Managing directors, 66
Marini, Rick, 7
Maris, Bill, 118, 119
Markkula, Mike, 43
M&As (mergers and acquisitions), 165–170
Mashinsky, Alex, 18–20
Massolution, 31
Matthews, Joe, 207
Maverick, 176

Mayfield, 86
McGuire Woods, 163, 176
McIntosh, Rob, 185
McMillan, Eoin, 27
Mehra, Vivek, 46, 47
Mendelson, Jason, 192
Mentors, 22–23, 46
Mergers and acquisitions (M&As), 165–170
Michel, Chris, 10
Microloans, peer-to-peer, 29
Microsoft, 2
Micro-VCs, 20
Milestones, 92
Military.com, 10
Milner, Yuri, 24
Minimum draw amount, 93
Minimum investment, 38
Mirror neurons, 50
MIT, 97
Mohr Davidow Ventures, 124
Money people, 46
Monster Worldwide, 8
Montgomery, John, 44–51, 140–142
Montgomery & Hansen LLP, 44, 140
Montgomery Securities, 210
Moore's Law, 79
Morgan, J. P., 165
Morgan Stanley, 166
Morgenthaler Ventures, 43, 69, 103
Morihiro, Koji, 48
Morin, Dave, 10
Moritz, Mike, 52
Mosaic, 13
Movetis, 176
MTV, 8
Mullenweg, Matt, 10
Murdoch, Rupert, 154

Napster, 10, 150
NASDAQ, 69, 70, 73
National Venture Capital Association, 73
NBPs (non-bank providers), 88–89
NDAs (nondisclosure agreements), 128, 167

Negotiating with VCs, 124–128
    confidentiality and, 127–128
    "gamification" in, 125–126
    nondisclosure agreements and, 128
    preparation for, 125
    valuation in, 126
NetMind Technologies, 45, 47–49
Netscape, 13
Networking, 58–59
    events for, 42–43
    social, 18
Neurons, 50–51
New Century Bank, 164
News Corporation, 153
Nishar, Deep, 163
Noble, Alan, 47
Non-bank providers (NBPs), 88–89
Nondisclosure agreements (NDAs), 128, 167
Non-solicit agreements (NSAs), 167
Norwest Venture Partners, 9, 10
NSAs (non-solicit agreements), 167

Obama, Barack, 29–30
Offers, refusing, 202–203
Omniture, 163
Online funding, resources for, 28
Open Systems, 13
Open Systems Today, 14
Open Table, 157–159
Operating cash flow, 106
Oracle, 80
Organizational behavior, 50
Orr, Mark, 46
Orrick, 40, 55, 211
Out-of-control licensees, 201–202

Palantir Technologies, 208
Pandora, 152, 208
Papiernik, Antoine, 174–176, 191
Parker, Sean, 9, 10
Partech International, 130
Partners, 66
Passive investors, 81
Patel, Parag, 186

Path, 10
Patricot, Alan, 70–71
Pavey, Bob, 43, 69, 103
Payne, Gordon, 185
PayPal, 157–158
Peer-to-peer microloans, 29
Pension funds, 69
Percentage to new investors, 197
Perkins, Tom, 52
Pitches:
    to lawyers, 53–54
    materials for, 116–119
    venture capitalists' feedback on,
        118–119
Plattner, Hasso, 130
Pledge funds, 58
Poggled, 207
Polis, Jared, 25
Porter Five Forces Model, 77
Post-money valuation, 197
Pre-money valuations, 53, 197
Prepayment (of venture debt), 94
Presentation materials (see Investment
    materials)
Priced round, convertible notes vs., 37–40
Principles, 66
Private equity:
    and cycle between venture capital, 3
    venture capital vs., 81–85
Product, distribution vs., 149–150
ProFlowers, 25
Pulitzer, Joseph, 29

Qualcomm, 60
Questions, answering, 118
Quilici, Leo, 144

Raschle, Bruno, 96–97
Rathmann, George, 73–76
Ravikant, Naval, 10
Rebate Networks, 209
Recession (1973-74), 5
Recession (1991), 5
Recession (2008-), 5
Refusing offers, 202–203

Reg. D offerings, 33
Reses, Jackie, 185
Reuters Venture Capital, 69
Rewards-based crowdfunding, 30–32
Reyn, Dirk, 176
Richards, Mark, 47–48
Ries, Eric, 104
RJR Nabisco, 5
Robertson-Stephens, 210
Rock, Arthur, 5
Romans, Andrew, 186–187
Romans Five Forces Analysis, 78–79
Romney, Mitt, 35
Rosoff, Matt, 118
Rothrock, 118
Round size, 197
Runa Capital, 51

Salesmen, 45
San Francisco Opera, 73
Sand Hill Road, 9
SAP Ventures, 80
Satusky, Elton, 44
SBICs (Small Business Investment
    Companies), 72
Schlenker, Steve, 159–160
SEC (Securities and Exchange
    Commission), 30
Secondary market, 205–220
    and direct secondary funds, 213
    and equity diversification, 213–214
    and founder early liquidity, 211–213
    and Founders Club Equity Exchange
        Fund Model, 214–217
    and start-ups, 208–210
SecondMarket, 212–213
Securities and Exchange Commission
    (SEC), 30
Seed stage, 19
Seedcamp, 121
Segregated accounts, 101
Sellers, Scott, 47
Semanta, 121–122
Senior associates, 66
Senkut, 118

Sensitivity analysis, 111–112
Sequoia, 52, 209
Series A venture capital financings, 6
Service agreements, 101
Services, 100
SharesPost, 212
Siemens, 86
Sigma Partners, 97
Silicon Valley, 6
Silver, Jonathan, 2
Simplicity, 113
Singtel, 209
Slide decks, investor, 105–106
Small Business Investment Act of 1958, 72
Small Business Investment Companies
    (SBICs), 72
Smeet, 130
Smith, Nate, 8
Smith, Ross Q., 47
Social intelligence, 49–51
Social media, 150–156
Social networking, 18
Social neuroscience, 49
Sofinnova Partners, 174, 191
Sony, 8
Sony PlayStation, 48
Specific Media, 156
Sperling, Jörg "George," 83–85
Spetic, Ales, 121–123
Spindle neurons, 50–51
Spreadsheet models, 109–114
    and clarity of building competitve
        advantage, 113–114
    and confidence in economic drivers,
        109–114
    investments vs. core economics in,
        112
    key economic drivers in, 110–111
    predictiveness in, 110
    real-world evaluation of, 113
    sensitivity analysis of, 111–112
Stanford Graduate School of Business, 73
Stanford University, 97, 124
Star Wars, 117
StartUp Bus, 27

Startups:
    and accelerators, 22–23
    "Cambrian explosion" of, 18–20
    legal fees for, 55–56
Startworks, 44, 140
Statue of Liberty, 28–29
Stevens, Jay, 153, 154
Stock market, 69
Storytelling, 118–119
Strategic assets, 169
Strategic investors, 59–60
Strategic purchasers, 170–171
StudiVZ.net, 209
Sun Microsystems, 15
Super angel, Ron Conway as, 20–21
SuperFan, 8
Sutter Hill Ventures, 72, 75
SV Angel, 20–21
Swanson, Bob, 74
SXSW, 27
Sylantro, 131
Syndicates, 37–38

Tarolli, Gary, 47
Team buys, 169
Team hires, 169
Teams, management (see Management
    teams)
TechCrunch, 8
Techfarm, 45, 48, 49
TechFund, 48
Technologists, 45
Technology buys, 169
TechStars, 24–26
"TechStars Demo Day," 26
Telenor, 131
Term (time), 93
Term sheets, 192–198
    anti-dilution, 195
    board control, 195–196
    exclusivity and costs, 197–198
    liquidation preference, 194–195
    protective provisions, 196
    valuation, 192–194
Thiel, Peter, 153

3Dfx Interactive, 45, 47, 49
Tickle.com, 8–10
Tiger Fund, 2
Timberlake, Justin, 156
Timing factors, 68
Tindell, Kip, 45
T-Mobile, 60
Trade sales:
    of private medical device companies,
        176
    working with, 175
Traits, 45
T-Ventures, 59–60
Twitter, 18, 20, 21, 39, 122, 151, 208

Ubidyne, 59
Ueberla, Joerg, 208
Union Square Ventures, 32, 122
Universal, 8
UNIX, 13
Up round, 78
U.S. Patent and Trademark Office, 164

Valuation(s):
    and angel funding, 41, 56
    and negotiating with VCs, 126
    pre-money, 53, 197
    ranges of, for pre-money caps on seed-
        stage convertible note financings,
        40–41
    in Romans Five Forces Analysis, 78
Value of your company, growing the,
    129–130
Vator.tv, 116
Venture capital, 61–101
    cycle between private equity
        and, 3
    life cycle of, 61–66
    old-school, 72–76
    private equity vs., 81–85
    stock market and, 69
    terminology related to, 61–62
    and venture fratricide, 132–133
    vintages of, 68
Venture capital funding, 121–133

and cash flow, 129–130
    fees for, 55
    negotiating key terms for, 123–124
Venture capitalists (VCs):
    arrogance of, 71
    and capital providers, 87
    corporate, 79–80
    and family offices, 80–81
    feedback of, on pitches, 118–119
    investment materials for (see Investment
        materials)
    and liquidity events, 65
    negotiating with, 124–127
    reaching your first-choice, 121–123
    sources of funding for, 69–71
    and syndication, 66
    titles of, 66–67
    working with, 175
Venture Deals (Feld and Mendelson), 192
Venture debt (venture lending), 85–96
    as asset class, 95–96
    choosing a provider for, 87–91
    modern, 86
    and term sheets, 91–95
    terminology for, 91–95
Venture debt providers:
    banks as, 87–88
    non-bank providers of, 88–89
    questions for, 90–91
Venture exits, 186–189
Venture fratricide, 132–133
Venture partners, 67
Venture returns, 68
Videos, 114–115
Vimeo, 115
Visionaries, 45
VMWare, 79, 186
Voice on the Net (VON), 150
Voice over IP (VoIP), 150
VPs, 66

Warner Music, 8
Warrants, 40, 94–95
Weaver, Sigourney, 117
Wellington Partners, 208

Western Association of Venture
    Capitalists, 73
WHEB Ventures, 83, 84
Whims, Jim, 48
Wikia, 159
Wikipedia, 159
Wilson, Fred, 32, 122, 123, 146–147
Wilson Sonsini Goodrich & Rosati,
    44
WordPress, 10
Wu, Mark, 46

Y Combinator, 24
Yahoo!, 185, 209
"You Think It's Hard to Raise Money for
    a Company?" (Alan Patricot), 71
YouTube, 115, 156

Zacconi, Riccardo, 160–161
ZipCar, 157–158
Zoll Data Systems, 25
Zuckerberg, Mark, 9, 108, 149, 152, 196
Zynga, 20, 21, 122, 208

About the Author

Andrew Romans is the author of *Masters of Corporate Venture Capital* and the co-founder and General Partner of Rubicon Venture Capital, an early stage VC fund with offices in San Francisco and New York City. Romans is an active VC investor and advises corporate executives on Corporate Venture Capital (CVC) programs. He is the Founder and President of The Global TeleExchange (The GTX), where he raised $50m from VCs and corporations, and built and managed a team of 90 people. Andrew was also a Managing Partner at both Georgetown Angels, a global angel group, and Georgetown Venture Partners (GVP), a venture-capital-focused boutique investment bank based in London, with offices in Europe, the US, and Israel. At The Founders Club, which focused on secondaries and equity exchange VC funds he served as a General Partner, and recruited 42 VCs from the US, Europe, and Israel to the advisory board. In addition, while working as Managing Director of EMEA at VC-backed Sentito Networks (acquired by Verso Technologies), he managed enterprise software sales at VC-backed Motive Communications (NASDAQ IPO), opening new markets in France, Benelux, Scandinavia, and Ireland. As country manager for fiber optic cable manufacturing and turn-key project construction company, Dura-Line, which has offices in the UK, Austria, Czech and Slovak Republics, Slovenia, Croatia, and Bosnia-Herzegovina, Romans opened new markets in these locations. He is also a frequent venture capital guest speaker on TV shows including MSNBC, CNBC, and ABC, as well as various TV channels in China and Russia. He was born in Japan, lived in Europe for 15 years, and is fluent in English, German, and French and can speak conversationally in Slovak. He began his career in 1993 working in the UNIX computing industry at Pencom Systems in New York, Silicon Valley, and Austin. He holds a BA from the University of Vermont and an MBA in finance from Georgetown University, which he completed on scholarship.